Microservices with Clojure

Develop event-driven, scalable, and reactive microservices
with real-time monitoring

Anuj Kumar

BIRMINGHAM - MUMBAI

Microservices with Clojure

Commissioning Editor: Richa Tripathi
Acquisition Editor: Aiswarya Narayanan
Content Development Editor: Akshada Iyer
Technical Editor: Abhishek Sharma
Copy Editor: Safis Editing
Project Coordinator: Prajakta Naik
Proofreader: Safis Editing
Indexer: Francy Puthiry
Graphics: Jason Monteiro
Production Coordinator: Deepika Naik

First published: January 2018

Production reference: 1230118

Published by Packt Publishing Ltd.
Livery Place
35 Livery Street
Birmingham
B3 2PB, UK.

ISBN 978-1-78862-224-0

www.packtpub.com

To my mother, Mrs. Indu Srivastava, my father, Mr. Dilip Kumar, and to my lovely wife, Aishwarya, for their continuous support and encouragement. All the time that I have spent on this book should have been spent with them. For trips that we canceled and for weekends that I spent at my desk.

To my family, teachers, and colleagues. They have extended their continuous support, provided critical feedback, and made it possible for me to focus on this book.

`mapt.io`

Mapt is an online digital library that gives you full access to over 5,000 books and videos, as well as industry leading tools to help you plan your personal development and advance your career. For more information, please visit our website.

Why subscribe?

- Spend less time learning and more time coding with practical eBooks and Videos from over 4,000 industry professionals

- Improve your learning with Skill Plans built especially for you

- Get a free eBook or video every month

- Mapt is fully searchable

- Copy and paste, print, and bookmark content

PacktPub.com

Did you know that Packt offers eBook versions of every book published, with PDF and ePub files available? You can upgrade to the eBook version at `www.PacktPub.com` and as a print book customer, you are entitled to a discount on the eBook copy. Get in touch with us at `service@packtpub.com` for more details.

At `www.PacktPub.com`, you can also read a collection of free technical articles, sign up for a range of free newsletters, and receive exclusive discounts and offers on Packt books and eBooks.

Contributors

About the author

Anuj Kumar is the co-founder and chief architect of FORMCEPT, a data analytics startup based in Bangalore, India. He has more than 10 years of experience in designing large-scale distributed systems for storage, retrieval, and analytics.

He has been in industry hacking, mainly in the area of data integration, data quality, and data analytics using NLP and machine learning techniques. He has published research papers at ACM conferences, got a few patents granted, and has spoken at TEDx.

Prior to FORMCEPT, he has worked with the Oracle Server Technologies division in Bangalore, India.

I would like to thank my technical reviewer, Michael Vitz, for his valuable feedback and the Packt editorial team for an excellent feedback loop to come up with good quality content. I would also like to thank my teachers and FORMCEPT team members, who have helped me on various topics covered in this book. And especially, I would like to thank my parents, my wife, and my entire family for their continuous encouragement.

About the reviewer

Michael Vitz has many years of experience building and maintaining software for the JVM. Currently, his main interests include microservice and cloud architectures, DevOps, the Spring Framework, and Clojure.

As a senior consultant for software architecture and engineering at INNOQ, he helps clients by building well-crafted and value-providing software.

He also is the writer of a column in the German magazine, JavaSPEKTRUM, where he publishes articles about JVM, infrastructure, and architectural topics every two months.

Packt is searching for authors like you

If you're interested in becoming an author for Packt, please visit `authors.packtpub.com` and apply today. We have worked with thousands of developers and tech professionals, just like you, to help them share their insight with the global tech community. You can make a general application, apply for a specific hot topic that we are recruiting an author for, or submit your own idea.

Table of Contents

Preface

The microservice architecture is sweeping the world as the de facto pattern for building scalable and easy-to-maintain web-based applications. This book will teach you common patterns and practices, showing you how to apply them using the Clojure programming language. It will teach you the fundamental concepts of architectural design and RESTful communication, and show you patterns that provide manageable code that is supportable in development and at scale in production. This book will provide you with examples of how to put these concepts and patterns into practice with Clojure.

Whether you are planning a new application or working on an existing monolith, this book will explain and illustrate with practical examples how teams of all sizes can start solving problems with microservices. You will understand the importance of writing code that is asynchronous and non-blocking, and how Pedestal helps us do this. Later, the book explains how to build Reactive microservices in Clojure, which adhere to the principles underlying the Reactive Manifesto. We finish off by showing you various techniques to monitor, test, and secure your microservices. By the end, you will be fully capable of setting up, modifying, and deploying a microservice with Clojure and Pedestal.

Who this book is for

If you are looking forward to migrate your existing monolithic applications to microservices or taking your first steps into microservice architecture, then this book is for you. You should have a working knowledge of programming in Clojure. However, no knowledge of RESTful architecture, microservices, or web services is expected.

What this book covers

Chapter 1, *Monolithic Versus Microservices*, introduces monolithic and microservice architecture and discusses when to use what. It also covers the possible migration plans of moving from monolithic applications to microservices.

Chapter 2, *Microservices Architecture,* covers the basic building blocks of microservice architecture and its related features. It discusses how to set up messaging and contracts, and manage data flows among microservices.

Chapter 3, *Microservices for Helping Hands Application*, introduces a sample Helping Hands application and describes the steps that will be taken in the rest of the book to build the application using microservices. Further, the chapter compares and contrasts the benefits of using a microservices-based architecture compared with a monolithic one.

Chapter 4, *Development Environment*, covers Clojure and REPL at a high level and introduces the concepts of Leiningen and Boot—the two major build tools for any Clojure project. The emphasis will be on Leiningen with a basic introduction to Boot on how to set up a Clojure project for implementing microservices.

Chapter 5, *REST APIs for Microservices*, covers the basics of the REST architectural style, various HTTP methods, when to use what, and how to give meaningful names to RESTful APIs of microservices. It also covers the naming conventions for REST APIs using the Helping Hands application as an example.

Chapter 6, *Introduction to Pedestal*, covers the Clojure Pedestal framework in detail with all the relevant features provided by Pedestal, including interceptors and handlers, routes, WebSockets, server-sent events, and chain providers.

Chapter 7, *Achieving Immutability with Datomic*, gives an overview of the Datomic database along with its architecture, data model, transactions, and Datalog query language.

Chapter 8, *Building Microservices for Helping Hands*, is a step-by-step, hands-on guide to build and test microservices for the Helping Hands application using the Pedestal framework.

Chapter 9, *Configuring Microservices*, covers the basics of microservices configuration and discusses how to create configurable microservices using frameworks such as Omniconf. It also explains the steps to manage the application state effectively using available state-management frameworks such as Mount.

Chapter 10, *Event-Driven Patterns for Microservices*, covers the basics of event-driven architectures and shows how to use Apache Kafka as a messaging system and event store. Further, it discusses how to use Apache Kafka brokers and set up consumer groups for the effective coordination of microservices.

Chapter 11, *Deploying and Monitoring Secured Microservices*, covers the basics of microservices authentication using JWT and how to set up a real-time monitoring system using the ELK Stack. It also explains the basic concepts of containers and orchestration frameworks such as Kubernetes.

To get the most out of this book

The Java Development Kit (JDK) is required to run and develop applications using Clojure. You can get the JDK from `http://www.oracle.com/technetwork/java/javase/downloads/index.html`. It is also recommended that you use a text editor or an integrated development environment (IDE) of your choice for implementation. Some of the examples in the chapters require Linux as an operating system.

Download the example code files

You can download the example code files for this book from your account at `www.packtpub.com`. If you purchased this book elsewhere, you can visit `www.packtpub.com/support` and register to have the files emailed directly to you.

You can download the code files by following these steps:

1. Log in or register at `www.packtpub.com`.
2. Select the **SUPPORT** tab.
3. Click on **Code Downloads & Errata**.
4. Enter the name of the book in the **Search** box and follow the onscreen instructions.

Once the file is downloaded, please make sure that you unzip or extract the folder using the latest version of:

- WinRAR/7-Zip for Windows
- Zipeg/iZip/UnRarX for Mac
- 7-Zip/PeaZip for Linux

The code bundle for the book is also hosted on GitHub at `https://github.com/PacktPublishing/Microservices-with-Clojure`. We also have other code bundles from our rich catalog of books and videos available at `https://github.com/PacktPublishing/`. Check them out!

Conventions used

There are a number of text conventions used throughout this book.

`CodeInText`: Indicates code words in text, database table names, folder names, filenames, file extensions, pathnames, dummy URLs, user input, and Twitter handles. Here is an example: "The persistence protocol `ServiceDB` consists of `upsert`, `entity`, and `delete` functions."

A block of code is set as follows:

```
{
  "query": {
    "term": {
      "status": "O"
    }
  }
}
```

When we wish to draw your attention to a particular part of a code block, the relevant lines or items are set in bold:

```
(defn home-page
  [request]
  (log/counter ::home-hits 1)
  (ring-resp/response "Hello World!"))
```

Any command-line input or output is written as follows:

```
% lein run
Noname | Hello, World!

% lein run Clojure
Clojure | Hello, World!
```

Bold: Indicates a new term, an important word, or words that you see onscreen. For example, words in menus or dialog boxes appear in the text like this. Here is an example: "Click on the **Create a visualization** button."

Warnings or important notes appear like this.

Tips and tricks appear like this.

Get in touch

Feedback from our readers is always welcome.

General feedback: Email `feedback@packtpub.com` and mention the book title in the subject of your message. If you have questions about any aspect of this book, please email us at `questions@packtpub.com`.

Errata: Although we have taken every care to ensure the accuracy of our content, mistakes do happen. If you have found a mistake in this book, we would be grateful if you would report this to us. Please visit `www.packtpub.com/submit-errata`, selecting your book, clicking on the Errata Submission Form link, and entering the details.

Piracy: If you come across any illegal copies of our works in any form on the Internet, we would be grateful if you would provide us with the location address or website name. Please contact us at `copyright@packtpub.com` with a link to the material.

If you are interested in becoming an author: If there is a topic that you have expertise in and you are interested in either writing or contributing to a book, please visit `authors.packtpub.com`.

Reviews

Please leave a review. Once you have read and used this book, why not leave a review on the site that you purchased it from? Potential readers can then see and use your unbiased opinion to make purchase decisions, we at Packt can understand what you think about our products, and our authors can see your feedback on their book. Thank you!

For more information about Packt, please visit `packtpub.com`.

1
Monolithic Versus Microservices

"The old order changeth yielding place to new"

- Alfred Tennyson

A well-designed **monolithic architecture** has been the key to many successful software applications. However, microservices-based applications are gaining popularity in the age of the internet due to their inherent property of being autonomous and flexible, their ability to scale independently, and their shorter release cycles. In this chapter, you will:

- Learn about the basics of monolithic and microservices architectures
- Understand the monolithic-first approach and when to start using microservices
- Learn how to migrate an existing monolithic application to microservices
- Compare and contrast the release cycle and deployment methodology of monolithic and microservices-based applications

Dawn of application architecture

Ever since Ada Lovelace (https://en.wikipedia.org/wiki/Ada_Lovelace) wrote the first algorithm for Analytical Engine (https://en.wikipedia.org/wiki/Analytical_Engine) in the 19th century and Alan Turing (https://en.wikipedia.org/wiki/Alan_Turing) formalized the concepts of algorithm and computation via the Turing machine (https://en.wikipedia.org/wiki/Turing_machine), software has gone through multiple phases in its evolution, both in terms of how it is designed and how it is made available to its end users. The earlier software was designed to run on a single machine in a single environment, and was delivered to its end users as an isolated standalone entity. In the early 1990s, as the focus shifted to application software, the industry started exploring various software architecture methodologies to meet the demands of changing requirements and underlying environments. One of the software architectures that was widely adopted was multitier architecture, which clearly separated the functions of data management, business logic, and presentation. When these layers were packaged together in a single application, using a single technology stack, running as a single program, it was called a monolithic architecture, still in use today.

With the advent of the internet, software started getting offered as a service over the web. With this change in deployment and usage, it started becoming hard to upgrade and add features to software that adopted a monolithic architecture. Technology started changing rapidly and so did programming languages, databases, and underlying hardware. Companies that were able to disintegrate their monolithic applications into loosely-coupled services that could talk to each other were able to offer better services, better integration points, and better performance to their users. They were not only able to upgrade to the latest technology and hardware, but also able to offer new features and services faster to their users. The idea of disintegrating a monolithic application into loosely-coupled services that can be developed, deployed, and scaled independently and can talk to other services over a lightweight protocol, was called microservices-based architecture (https://en.wikipedia.org/wiki/Microservices).

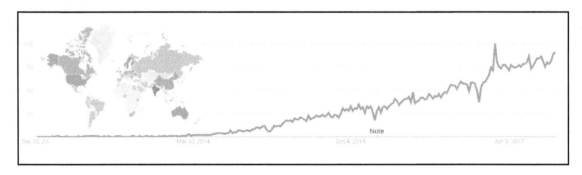

Companies such as Netflix, Amazon, and so on have all adopted a microservices-based architecture. If you look at Google Trends in the preceding screenshot, you can see that the popularity of microservices is rising day by day, but this doesn't mean that monolithic applications are obsolete. There are applications that are still suited for monolithic architecture. Microservices have their advantages, but at the same time they are hard to deploy, scale, and monitor. In this chapter, we will look at both monolithic and microservices-based architectures. We will discuss when to use what and also talk about when and how to migrate from a monolithic to a microservices-based architecture.

Monolithic architecture

Monolithic architecture is an all-in-one methodology that encapsulates all the required services as a single deployable artifact. It works on a single technology stack and is deployed and scaled as a single unit. Since there is only one technology stack to master, it is easy to deploy, scale, and set up a monitoring infrastructure for monolithic applications. Each team member works on one or more components of the system and follows the design principle of **Separation of Concerns (SoC)** (https://en.wikipedia.org/wiki/Separation_of_concerns). Such applications are also easier to refactor, debug, and test in a single standalone development environment.

Applications based on monolithic architecture may consist of one or more deployable artifacts that are all deployed at the same time. Such a monolithic architecture is often referred to as a *Distributed Monolith*.

For example, a very common monolithic application is a word processing application; Microsoft Word is installed via a single deployable artifact and is entirely built on Microsoft .NET Framework (https://www.microsoft.com/net/). There are various components within word processing application, such as templates, import/export, spell-checker, and so on, that work together to help create a document and export it the format of choice.

Monolithic architecture applies not only to standalone applications, but also to client-server based applications that are provided as a service over the web. Such client-server based applications have a clearly defined multitier architecture that provides the relevant services to its end users via a user interface.

The user interface talks to application endpoints that can be programmed using well-defined interfaces.

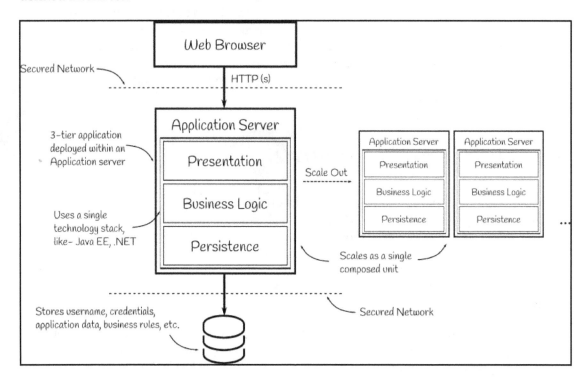

A typical client-server application may adopt a three-tier architecture to separate the **presentation, business logic**, and **persistence** layer from each other, as shown in the preceding diagram. Components of each layer talk strictly to the components of the layer below them. For example, the components of the **presentation** layer may never talk to the **persistence** layer directly. If they need access to data, the request will be routed via the **business logic** layer that will not only move the data between the **persistence** layer and the **presentation** layer, but also do the required processing to serve the request. Adopting such a component-based layered architecture also helps in isolating the effect of change to only the components of dependent layers instead of the entire application. For example, changes to the components of the **business logic** layer may require a change in the dependent components of the **presentation** layer but components of the **persistence** layer may remain intact.

Even though a monolithic application is built on SoC, it is still a single application on a single technology stack that provides all required services to its users. Any change to such an application requires to be compatible with all the encapsulated services and underlying technology stack. In addition to that, it is not possible to scale each service independently. Any scaling requirement is met by deploying multiple instances of the entire system as a single unit. A team working on such a monolithic application scales over time and has to adapt to newer technologies as a whole, which is often challenging due to the rapidly changing technology landscape. If they do not change with the technology, the entire software becomes obsolete over time and is discarded due to incompatibility with newer software and hardware, or a shortage of talent.

Microservices

Microservices are a functional approach well applied to software. It tries to decompose the entire application functionally into a set of services that can be deployed and scaled independently. Each service does only one job and does it well. It has its own database, decides its own schema, and provides access to datasets and services through well-defined application programming interfaces that are better known as APIs, often paired with a user interface. APIs follow a set communication protocols, but services are free to choose their own technology stack and can be deployed on hardware of choice.

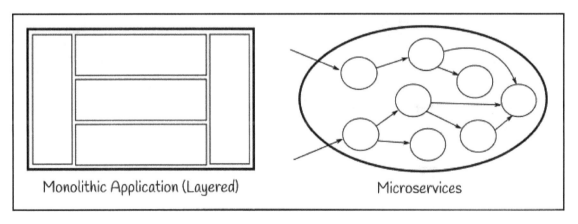

Monolithic Application (Layered)   Microservices

In a microservice environment, as shown in the preceding diagram, there are no layers like in monoliths; instead, each service is organized around a bounded context (`https://en.wikipedia.org/wiki/Domain-driven_design#Bounded_context`) that adds a business capability to the application as a whole. New capabilities in such an application are added as new services that are deployed and scaled independently. Each user request in a microservices-based application may call one or more internal microservice to retrieve data, process it, and generate the required response, as shown in the following diagram. Such software evolves faster and has low technology debt. They do not get married to a particular technology stack and can adopt a new technology faster:

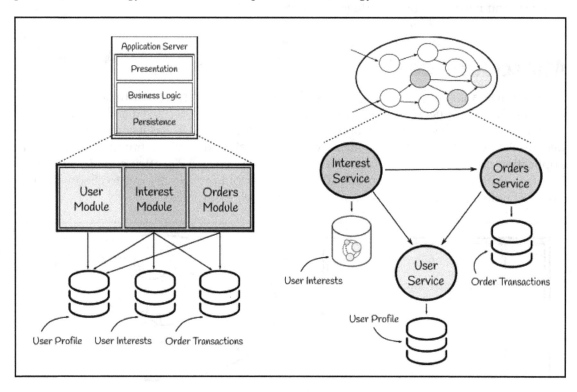

Data management

In a microservices-based application, databases are isolated for each business capability and are managed by only one service at a time. Any request that needs access to the data managed by another service strictly uses the APIs provided by the service managing the database. This makes it possible to not only use the best database technology available to manage the business capability, but also to isolate the technology debt to the service managing it. However, it is recommended for the calling service to cache responses over time to avoid tight coupling with the target service and reduce the network overhead of each API call.

For example, a service managing user interests might use a graph database (https://en.wikipedia.org/wiki/Graph_database) to build a network of users, whereas a service managing user transactions might use a relational database (https://en.wikipedia.org/wiki/Relational_database) due to its inherent ACID (https://en.wikipedia.org/wiki/ACID) properties that are suitable for transactions. The dependent service only needs to know the APIs to connect to the service for data and not the technology of the underlying database.

This is contrary to a monolithic layered architecture, where databases are organized by business capability, which may be accessed by one or more persistence modules based on the request. If the underlying database is using a different technology, then each of the modules accessing the databases have to comply with the same technology, thus inheriting the complexity of each database technology that it has access to.

 Database isolation should be done at the database level and not at the database technology level. Avoid deploying multiple instances of the same relational database or graph database as much as possible. Instead, try to scale them on demand and use the isolation capability of these systems to maintain separate databases within them for each service.

The concept of microservices is very similar to a well-known architecture called **service-oriented architecture (SOA)** (`https://en.wikipedia.org/wiki/Service-oriented_architecture`). In microservices, the focus is on identifying the right bounded context and keeping the microservices as lightweight as possible. Instead of using a complex message-oriented middleware (`https://en.wikipedia.org/wiki/Message-oriented_middleware`) such as ESB (`https://en.wikipedia.org/wiki/Enterprise_service_bus`), a simple mode of communication is used that is often just HTTP.

> *"Architectural Style [of Microservices] is referred to as fine-grained SOA, perhaps service orientation done right"*
>
> *- Martin Fowler on microservices*

When to use what

The monolithic layered architecture is one of the most common architectures in use across the software industry. Monolithic architectures are well suited for transaction-oriented enterprise applications that have well-defined features, change less often, and have complex business models. For such applications, transactions and consistency are of prime importance. They require a database technology with built-in support for ACID properties to store transactions. On the other hand, microservices are suited better for Software-as-a-Service, internet-scale applications that are feature-first applications with each feature focused on a single business capability. Such applications change rapidly and are scaled partially per business capability on demand. Transactions and consistency in such applications are hard to achieve due to multiple services, as compared to monoliths that are implemented as single applications.

It is recommended to start with a well designed, modular monolithic application irrespective of the domain complexity or transactional nature. Generally, all applications start as a monolithic application that can be deployed faster as a single artifact and later split into microservices when the application's complexity begins to outweigh the productivity of the team.

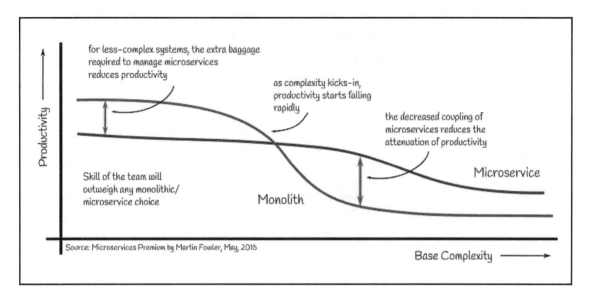

The productivity of the team may start decreasing when changes to the monolithic application start affecting more than one component, as shown in the preceding diagram. These changes may be a result of a new feature being added to the application, a database technology upgrade, or the refactoring of existing components. Any changes made to the application must keep the entire team in-sync, especially the deployment team, if there are any changes required in the deployment processes. Communicating such changes in a large team often results in a coordination nightmare, multiple change requests, and in-turn, reduces the overall productivity of the team working on the application.

Productivity also depends on the initial choices made with respect to the technology stack and its flexibility of implementation. For example, if a new feature requires a library that is readily available with a different technology stack or a programming language, it becomes challenging to adopt as it does not conform to the existing technology stack of the application components. In such cases, the team ends up implementing the same feature set for the current technology stack from scratch, and that in turn reduces productivity and further adds to the technology debt.

Before starting with microservices, first set up best design principles among team members. Next, try to evaluate the existing monolith with regard to components and their interaction. If refactoring can help reduce the dependency between the components, do that first instead of disintegrating your application into microservices.

Monolithic applications to microservices

Most applications start as a monolith. Amazon (`http://highscalability.com/amazon-architecture`) started with a monolithic Perl (`https://en.wikipedia.org/wiki/Perl`) /C++ (`https://en.wikipedia.org/wiki/C%2B%2B`) application, and Twitter (`http://highscalability.com/blog/2013/7/8/the-architecture-twitter-uses-to-deal-with-150m-active-users.html`) started with a monolithic Rails (`https://en.wikipedia.org/wiki/Ruby_on_Rails`) application. Both organizations have not only gone through more than three generations of software architectural changes, but have also transformed their organizational structures over time. Today, all of them are running on microservices with teams organized around services that are developed, deployed, scaled, and monitored by the same team independently. They have mastered continuous integration and continuous delivery pipelines with automated deployment, scaling, and monitoring of services for real-time feedback to the team.

Identifying candidates for microservices

The top-most challenge in migrating from a monolithic application to microservices is to identify the right candidates for microservices. A well structured and modularized monolithic application already has well-defined boundaries (bounded contexts) that can help disintegrate the application into microservices. For example, the *User*, *Orders*, and *Interest* modules already have well-defined boundaries and are good candidates to create microservices for. If the application does not have well-defined boundaries, the first step is to refactor the existing application to create such bounded contexts for microservices. Each bounded context must be tied to a business capability for which a service can be created.

Another approach in identifying the right candidates for microservices is to look at the data access patterns and associated business logic. If the same database is being updated by multiple components of a monolithic application, then it makes sense to create a service for the primary component with associated business logic that manages the database and makes it accessible to other services via APIs. This process can be repeated until databases and the associated business logic are managed by one and only one service that has a small set of responsibilities, modeled around a business capability.

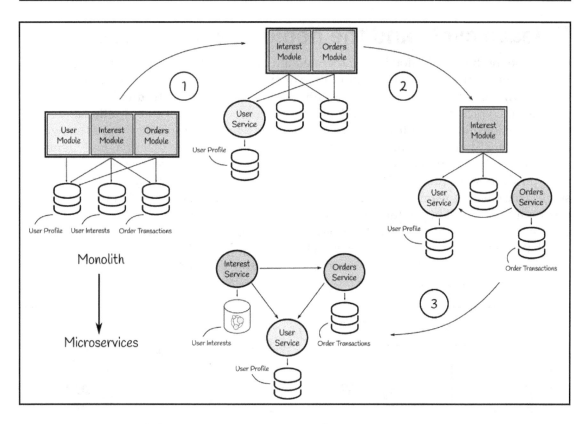

For example, a monolithic application consisting of *User*, *Interest*, and *Orders* components can be migrated into microservices by picking one component at a time and creating a microservice with an isolated database, as shown in the preceding diagram. To start with, first pick the one with the least dependency, the *User* module, and create the *User Service* service around it. All other components can now talk to this new *User Service* for *User Management*, including authentication, authorization, and getting user profiles. Next, pick the *Orders* module based on the least dependency logic, and create a service around it. Finally, pick the *Interest* module as it is dependent on both the *User* and *Orders* modules. Since we have the databases isolated, we can also swap out the database for *Interest* with maybe a graph database that is efficient to store and retrieve user interests due to its inherent capability of storing relationships as a graph.

> In addition to organizing your microservices around business capabilities and database access patterns, look for common areas, such as authentication, authorization, and notification, that can be perfected once as a service and can be leveraged by one or more microservices later.

Release cycle and the deployment process

Once a monolithic application is disintegrated into microservices, the next step is to deploy them into production. Monolithic application are mostly deployed as a single artifact (JARs, WARs, EXEs, and more) that are released after extensive testing by the **quality assurance (QA)** team. Typically, developers work on various components of the application and release versions for the QA team to pick and validate against the specification, as shown under the Org Structure of monolithic architecture in the following diagram. Each iteration may involve the addition or removal of features and bug fixes. The release goes through multiple **developers** (**dev**) and QA team iterations until the QA team flags off the release as stable. Once the QA team flags off the release, the released artifact is handed over to the IT ops team to deploy it in production. If there are any issues in production, the IT ops team asks the dev team to fix them. Once the issues are fixed, the dev team tags a new release for QA that again goes through the same dev-QA iterations before being marked as stable and eventually handed over to IT/ops. Due to this process, any release for a monolithic applications may easily take up to a month, often three months.

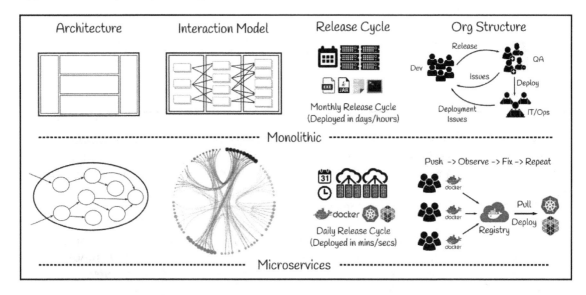

On the other hand, for microservices, teams are organized into groups that fully own a service. The team is responsible for not only developing the service, but also for putting together automated test cases that can test the entire service against each change submitted for the service. Since the service is to be tested in isolation for its features, it is faster to run entire test suites for the service for each change submitted by the developers. Additionally, the team itself creates deployable binaries often packaged into containers (`https://en.wikipedia.org/wiki/Linux_containers`), such as Docker (`https://en.wikipedia.org/wiki/Docker_(software)`), that are published to a central repository from where they can be automatically deployed into production by some well-known tools, such as Kubernetes (`https://en.wikipedia.org/wiki/Kubernetes`). The entire development to production timeline is cut short to days, often hours, as the entire deployment process is automated. We will learn more about deploying microservices in production and how to use these deployment tools in *Part-4*, the last part of this book.

There is a reason why a lot of microservice projects fail and only a few succeed. Migrating from a monolithic architecture to microservices must not only focus on identifying the bounded contexts, but also the organizational structure and deployment methodologies. Teams must be organized around services and not projects. Each team must own the service right from development to production. Since each team owns the responsibility for testing, validation, and deployment, the entire process should be automated and the organization must master it. Development and deployment cycles must be short with immediate feedback via fine-grained monitoring of the deployed microservices.

 Automation is key for any successful microservices project. Testing, deployment, and monitoring must be automated before moving microservices to production.

Summary

In this chapter, we learned about monolithic and microservices architectures and why microservices are becoming popular in the industry, especially with web-scale applications. We learned about the importance of database isolation with microservices and how to migrate a monolithic application to microservices by observing the database access pattern. We also discussed the importance of the monolith-first approach and when to move towards microservices. We concluded with a comparison of monolithic and microservices architectures with regard to the release cycle and deployment process.

The next chapter of this book will talk about microservice architecture in detail; we will learn more about domain-driven design and how to identify the right set of microservices. In Chapter 3, *Microservices for Helping Hands Application*, the last chapter of *Part-1*, we will pick a real-life use case for microservices and discuss how to design it using the principles of microservice architecture.

2
Microservices Architecture

"Gather together the things that change for the same reasons. Separate those things that change for different reasons."

- Robert Martin, Single Responsibility Principle

Software architecture plays a key role in identifying the behavior of the system before it is built. A well-designed software architecture leads to flexible, reusable, and scalable components that can be easily extended, verified, and maintained over time. Such architectures evolve over time and help pave the way for the adoption of next-generation architectures. For example, a well-designed monolithic application that is built on the principles of **Separation of Concern (SoC)** is easier to migrate to microservices than an application that does not have well-defined components. In this chapter, you will:

- Learn a systematic approach to designing microservices using the bounded context
- Learn how to set up contracts between microservices and isolate failures
- Learn how to manage data flows and transactions among microservices
- Learn about service discovery and the importance of automated deployment

Domain-driven design

Ideal enterprise systems are tightly integrated and provide all business capabilities as a single unit that is optimized for a particular technology stack and hardware. Such monolithic systems often grow so complex over time that it becomes challenging to comprehend them as a single unit by a single team. Domain-driven design advocates disintegrating such systems into smaller modular components and assigning them to teams that focus on a single business capability in a bounded context (`https://en.wikipedia.org/wiki/Domain-driven_design#Bounded_context`). Once disintegrated, all such components are made a part of an automated **continuous integration** (**CI**) process to avoid any fragmentation. Since these components are built in isolation and often have their own data models and schema, there should be a well-defined contract to interact with the components to coordinate various business activities.

 The term *Domain-driven design* was first coined by Eric J. Evans as the title of his book in 2003. In *Part-IV*, Evans talks about the bounded context and the importance of continuous integration, which forms the basis of any microservices architecture.

Bounded context

A domain model is a conceptual model of a business domain that formalizes its behavior and data. A single unified domain model tends to grow in complexity with business capabilities and increases the collaboration overhead among the team due to high coupling. To reduce coupling, domain-driven design recommends defining a model for each business capability with a well-defined boundary to separate the domain concepts within the model from the ones outside. Each such model then focuses on the behavior and data confined to a single business capability, and thus gets bounded by a single application context, called a bounded context. Monolithic applications tend to have a unified domain model for the entire business domain, whereas for microservices, domain models are defined for each identified bounded context.

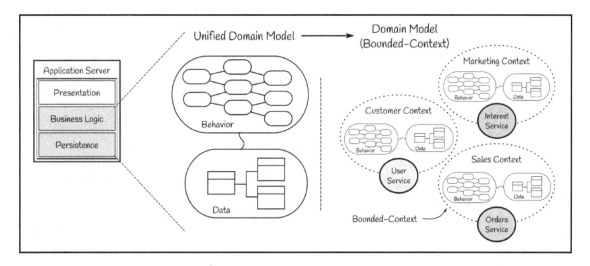

For example, instead of defining a single unified domain model for an e-commerce application, it is better to divide the application into bounded contexts of *Customer*, *Sales*, and *Marketing* and define a domain model for each of these contexts, as shown in the preceding diagram. Such focused domain models can then conquer each context based on business capabilities. For example, **Customer Context** can focus only on user and profile management, **Sales Context** can handle orders and transactions, and **Marketing Context** can keep track of user interests for focused marketing.

Identifying bounded contexts

One of the most challenging tasks in designing a microservices-based architecture is to get the bounded context right for each microservice. It is an iterative process that requires a thorough understanding of business capabilities and business domain. Business capabilities must not be confused with business functions or processes. Business capabilities target the what part of a business and have an outcome, whereas a business process targets the how part. For example, *alerting* is a business capability, whereas *sending an email* is a business process. A business capability may incorporate one or more business processes.

Bounded contexts must target business capabilities and not business processes. To identify the right bounded contexts, it is recommended to start with a monolithic application with a single unified model and analyze it iteratively over time for high coupling areas. Often, high coupling areas are good target points to split the domain model into sub-domain models that can interact using fixed contracts and help reduce tight coupling. However, such sub-domains must be further validated against business capabilities to make sure that they target only one business capability.

Microservices must be organized around a business capability within a bounded context and own their presentation, business domain, and persistence layer. They must take responsibility for the end-to-end development stack including functions, data model, persistence, user interface, and the contract to access the service using APIs, often over HTTP(S).

Organizing around bounded contexts

> *"Any organization that designs a system (defined broadly) will produce a design whose structure is a copy of the organization's communication structure"*

> *- Melvyn Conway, 1967*

Generally, the organization structure contributes heavily to the design of the application. Therefore, bounded contexts should never be identified on the basis of the existing structure of the organization. Instead, the organization must be structured around bounded contexts such that the entire team can work on a service in isolation.

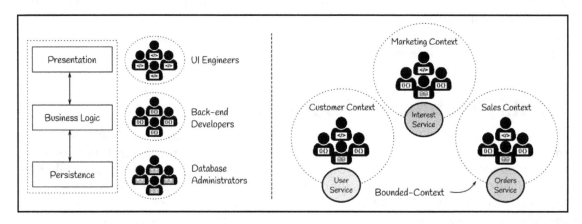

A typical organization, working on a monolithic application, is built around layers of **presentation**, **business logic**, and **persistence**, as shown in the preceding diagram. They tend to have a separate team of UI designers and UI/UX experts for the **presentation** layer, a team of backend developers to implement the domain model, and a team of database administrators to create a database for developers to access. Such an organization structure is ideal for an application with a smaller set of business capabilities.

Once the application grows, any changes to the application require communication to be made across the team of UI engineers, backend developers, and database administrators. Often, such communication leads to so many back-and-forth exchanges involving design documents and specification changes that it becomes overwhelming for the teams to translate the requirements correctly to the implementation. Such communication overhead adds delays to the project and brings down the productivity of the entire team working on the product as a whole.

Bounded context, if identified correctly, solves this problem by localizing the team of UI developers, backend developers, and database administrators to focus on a single business capability. Such boundaries make sure that the communication between the teams is bounded by a fixed contract that is set at the service level. This makes it possible to reduce a considerable communication overhead, as any changes made to a service are confined within the team working on the service. For example, the localized team of **User Service** and **Orders Service** will communicate only to discuss the service APIs that the user service is exposing for **Orders Service** to get the customer details. Since any changes to the customer schema or the orders schema should not impact each other as per the definition of bounded context, it is not required to communicate such changes to the other service.

Components

Once the bounded contexts are identified for microservices and the organization structure is aligned, each microservice must be considered as a product that is tested, deployed, and scaled in isolation by the same team that developed it. A well-designed microservice must never expose its internal data model to the outside world directly. Instead, it must maintain a service contract that maps to its internal model such that it can evolve over time without affecting the dependent microservices.

Component-based software engineering (`https://en.wikipedia.org/wiki/Component-based_software_engineering`) defines a component as a reusable module that is based on the principles of SoC and encapsulates a set of related functions and data. In the context of microservices architecture, it is recommended to implement each service as a component that is independently swappable and deployable without affecting any other microservices.

Hexagonal architecture

Hexagonal architecture (`http://alistair.cockburn.us/Hexagonal+architecture`), also known as the ports and adapters pattern, aims to decouple business logic from other parts of the component, especially the persistence and services layers. A component, built on the ports and adapters pattern, exposes a set of ports to which one or more adapters can be added as necessary. For example, to test and verify the core business logic in isolation, a mock database adapter can be plugged in and later replaced with a runtime database adapter in production.

A **port** is an entry point that is provided by the core business logic to interact with other parts of the component. An adapter is an implementation of a port, and there may be more than one adapter defined for a single port based on the requirement. For example, a **REST adapter** is used to accept requests from external users or other microservices components. It internally calls the **service API port** defined by the **core business logic** that performs that requested operation and generates a response. Similarly, a **database adapter** is used by the **core business logic** to interact with the external database via its **database port**, as shown in the following diagram:

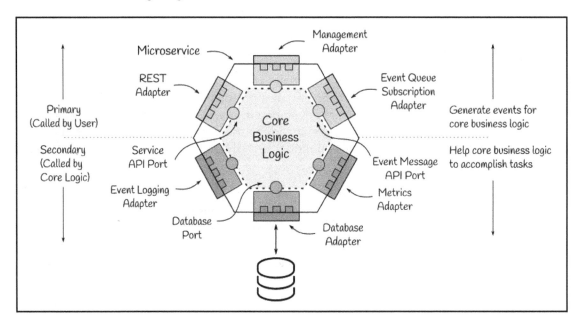

Based on their applicability and usage, the **REST adapter** and **database adapter** are often referred to as primary and secondary adapters respectively. Similarly, the **service API port** and **database port** are referred to as primary and secondary ports respectively. Primary ports are called by the primary adapters and they act as the main interface between the **core business logic** and its users, whereas secondary ports and secondary adapters are used by the **core business logic** to generate events or interact with external services, like a database. Primary adapters help validate service requests with respect to a service schema and call core business logic functions, whereas the **core business logic** calls the functions of secondary adapters to help translate the application schema to the external service schema, like that of a database. Primary adapters are initialized with the application, but references to the secondary adapters are passed to the **core business logic** via dependency injection.

 The name hexagonal architecture is derived from the structure of a component that has six ports, but that is not a rule. The idea of representing the architecture as a hexagon is just to remove the notion of one-dimensional layered architecture and have room to insert ports and adapters as required.

Messaging and contracts

In monolithic applications, messaging between components is mostly achieved using function calls, whereas for microservices, it is achieved using lightweight messaging systems, often HTTP(S). Using a lightweight messaging system is one of the most promising features of microservices and makes it easier to adopt and scale, as compared to **service-oriented architecture** (**SOA**) that uses a complex messaging system with multiple protocols. Microservices are more about keeping the endpoints smart and the communication channels as simple as possible.

In a microservices architecture, often multiple microservices need to interact with each other to achieve a particular task. These interactions can be either direct, via request-response-based (https://en.wikipedia.org/wiki/Request-response) communication, or through a lightweight **message-oriented middleware** (**MOM**) (https://en.wikipedia.org/wiki/Message-oriented_middleware). Direct messaging is synchronous, that is, the requester waits for the response to be returned, whereas a message-oriented middleware is primarily used for asynchronous communication.

Direct messaging

In direct messaging, each request is sent directly to the microservice on its API endpoint. Such requests may be initiated by users, applications, or by other microservices that integrate with the target microservice to complete a particular task. Mostly the endpoints to handle such requests are implemented using REST (`https://en.wikipedia.org/wiki/Representational_state_transfer`), which allows resource identifiers to be addressed directly via HTTP based APIs with a simple messaging style.

 REST is an architectural style with predefined operations based on HTTP request methods, such as `GET`, `PUT`, `POST`, and `DELETE`. The stateless nature of REST makes it fast, reliable, and scalable with multiple components.

For example, in a typical microservices-based e-commerce application, an administrative user may wish to create, update, or manage users via the User Service's REST endpoint. In that case, the user can directly call the REST API of the **User Service**, as shown in the following diagram:

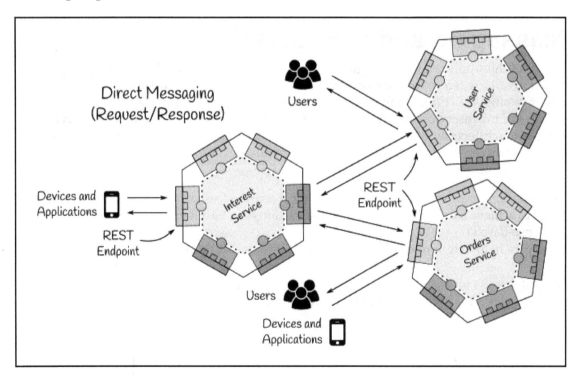

Similarly, a mobile application may want to query user interests via Interest Service's REST endpoint of the e-commerce application. Since the **Interest Service** depends on both the **User Service** and the **Orders Service**, it may further initiate two separate calls to the REST endpoint of these two services to get the desired response which it can merge with the user interests data and generate the response for the requesting application. Mostly, all these kinds of request-response are synchronous in nature as the sender expects a response with the results in the same call. Asynchronous requests are mostly used to send alerts or messages to record an operation, and in those cases, the sender doesn't wait for the response and expects the action to be taken eventually.

Avoid building long chains of synchronous calls as that may lead to high latency and an increased possibility of failure due to multiple hops of intermediate requests and network round-trips among the participating services.

Message formats used with REST endpoints are mostly text-based message formats such as JSON, XML, or HTML, as supported by the endpoint implementation. Binary message formats such as Thrift (https://en.wikipedia.org/wiki/Apache_Thrift), ProtoBuf (https://en.wikipedia.org/wiki/Protocol_Buffers), and Avro (https://avro.apache.org/) are also popular due to their wide support across multiple programming languages.

Use direct messaging only for smaller microservices-based deployments. For larger deployments, it is advisable to go with API gateways that act as the main entry point for all clients. Such API gateways help monitor requests for microservices and also assist in the maintenance and upgrade operations.

Observer model

The observer model uses a message broker (https://en.wikipedia.org/wiki/Message_broker) at its core to send messages among microservices. A message broker provides content and topic-based routing using the publish-subscribe pattern (https://en.wikipedia.org/wiki/Publish-subscribe_pattern), which makes the sender and receiver independent of each other. All observing microservices subscribe to one or more topics through which they can receive the messages and also connect to topics on which they can publish the messages for other observers. All interactions done via message brokers are asynchronous in nature and do not block the sender. This helps in scaling both the publishers and subscribers independently. A microservices architecture that is built on only asynchronous and non-blocking interactions using message broker scales very well.

Message brokers are also used to manage workloads in scenarios where the rate of published messages is higher than the rate at which the subscriber is able to process the messages. Message brokers also provide reliable storage, multiple delivery semantics (at least once, exactly once, and so on), and also transaction management that is useful for data management across microservices. Binary message formats such as Thrift, ProtoBuf, and Avro are preferred over text formats for message brokers.

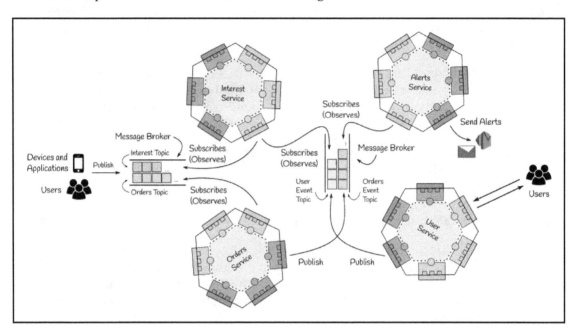

In the observer model, all the requests generated by users, applications, or microservices are published on a topic to which one or more microservices can subscribe and receive the message for processing, as shown in the preceding diagram. The generated results can also be written back to a topic that can be later picked by another microservice, which may either report the response back to the application or persist it within a data store. If a subscriber fails, the message broker can replay the message. Similarly, if all subscribers are busy, the message broker can accumulate the messages until they are processed by the subscribers.

The observer model helps to achieve better scalability as compared to direct messaging at the expense of a single point of failure of the message broker.

Service contracts

Contracts are required for entities to interact with each other. They define the message format and medium of communication for the participating entities. In a monolithic environment, it is simpler for components to interact with the target components using the interfaces and functions exposed by them. Since a function clearly defines its message format as input parameters, the message passing between the components can be done by just a function call with the required input parameters. Function calls are further simplified in a monolith due to a common underlying technology stack. Contracts are also easier to maintain for monolithic applications because any change done to the contract is tested and verified across components for compatibility. Such applications are also versioned as a whole and not per-component. The following table compares and contrasts monolithic and microservice architectural styles:

	Monolithic architecture	Microservices
Entity	Components	Services by capability
Endpoint	Interfaces and functions	REST URIs (HTTP)/Thrift/Avro/Protobuf
Medium	Function calls	HTTP/publish-subscribe via message broker (observer)
Contract	Function definition	API specification (Swagger, RAML)/message serialization (Thrift IDL, Avro Schema)
Version	Single version	Separate versions for each service
Technology	Single	Polyglot

As compared to a monolith, in a microservices-based environment, there is a service deployed for each business capability that may or may not be using the same technology stack. In such cases, service contracts become absolutely mandatory for microservices to understand the message formats and communication medium accepted by other microservices and interact with them. Moreover, these message formats need to be language-agnostic to allow any microservice to communicate irrespective of the technology stack in which they are implemented.

Microservices should never expose their internal data model directly as a part of a message contract to the external world. The internal data model must be decoupled from the external service contract and there should be a way to convert and validate the contract at entry and exit. This helps to evolve the data model of a microservice in isolation without affecting the contract with other microservices. If there is a change required in the service contract, it must be versioned and each version of the contract must be supported by the microservice as long as it is in use by any external service. A version should be discarded only when there are no other services using the obsolete version and there is no longer a need to roll back the service to its previous version.

 Avoid multiple versions of service contracts (and message formats) as much as possible. Choose a flexible message format that can evolve over time without breaking previous versions.

Microservices that expose REST APIs primarily use the REST API definition and HTTP verbs (`https://en.wikipedia.org/wiki/Hypertext_Transfer_Protocol#Request_methods`) to define well-formed URIs. Service contracts for REST-based APIs are defined using frameworks such as Swagger (`https://swagger.io/`) and RAML (`https://raml.org/`). Microservices that use the observer pattern tend to accept messages in Thrift, Avro, or ProtoBuf formats. Each of these frameworks has a way to define language-agnostic specifications and supports most of the popular programming languages.

Service discovery

All the APIs exposed by a microservice are accessible via the IP address and port of the host machine on which the microservice is deployed. Since microservices are deployed in a virtual machine or a container that has a dynamic IP, it is quite possible that the IPs and ports that are allocated to the microservice APIs may change over time. Therefore, IP addresses and ports of services should never be hardcoded by the depending microservice. Instead, there should be a common database of all the services that are active for the current application. Such a database of services is called the **service registry** in microservices architecture and is always kept up to date with the location of the microservices. It keeps the details of all the active microservices including their current IP address and port. Microservices then query this service registry to discover the current location of the required microservices and connect to them directly.

Service registry

The service registry acts as a database of microservices. It must have a dedicated static IP address or a fixed DNS name that must be accessible from all the clients, as shown in the following diagram. Since all the clients depend on a service registry to look up the target services, it also becomes a single point of failure for the entire microservices architecture. Therefore, the implementation of the service registry must be extremely lightweight and should support high availability by default. Some common tools that can be used as a service registry are Apache Zookeeper (`http://zookeeper.apache.org/`), etcd (`https://github.com/coreos/etcd`), and consul (`https://www.consul.io/`):

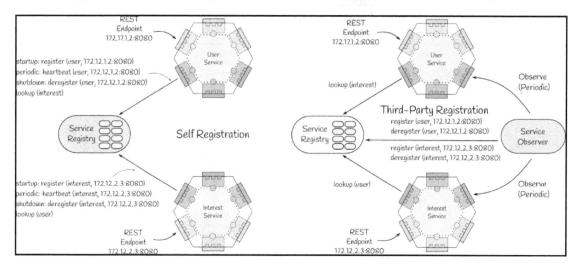

To keep the registry up to date, microservices should either implement the startup/shutdown event to register/deregister with the service registry themselves or there should be an external service configured to keep track of services and keep the registry up to date. Some orchestration tools, such as Kubernetes (`https://kubernetes.io/`), support service registry out of the box and maintain the registry for the entire infrastructure.

> Clients must cache the location of frequently used microservices to reduce dependency on the service registry, but the location must be synced periodically with the service registry for up-to-date information.

Service discovery patterns

Microservices-based applications may often scale to such a large number of services that it may not be feasible for each microservice to keep a track of all other active service locations. In such scenarios, the service registry helps in discovering microservices to perform a particular task. There are primarily two patterns for service discovery—client-side discovery and server-side discovery, as shown in the following diagram.

In the **client-side discovery** pattern, the responsibility for determining the location of services by querying the **service registry** is on the client. Therefore, the **service registry** must be accessible to the client to look up the location of the required services. Also, each client must have service discovery implementation built-in for this pattern to work.

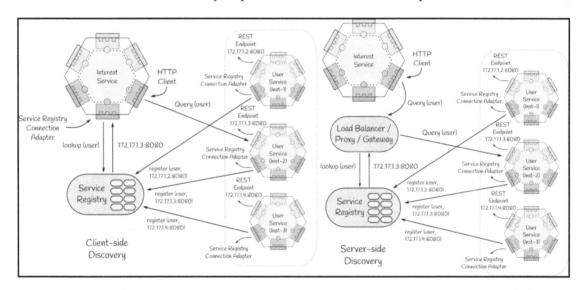

On the other hand, in the **server-side discovery** pattern, the responsibility for connecting with the **service registry** and looking up the location of services is of a router or a gateway that acts as a load balancer as well. Clients just need to send a request to a router and the router takes care of forwarding the request to the required service. Orchestration tools such as Kubernetes support server-side discovery using proxies.

The server-side discovery pattern must be preferred for a large-scale deployment. It can also be used as a circuit breaker to prevent resource exhaustion by controlling the number of open requests to a service that has encountered consecutive failures or is not available.

Data management

In a microservices-based architecture, the data model and schema must not be shared among bounded contexts. Each microservice must implement its own data model backed by a database that is accessible only through the service endpoints. Microservices may also publish events that can be considered as a log of the changes the service applies to its isolated database. Keeping application data up to date across microservices may also add to the network overhead and data duplication.

Direct lookup

Although microservices have their own isolated persistence, an application implemented using microservices may need to share data among a set of services to perform tasks. In a monolithic environment, since there is a common database, it is easier to share data and maintain consistency using transactions. In a microservices environment, it is not recommended to provide direct access to the database managed by a service, as shown in the following diagram:

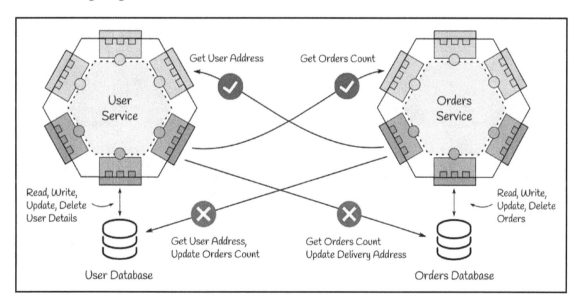

For example, when a user places a new order, the **Order Service** may need access to the delivery address; that is, the user address from the **User Service**. Similarly, once the order is placed, the **User Service** would like to update the total orders placed till date by the user in its database. Since the user database is maintained by the **User Service** and the **Orders Database** is maintained by the **Orders Service**, these two services will get the required details via the APIs exposed by the other service only. They should not be allowed to directly update or access databases maintained by another service. This helps in always maintaining a single copy of the user and order databases that is not accessible to any other microservice directly.

Asynchronous events

Getting data via service endpoints synchronously may become overwhelming for services that maintain a widely used database, like the users database. Therefore, it is recommended for services to maintain a read-only cache for such databases and keep it up to date asynchronously using events, as shown in the following diagram:

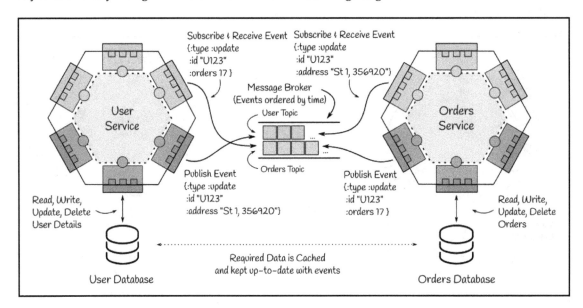

For example, instead of looking up the address or order count using service endpoints synchronously, services such as **User Service** and **Orders Service** can publish the events of interest on a message queue in order of occurrence. The **User Service** can then receive the orders event from the **Orders Service** via the **Message Broker** and update its database with the orders count or cache it. Similarly, the **Orders Service** can receive any address update event from the **User Service**, keep the address up to date for the user within its cache, and refer to it as and when required to generate orders for users.

> Microservices should always have an isolated database, but it is not recommended to create separate services to isolate immutable databases such as geolocations, PIN codes, domain knowledge, and so on. Since these database do not change that often, it is fair enough to share and cache these across microservices.

Combining data

In a monolithic environment, combining data is easy; you need to just join two tables to create the required view. In microservices, datasets are distributed across microservices and combining them requires moving the data across microservices, which may involve significant network and storage overhead. It also becomes challenging to keep the combined data up to date. There are multiple ways to solve the problem of combining data or joins in a microservices architecture based on the scope of the request.

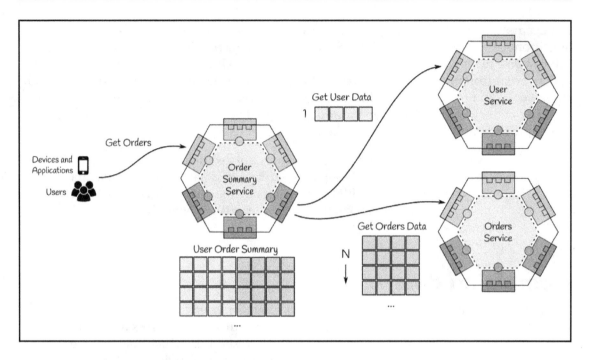

For example, if you wish to build an order summary page for a particular user, you need to get only that user's data from the **User Service** and all the orders for that user from the **Orders Service**. These can be obtained independently and joined at the requesting service level to generate the order summary, as shown in the preceding diagram. These kinds of join work well for 1:*N* joins.

Real-time joins work well for limited datasets, but it is expensive to combine data in real time for each request. Imagine tens of thousands of similar requests hitting the **Order Summary Service** every second. In such scenarios, services should instead keep denormalized (https://en.wikipedia.org/wiki/Denormalization) combined data in a cache that is kept up to date using the events generated by the source services. The service can then respond to the requests by just looking up this denormalized data cache in real time. This approach scales well at the expense of data being near real time. The data in the cache might be off by the time source service generates the event and target service picks it up and makes changes to its cache.

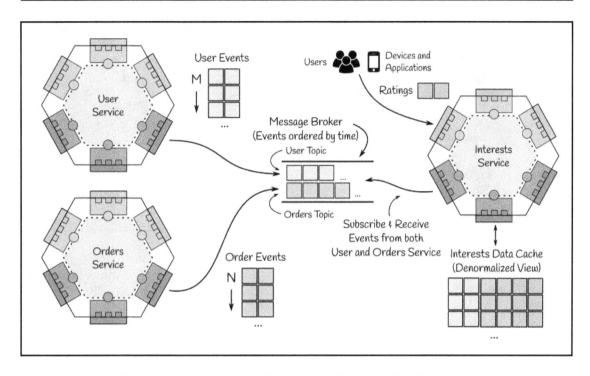

For example, as shown in the preceding diagram, an **Interest Service** may receive user interests via its API endpoint, but it may need the user and order details from the **User** and **Orders** services respectively. Instead of directly looking up details for each user interest, the **Interest Service** may subscribe to the events generated by the user and orders service and internally keep a denormalized cache view of interest data that is readily available with all the required details of users and orders.

Transactions

Each microservice can use a database of its choice. The chosen databases may or may not have the ACID property (https://en.wikipedia.org/wiki/ACID) and support transactions. This is one of the reasons why distributed transactions are hard to implement with microservices. However, business transactions involving changes across multiple business entities cannot be omitted entirely, and therefore microservices implement distributed transactions by using data workflows, as shown in the following diagram:

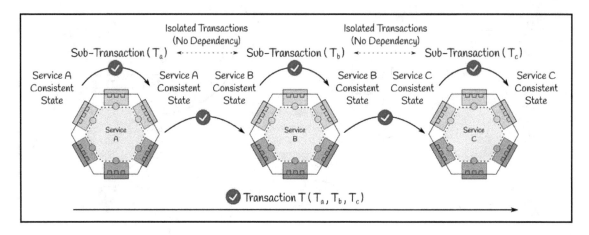

Microservices publish events whenever they make a change to the database. The events contain the type of change along with immutable data about the business entities that were affected by this change. Other services then listen to these events asynchronously and perform the changes strictly in the order in which events were published. A single transaction may contain one or more events that may result in cascading events generated by the microservices that are affected by it. Due to the asynchronous nature of the event flow, the consistency achieved across microservices in this case is eventual (`https://en.wikipedia.org/wiki/Eventual_consistency`).

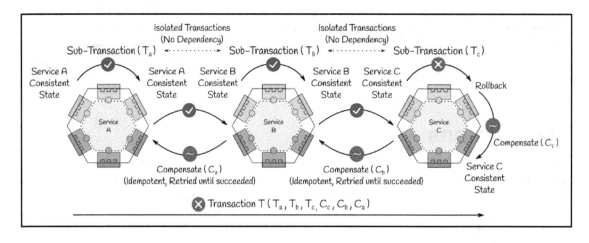

If a transaction fails, the service that encounters the failure generates compensatory events to nullify the changes made across microservices that have already processed the transaction events in the chain. The compensatory events flow backwards towards the origin of the transaction, as shown in the preceding diagram. Compensatory events are idempotent in nature and retried until they succeed.

 The transaction pattern for microservices is inspired by *Sagas* (`http://www.cs.cornell.edu/andru/cs711/2002fa/reading/sagas.pdf`) and was proposed by *Hector Garcia-Molina* and *Kenneth Salem*, as published in an ACM paper in 1987. *Sagas* may be implemented as a set of workflows, where at each step of failure a compensating action is triggered to bring the system back to its original state as it was before the workflow was triggered.

Automated continuous deployment

The core philosophy of a microservice environment must be based on the *You build it, you run it* (`https://queue.acm.org/detail.cfm?id=1142065`) model; that is, the team working on the microservice must own it end to end, right from development to deployment. The infrastructure required for the team to integrate, test, and deploy any changes must be completely automated. This makes it possible to build a continuous integration and **continuous delivery** (**CD**) pipeline, which is the backbone of microservices-based architectures.

CI/CD

The term CI/CD combines the practices of CI and CD together as a seamless process. In a typical microservices-based setup, the team continuously works on enhancing the features of the microservice and fixing the issues that are encountered in production.

The entire cycle from development to deployment has three major phases, as shown in the following diagram:

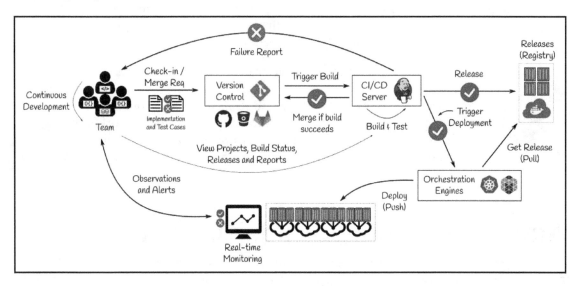

In the first phase, the team commits the changes to a version control repository. The version control repository used for microservices should be common for all the services and applications. Consolidating all the implementations in a single version control system helps in automation and running application-wide integration and acceptance tests. Some version control services also support a fine-grained collaboration system that allows the developers to not only share their changes with a group of developers, but also have active reviews and a feedback system within the team before the changes are committed.

 Version control systems like Git are ideal for a distributed team working on multiple microservices due to its inherent features. Service like GitHub and Bitbucket are some cloud hosting providers for Git that also have the capability to build triggers for CI/CD systems.

In the second phase, a CI/CD system such as Jenkins is used to build the changes and run the unit tests for the microservice for which the change is committed. Running the tests for each change request helps in detecting issues before the changes are integrated with the rest of the application. It also helps to detect any regressions (https://en.wikipedia.org/wiki/Software_regression) that might have been introduced due to the recent changes. If there are any test failures, an alert is sent back to the team, especially the committer who submitted the change request.

The team then fixes the tests and sends the change request again to the version control system that in-turn triggers the build to retest the changes. This process repeats until all the tests succeed. Once the tests succeed, the CI/CD system merges the changes with the mainline and prepares a release artifact for the service. Artifacts for microservices are often packaged as containers that are readily deployable by orchestration tools. Packaging microservices in a container also helps in automating the deployment and scaling of the services on-demand.

 Docker is one preferred technology for packaging microservices. It has seamless integration with multiple orchestration tools such as Kubernetes and Mesos (`http://mesos.apache.org/`).

In the third phase, the CI/CD system publishes the releases to a central repository and instructs the orchestration tools to pick the latest version of the microservice that contains the recent changes. The orchestration engine then pulls the latest release from the repository and deploys it in production. All the instances in production are monitored by automated tools that generate alerts for the team if there are any issues. If there are any issues encountered by the team, the team fixes the issues and submits the change request to the version control system that triggers the build and the entire process repeats to push the changes to production.

 Generally, the orchestration engine does a rolling upgrade of the service while deploying updates, but some teams prefer to do the A/B testing by upgrading only a subset of deployed service instances and roll-out only when the tests succeed for that subset. Such deployments are often referred to as BlueGreenDeployment (`https://martinfowler.com/bliki/BlueGreenDeployment.html`).

Such an automated environment helps the team cut short the entire development-to-deployment cycle from months to days and days to hours. Large companies such as Google, Facebook, Netflix, Amazon, and so on are now able to push multiple releases in a day due to such automated environments and robust testing processes.

Scaling

The Art of Scalability (http://theartofscalability.com/) book uses a *scale cube* model to describe three primary scaling patterns for an application, as shown in the following diagram. The *x*-axis of the cube represents horizontal scaling; that is, deploying the same instance of the application by just cloning them and front-ending by a load balancer to distribute the load evenly among the instances. This scaling pattern is quite common for handling a high number of service requests. The *z*-axis of the cube addresses scaling by data partitioning. In this case, each application instance deals with only a subset of data. This scaling pattern is particularly useful for applications where the persistence layer becomes a bottleneck:

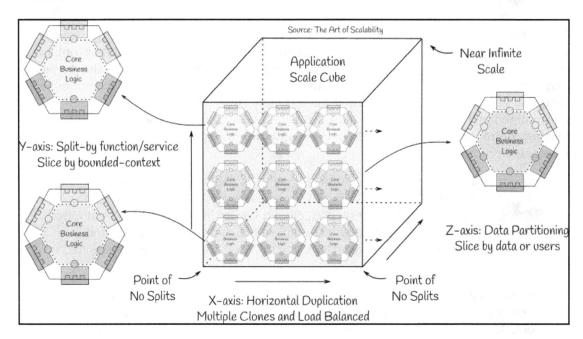

The *y*-axis of the cube addresses scaling by splitting the application by function or service. This pattern relates directly to the microservices pattern. The face of the cube created using the *xy*-axis combines the best practices of scaling for microservices-based architecture. Microservices are identified by splitting an application by bounded contexts (*y*-axis) and scaled by cloning each instance (*x*-axis). For microservices, cloning is done by deploying multiple instances of a service container.

Summary

In this chapter, we learned about domain-driven design and the importance of identifying the right bounded context for microservices. We learned about the hexagonal architecture for microservices and various messaging patterns. We also discussed data management patterns for microservices and how to set up service registries to discover microservices. We concluded with the importance of automating the entire microservice deployment cycle including testing, deployment, and scaling. In the next chapter, we will introduce a real-life use case for microservices and learn how to design an application using the concepts learned in this chapter.

3
Microservices for Helping Hands Application

"We learn by example and by direct experience because there are real limits to the adequacy of verbal instruction."

- Malcolm Gladwell, Blink: The Power of Thinking Without Thinking

Microservices are gaining popularity for internet-scale applications that target consumers. In this chapter, you will learn how to apply principles of microservices architecture to design a similar, internet-scale, fictitious application called **Helping Hands** that connects household service providers with consumers of services such as home cleaning, appliance repair, pest control, and so on. In this chapter, you will:

- Learn how to gather requirements and capture user stories to design the Helping Hands application
- Learn the importance of monolithic-first design
- Learn how to move towards a microservices-based design
- Learn how to use event-driven architecture with microservices

Design

One of the best ways to design a software system is to capture the business domain, its users, and their interaction with the system as a user story (https://en.wikipedia.org/wiki/User_story). User stories are an informal way of capturing the requirements of a software system. In user stories, the focus is on the end users and the interactions that are possible between the users and the system.

Users and entities

The first step in writing user stories for the Helping Hands application is to understand the users and entities of the system. Primarily, there are two users of the system—**Service Consumers** and **Service Providers**, as shown in the following diagram. **Service Consumers** subscribe to one or more services provided by the **Service Providers**. The core entity of the application is the service. A service is an intangible, temporal, and limited asset that providers own and provide to the consumers on-demand at a price.

Service Providers register one or more services with the system that can be subscribed to by the consumers. All services are registered with available time slots and the duration for which they can be offered. Each service duration and time slot has an associated price that the **Service Consumer** has to pay to make use of the service. **Service Providers** are also responsible for maintaining the availability status of the services with the system. **Service Consumers** can search for services available from a set of providers and can pick a provider of their choice. Once chosen, the **Service Consumer** can schedule a service from the **Service Provider** based on availability.

User stories

The next step is to list the user stories that will be supported by the Helping Hands application. Here are the user stories for the application:

- As a *Service Consumer*, I can create an account so that I can search for services and book them
- As a *Service Consumer*, I can search for required services so that I can book one for my task
- As a *Service Consumer*, I can subscribe to one or more services so that I can get my task done on a regular basis
- As a *Service Consumer*, I would like to rate the services offered so that others can benefit from the feedback and choose the best services offered for a particular task
- As a *Service Consumer*, I want to get notifications so that I can get reminded of the service schedule
- As a *Service Provider*, I can create an account so that I can register one or more services for consumers
- As a *Service Provider*, I want to register one or more services so that I can get service requests
- As a *Service Provider*, I want to specify the service location area so that I can get only service requests that are near to my place
- As a *Service Provider*, I want to specify the price and availability so that I can get only service requests that are feasible to serve and the ones I am interested in
- As a *Service Provider*, I want to get notifications when a service request is placed so that I can attend to it

Apart from user stories, there are some non-functional requirements (https://en.wikipedia.org/wiki/Non-functional_requirement) as well that must be addressed by the Helping Hands application:

- All the implementations must be tracked and versioned in a revision control system. The Helping Hands application will use the external hosting service GitHub to track the code base.
- All the dependencies must be explicitly declared. The Helping Hands application will be implemented using Clojure (https://clojure.org/) with Leiningen (https://leiningen.org/) for dependency management.
- All services must have authentication and authorization built in.
- Configurations must be specified externally and not hardcoded in the application.
- All events must be logged to understand the state of the application and monitor it in production.

Non-functional requirements are a part of twelve-factor methodology (https://12factor.net/), which covers twelve different aspects that must be addressed by the application. *Part-3* and *Part-4* of this book address some of these important aspects for the Helping Hands application in detail.

Domain model

Based on the user stories, **Service Order** and **Service** (catalog) are the two core domains of the Helping Hands application. Apart from these two domains, user accounts, provider accounts, and notifications are the generic domains that form the Helping Hands application. **Service Consumer**, **Service Provider**, **Service**, and **Service Order** are entities of the Helping Hands application. These are shown along with their fields in the following diagram:

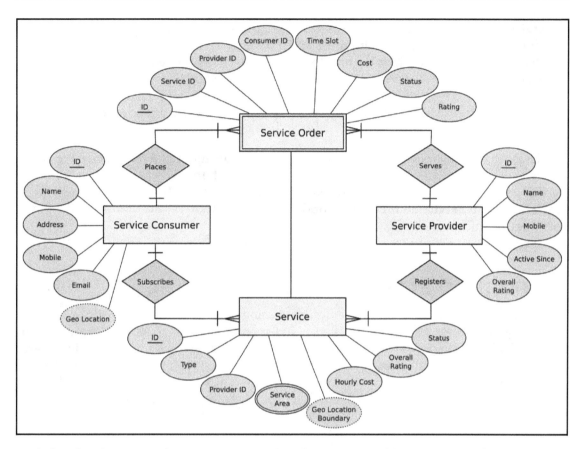

Each **Service Consumer** has an **ID** assigned in the system and has **Name**, **Address**, **Mobile**, and **Email** defined as some of the attributes. The **Geo Location** of each consumer is derived from the address information. Each **Service Provider** also has an **ID** assigned in the system with **Name**, **Mobile**, **Active Since**, and **Overall Rating** as some of the attributes. A **Service** is registered by the **Service Provider** and has a unique **ID** defined in the system. It is registered against a **Service Type** and has one or more **Service Areas** defined. Based on the **Service Areas**, the system derives the **Geo Location Boundary** where the service is offered to the consumers. A **Service** also has an **Hourly Cost** set by the **Service Provider** and keeps an **Overall Rating** based on the previous orders.

A **Service Consumer** subscribes to the **Service** and places a **Service Order** for the **Service Provider** to fulfill. Each **Service Order** has an **ID** defined in the system and has an associated **Service ID**, **Provider ID**, and **Consumer ID**. Each order entry has an associated **Time Slot** based on which the **Cost** is determined by the system. The **Service Order** also has a status that is updated by the **Service Provider** once the order is completed. The order also keeps a **Rating** between 1 and 5, as rated by the consumer for the service provided.

The Helping Hands application also alerts the **Service Consumer** and the **Service Provider** with respect to the related **Service Order**. Any change in **Status** is notified to both the participants via SMS sent over the registered mobile number. The **Service Consumer** can also subscribe to **Service** and receive all updates with respect to service status, availability, cost changes, and so on.

Monolithic architecture

The Helping Hands application can be designed using a three-layered architecture of presentation, business logic, and persistence. Based on the domain model, there can be four main tables in the Helping Hands application database corresponding to each entity. There will be a single database that will store all the data in the designated table. The database must be accessible to all the components of the system. The business logic layer will have well-defined components based on the principle of **Separation of Concerns** (**SoC**). Components will address all user stories for the Helping Hands application.

Application components

To address the user stories, there will be three main components and two helper components, as shown in the following diagram. The **Registration Component** will manage all the user accounts and related CRUD operations. The **Service Component** will handle all service-related operations such as create, update, and lookup. The **Order Component** will help place the orders, search for the historical order, and also rate the services. It will also help to maintain a status for the service order and generate relevant alerts in the form of SMS and email using an external service:

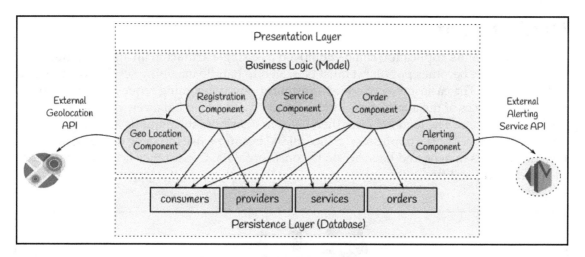

There will be two helper components—**Geo Location** and **Alerting**. These components will help connect the application to external services to get geolocation tags and send alerts in the form of SMS and email via provided APIs. Components, their responsibilities, and related databases are summarized in the following table:

Component	Responsibilities	Component	Database
Registration Component	• Create/update/delete account for service consumers • Create/update/delete account for service providers	• *Geo Location Component* to get the longitude and latitude based on the address	• Consumers • Providers
Service Component	• Create/update/delete services • Search for services by keywords, types, location, and so on	• *Geo Location Component* to get the longitude and latitude based on service area	• Services • Consumers (to support search by location) • Providers
Order Component	• Create/update orders • Search for orders by keywords, types, timespan	• *Alerting Component* to generate alerts with respect to orders	• Orders • Consumers • Providers • Services
Geo Location Component	• Lookup longitude and latitude by address	• *External Service* (API)	-
Alerting Component	• Send email and SMS alerts	• *External Service* (API)	-

Components such as authentication and users such as administrators and so on have been intentionally omitted from the explanation to focus only on the core components and features of the application.

Deployment

The Helping Hands application can be deployed as a single artifact in an application server. Once the service becomes popular it must be scaled to handle incoming service lookups and order requests. The easiest way to scale the application for incoming requests is to deploy multiple instances of the application and frontend it with a load balancer, as shown in the following diagram. The load balancer then helps to distribute the requests among the deployed instances of the application. Since all the instances use the same database, all of them are always in-sync and have access to consistent data. Consistency is achieved due to the inherent capabilities of the database used for the application; it supports ACID transactions:

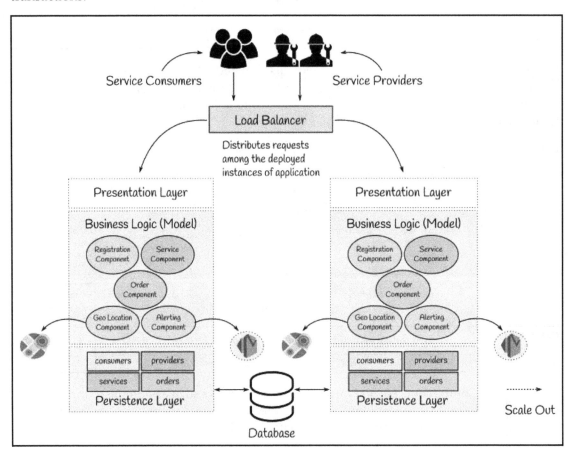

Limitations

Although a monolithic architecture for the Helping Hands application fulfills the purpose, it has some inherent limitations. There is a high coupling of the components with the *consumers* and *providers* table. Any change in these two tables will affect almost all the components of the system and will require redeployment of the entire application.

The Helping Hands application also depends on two external services. Suppose one of these services shuts down or there is a requirement to move to a better service; the corresponding geolocation or alerting component will be changed and will result in the redeployment of all the instances of the application, even though there was no change in the core functionality and services of the application. This adds to the deployment overhead for simple changes as well.

Since the entire application is deployed as a single artifact, scaling an application scales all the components of the application equally. For example, to scale with incoming order and service lookup requests, the *Registration Component* is unnecessarily scaled with the order and service components. This also increases the load on the database that is handling all the incoming requests from the components. Often, requests from one component can affect the database performance for other components as well and reduce the performance of the entire application.

Another limitation of the current monolithic architecture of the Helping Hands application is its dependency on a single database technology. In practice, a fuzzy search for services using tags and lookup using geolocations can be supported better by databases such as Elasticsearch (`https://www.elastic.co/products/elasticsearch`) as compared to relational databases such as MySQL (`https://www.mysql.com/`). Relational databases are better suited for transactional operations such as creating service orders and maintaining user accounts. With the current architecture, there is only one database technology, and that affects the efficiency of the application and makes it less flexible.

Moving to microservices

The limitations of a monolithic architecture for Helping Hands can be addressed by separating out the components along with the database as a microservice. These services can then make informed choices about the technology stack and database that suit them well. These services can be developed, changed, and deployed in isolation as per the concepts of a microservices-based architecture. To identify the bounded context for the components of an existing monolithic application, it is recommended to look at the database access pattern and related business logic first, isolate them, and then look at the possibilities to isolate the components further based on business capabilities.

Isolating services by persistence

In the existing monolithic application of Helping Hands, the *consumers* and *providers* database tables are accessed by all the core components of the system, as shown in the following diagram. These tables are prime candidates for being wrapped around a service and isolated in a separate database that is accessible only to the corresponding service directly. All other services must talk to the **Service Consumer** service and the **Service Provider** service for any details instead of directly accessing the **consumers** and **providers** databases.

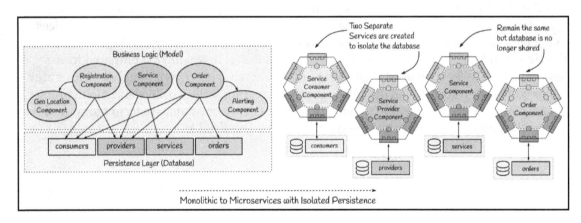

Monolithic to Microservices with Isolated Persistence

Since there is a separate service created to handle the requests for **consumers** and **providers**, there is no need to have a service corresponding to the **Registration Component**. The **Service Consumer** service and **Service Provider** service can now handle all the requests to register, modify, or delete consumers and providers, respectively. Similarly, the service and order services can now handle all the requests related to services and orders, respectively, by isolating the corresponding databases. The **order** service can now talk to **Service Consumer**, **Service Provider**, and **Service** to get the required details for the order.

The Helping Hands application will be using a combination of the Datomic (`http://www.datomic.com/`) and Elasticsearch (`https://www.elastic.co/products/elasticsearch`) databases for various microservices. *Part-3* of this book discusses the persistence layer in detail, and the last chapter of *Part-2* introduces Datomic.

Isolating services by business logic

Once persistence-based services are isolated, the next step is to evaluate existing components for microservices with respect to business logic. Apart from dropping the *Registration Component* in favor of separate services for consumer and provider, a new service called lookup can be created to consolidate all the search operations into one service and allow users to search across application entities, as shown in the following diagram. Since databases of consumers, providers, services, and orders cannot be shared with lookup services, it can keep a denormalized (`https://en.wikipedia.org/wiki/Denormalization`) view of these databases containing only the fields that need to be searched.

Geolocation-based queries will also be limited to lookup services, so there is no need to maintain a separate geolocation service; instead, the **Lookup Service** itself can query for the geolocation.

Since geolocations rarely change, the **Lookup Service** can cache them and maintain a database of well-known and already queried geolocations as well for better performance.

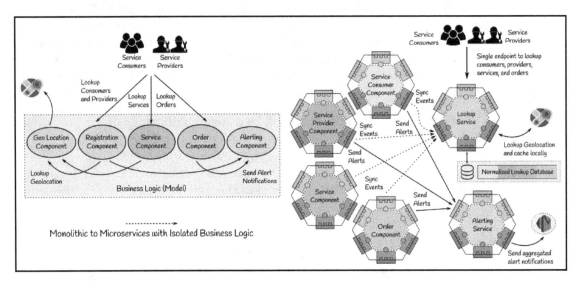

The **Alerting Component** can be isolated as a separate service as it will be required by multiple services, including **Order**, **Service Consumer**, and **Service Provider**, to send alerts to the users. Alerts may be sent via SMS or email, and the **Alerting Service** can use external services to send the alerts. Since alerts must not be overwhelming for users, the *Alerting Service* can group by user all the alerts that are requested in a short period of time and send them as a single notification message.

Do not attempt to aggressively start disintegrating your components into microservices. Focus on the business capabilities and not on features and use cases. For example, instead of creating a separate service for sending emails and sending SMS, it is recommended to create a single *Alerting Service* with both capabilities.

Messaging and events

The next step for the Helping Hands application is to define the interactions between the identified microservices. Microservices can either interact by directly sending the messages to other service endpoints synchronously or they can subscribe to the events generated by other microservices and receive the messages asynchronously. Asynchronous messages rely on the underlying message broker and its durability. Message brokers not only help to scale the application by holding the messages yet to be processed in the queue, but also support durable deliveries. Even if a service fails, it can be restored and allowed to start processing pending messages from the point where it left off. Combining both synchronous and asynchronous message patterns for the Helping Hands application gives us a flexible and performant architecture to accomplish a given task, as shown in the following diagram:

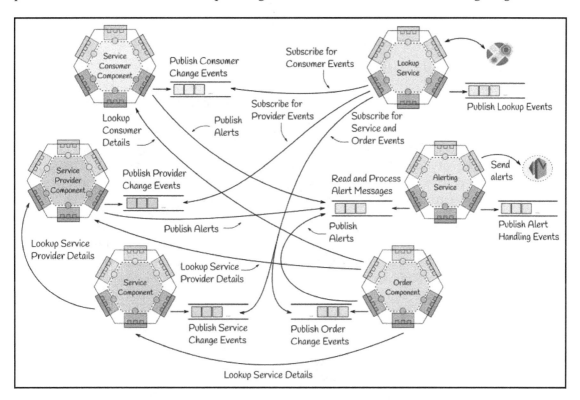

All the services of the Helping Hands application must publish change log events related to the business entities on a message queue that can be read by any service that subscribes to it. The published events must be retained by the message queue for a configured amount of time, beyond which the events may be discarded. For example, all the core services—**Service Consumer**, **Service Provider**, **Service**, and **Order**—publish events on their designated message queues at the allocated topic.

The **Lookup Service** must subscribe to all the events published by the **Consumer**, **Provider**, **Service**, and **Order** services to maintain a local denormalized database to support search queries. It must add geolocation details by querying the external service and caching the results locally. Any changes done to the *consumers*, *providers*, *services*, and *orders* databases must be communicated to the **Lookup Service** via events, asynchronously. The **Lookup Service** may also publish events to its designated message queue for other services to consume. These events are often useful to analyze the number of search queries received, trending services, and so on.

Services such as **Alerting** are best suited for such asynchronous messages. The **Alerting Service** should not only rely on the message broker for various delivery semantics, such as at-least or exactly-once delivery but must also read batches of alerts, combine alerts for the same user and send them as a single consolidated alert.

Services such as **Order Service** may also rely on direct messages to retrieve details of the consumer, provider, and the service before registering an order for the user. Once the order is registered, a change log event must be published by the **Order Service** for the **Lookup Service** to make the order available to be searched.

> Event logs are also useful to set up a deep monitoring and reporting infrastructure for microservices. *Part-4* of this book describes the monitoring and reporting pattern for the microservices architecture that is based on event logs.

Extensibility

A microservices-based architecture for the Helping Hands application not only makes it easier to deploy and scale but also makes it highly extensible. For example, by deploying a separate *Lookup Service* for search operations, it is now possible to use a database such as Elasticsearch only for search operations and Datomic for all other microservices that require consistent transactions.

In the future, if there is a better technology available, it will be easier to deploy services with a newer technology. Newer technology may also come with hardware challenges. For example, a database such as MapD (`https://www.mapd.com/`) runs on GPUs (`https://en.wikipedia.org/wiki/Graphics_processing_unit`). To use such databases, microservices need to run on specialized hardware. Since microservices can be deployed in isolation on the same or an entirely separate machine, it is possible to deploy services that need GPUs on machines that support GPUs without affecting the way they interact with other services. This is one of the advantages of microservices—you are not bound by the technology or underlying hardware and any changes done are localized within the bounded context of the service.

Data analytics is now an integral part of any web-based application. It not only helps us understand the usage patterns of the application, but also helps provide better services to the users. By generating event logs for all the changes done to entities, it is also possible to further extend the Helping Hands application to analyze usage patterns. For example, one can listen to events generated by the *Order Service* and study service usage patterns by demography. It should also be possible to analyze the popularity of services by location and provide customized offers to users as notifications.

Workflows for Helping Hands

Data workflows are the backbone of any microservices-based architecture. They define the sequence of messages and events that are generated among the services to accomplish a desired task. A workflow may consist of both synchronous and asynchronous messages.

Workflows shown in this section are only for explanatory purposes and do not conform to the exact semantics of sequence diagrams (`https://en.wikipedia.org/wiki/Sequence_diagram`). Details of authentication, authorization, validation, and error conditions have been omitted intentionally.

Service provider workflow

The service provider workflow consists of **Service Provider, Lookup Service**, and **Alerting Service**. The **Service Provider Component** exposes endpoints for users to create and update service providers for the Helping Hands application, as shown in the following diagram:

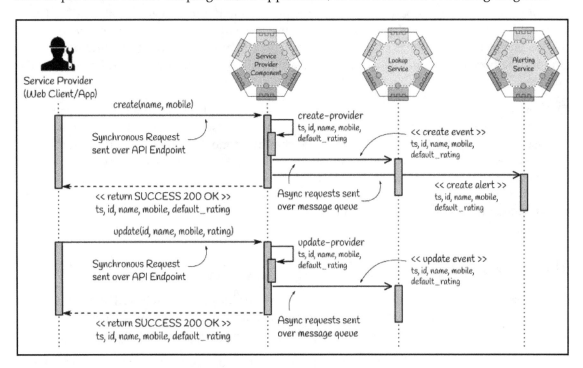

For the **create** operation, the **Service Provider** service first validates the input request for the required parameters and privileges, then starts a transaction to add a new service provider within the system. A new ID for the service provider is automatically generated by the **Service Provider**. Once the transaction is successful, it emits a **create event** on its event log queue for the **Lookup Service** and other subscribers to pick up, and publishes a **create alert** on the message queue of the **Alerting Service** for it to pick and send an alert to the interested users.

To update the service providers, the user sends the update request to the **Service Provider** and it initiates a new transaction to update its local database. Once the transaction is successful, it emits an **update event** on its event log queue for the **Lookup Service** to pick-up. Update operations are not sent as alerts or notifications to users. If this is a requirement, it can be enabled by publishing a message for the **Alerting Service** on its request queue.

Service workflow

The service workflow describes the message interaction among the **Service Component**, **Service Provider**, **Lookup Service**, and **Alerting Service**, as shown in the following diagram. The service exposes endpoints for users to create and update services for the Helping Hands application. Each service must have a service provider already defined for the application:

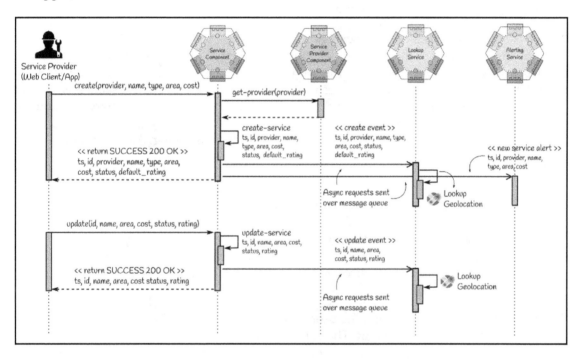

To create a new service, the user calls the API endpoint for **Service** with the required parameters. The provider ID must be specified to create a new service. Once the **Service Component** receives the request, it first sends a direct message to the **Service Provider** to validate the specified provider ID and make sure that the provider is already registered. If the provider is already registered, the Service Provider returns the provider details synchronously to the Service.

Once the provider is validated, the **Service Component** starts a transaction to add a new service into its local database. A new ID for the service is automatically generated by the **Service Component**. Once the transaction is successful, the **Service Component** emits a **create event** on its event log queue for the **Lookup Service** and other subscribers to pick up. The **Lookup Service** pulls the **create event**, looks up the geolocation corresponding to the service areas, and updates the service details in its local denormalized database. The **Service Component** also publishes a **new service alert** on the message queue of the **Alerting Service** to send an alert to the interested users.

To update the service details, the user sends an update request to the **Service Component** with the service ID. Since the update operation is performed only for existing services, the service provider is not validated in this case. The **Service Component** initiates a transaction to update the service details and updates the specified fields. Once the transaction is successful, it emits an **update event** on the event log queue for the **Lookup Service** to pick up. The **Lookup Service** then updates the local database with the changes and also updates the geolocations for the service areas if they are part of the changelog. Alerts are not sent for service updates.

Service consumer workflow

The service consumer workflow describes the message interaction among the *Service Consumer*, *Lookup*, and *Alerting Service*. The *Service Consumer* component exposes endpoints for users to create and update service consumers for the Helping Hands application, as shown in the following diagram.

To create a new service consumer, the user sends a request with valid parameters to the **Service Consumer Component**. The component then validates the request and if the request is valid, it starts a transaction to add a new consumer to the application. For each new consumer, an ID is automatically generated by **Service Consumer Component**.

Once the transaction is successful, the **Service Consumer Component** emits a **create event** on its event log queue for the **Lookup Service** and other subscribers to pick up. After receiving the **create event**, the **Lookup Service** looks up the geolocation corresponding to the address of the consumer and then stores the consumer details along with the geolocation in its local denormalized database. The **Service Consumer** component also publishes a **new consumer alert** on the message queue of the **Alerting Service** to send an alert to interested users:

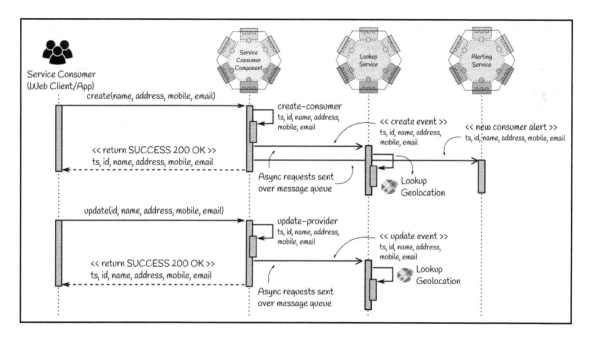

To update the consumer details, the user sends the update request to the **Service Consumer Component** along with the consumer ID. The **Service Consumer Component** initiates a transaction to update the consumer details and updates the specified fields. Once the transaction is successful, it emits an **update event** on the event log queue for the **Lookup Service** to pick up. The **Lookup Service** then updates the local database with the changes and also updates the geolocation for the consumer address if it is a part of the changelog. Alerts are not sent for consumer updates.

Order workflow

The order workflow involves most of the services in the Helping Hands application. The **Order Service** receives the request from the consumer to create a new order for the chosen service. The consumer sends the create request to the **Order Service** with the provider and service details along with the time slot. The **Order Service** then validates the order details by sending a direct synchronous request to the **Service Consumer, Service Provider**, and **Service**. If the details are valid, that is, the service is already registered by the specified provider and the consumer is a valid user in the system, then the **Order Service** sends a direct synchronous request to the **Lookup Service** to make sure that the service is available in the vicinity of the consumer location based on the geolocation of the consumer address and the service area.

If the service is feasible for the consumer address, the **Order Service** starts a transaction and creates a new order in the system, as shown in the following diagram:

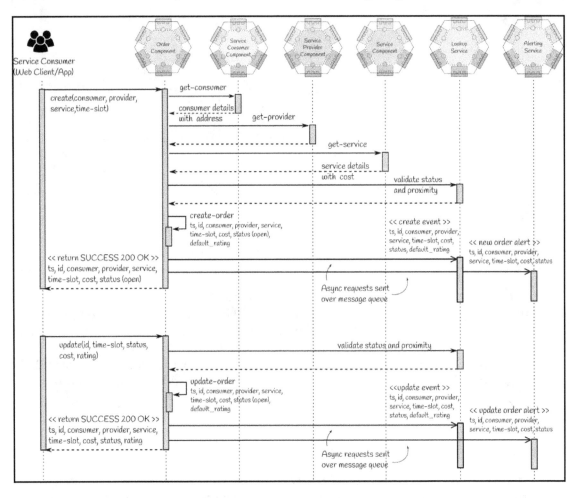

Once the transaction is successful, the **Order Service** emits a **create event** on its event log queue for the **Lookup Service**; it receives the events, updates the order list within its local database, and makes it available for users to search. The **Order Service** also publishes a **new order alert** on the message queue of the **Alerting Service** to send an alert to both the consumer and the provider of the service.

To update the order time slot, status, or rating, the user sends an update request to the **Order Service**. Since an update message requires an existing order ID, the **Order Service** does not validate the provider and consumer for the request, it just makes sure that it is an existing order. In addition to validating an existing order, the **Order Service** also sends a direct synchronous request to the **Lookup Service** to make sure that the requested time slot and service are still available for the consumer. If they are available, then the **Order Service** starts a transaction and updates its local database. Once the transaction is successful, it emits the **update event** on its event log queue for the **Lookup Service** and also sends an alert to the **Alerting Service** by publishing an **update order alert**. Any change made to the order is sent as an alert to both the consumer and provider of the service order.

 In practice, there will be separate services and workflows for authentication and authorization. Those workflows have been intentionally omitted from this chapter to focus only on the core services and workflows. *Part-4* of this book describes authentication and authorization services patterns in detail.

Summary

In this chapter, we designed an application called Helping Hands, using the best software engineering practices. We started with a monolithic architecture and argued why a microservices-based architecture is well suited for the Helping Hands application. In the next part of this book, we will first take a look at the basic development tools and libraries that we will be using to build our Helping Hands application.

4

Development Environment

"The mechanic that would perfect his work must first sharpen his tools."

- Confucius

The development environment consists of tools and libraries that are useful to implement, debug, and make changes to software systems. The efficiency of a development team is highly dependent on the development environment and technology stack at hand. In this chapter, you will learn how to set up a development environment for microservices using the Clojure ecosystem. This chapter will help you to:

- Learn the history of Clojure and functional programming
- Learn the importance of REPL
- Learn how to build your application using Clojure build tools
- Learn about well known **integrated development environments (IDEs)**

Clojure and REPL

Clojure (https://clojure.org/) is a dialect of the Lisp (https://en.wikipedia.org/wiki/Lisp_(programming_language)) programming language and primarily runs on a **Java virtual machine (JVM)**. The other target implementations include ClojureCLR (https://github.com/clojure/clojure-clr), which runs on **Common Language Runtime (CLR)**, and ClojureScript, which compiles to JavaScript. Although Clojure uses a JVM as its underlying runtime engine, it emphasizes a functional programming language with immutability at its core. All data structures of Clojure are immutable. Since Clojure is a dialect of Lisp, it also treats code as data and is known to be homoiconic. Its syntax is built on S-expressions (https://en.wikipedia.org/wiki/S-expression) that are first parsed as a data structure and then translated into constructs of the Java programming language before being compiled into Java bytecode. Clojure also supports metaprogramming with macro (https://en.wikipedia.org/wiki/Macro_(computer_science)).

 Clojure integrates well with existing Java applications due to its primary support for underlying JVMs and its entire ecosystem. All existing libraries that run on a JVM integrate seamlessly with Clojure, including Maven, Java's build system.

History of Clojure

Clojure is a functional programming language that treats functions as first-class objects; that is, it supports passing functions as arguments to other functions and also returning them as values from other functions. It also supports anonymous functions, assigning functions to variables and storing them in data structures.

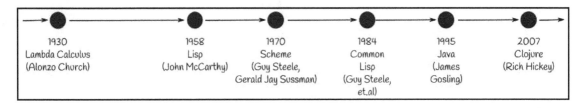

The timeline in the preceding diagram shows the evolution of functional programming that led to the development of Clojure. The concept of functional programming originated from a formal system called Lambda calculus that was introduced by Alonzo Church (https://en.wikipedia.org/wiki/Alonzo_Church) in 1930. Church proposed a universal model of computation that was based on function abstraction and its application using variable binding and substitution. Church's model laid the foundation of functional programming languages that are known today, including Clojure.

Almost three decades later in 1958, John McCarthy (https://en.wikipedia.org/wiki/John_McCarthy_(computer_scientist)) introduced the Lisp programming language, which was highly influenced by the notations of Lambda calculus. It was distinctive due to its fully parenthesized prefix notation. Its source code was made of lists, hence the name *LIS$_t$ P$_{rocessor}$*. LISP introduced many other concepts including tree data structure, dynamic typing, high-order functions, and **read-eval-print-loop** (**REPL**). Two widely popular Lisp dialects are Scheme (https://en.wikipedia.org/wiki/Scheme_(programming_language)) and Common Lisp (https://en.wikipedia.org/wiki/Common_Lisp), both invented by Guy Steele (https://en.wikipedia.org/wiki/Guy_L._Steele_Jr.). Scheme was introduced in 1970 followed by Common Lisp in 1984. Clojure is also one of the dialects of Lisp that was introduced in 2007 by Rich Hickey.

In addition to being a dialect of LISP, Clojure also chose JVM as its runtime due to its inherent advantages and matured ecosystem. Java was first introduced in 1994-1995 by James Gosling (https://en.wikipedia.org/wiki/James_Gosling). Java is an object-oriented language with a focus on concurrency. Java became widely popular in enterprises soon after its release due to its efficient dependency management and ability to *write once, and run anywhere* (https://en.wikipedia.org/wiki/Write_once,_run_anywhere). Java allowed developers to write their code once, compile it into bytecode, and then run it on all platforms that support JVM without recompiling the code.

Clojure inherited all the capabilities of JVM with the focus on immutability and LISP-like parenthesized prefix notation. It is built on the concepts of immutability and persistent data structures, which makes it highly concurrent. It uses the *Epochal Time Model*, which organizes programs by identities, where each identity is defined as a series of immutable states over time. Due to its highly concurrent nature, Clojure is best suited to building massively parallel software systems that are robust and utilize modern multiprocessor hardware to the fullest.

The Epochal time model was introduced by Rich Hickey in his keynote talk on *Are we there yet?* (`https://www.infoq.com/presentations/Are-We-There-Yet-Rich-Hickey`) at the *JVM Languages Summit* in 2009. He revisited it in his keynote talk on *Effective Programs - 10 Years of Clojure* (`https://www.youtube.com/watch?v=2V1FtfBDsLU`) at Clojure/Conj in 2017.

REPL

Read-eval-print-loop is an interactive programming environment that takes expressions as inputs from the user, parses them into a data structure for the programming language, evaluates them, and prints the result back to the user. Once done, it returns to the read state and waits for user input, thus forming a loop, as shown in the following diagram. REPL was pioneered by Lisp and is now available for other programming languages as well:

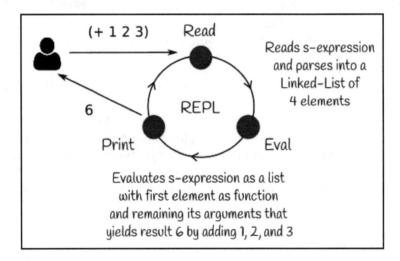

REPL is also the default interactive programming environment for Clojure. It compiles an expression into Java bytecode, evaluates it, and returns the result of the expression. To use Clojure REPL, download a Clojure release (1.8.0) from Clojure Downloads (`https://repo1.maven.org/maven2/org/clojure/clojure/1.8.0/clojure-1.8.0.zip`) and extract it. Since Clojure runs on JVM, you need to first make sure that you have Java 1.6+ or higher installed on your machine. To validate your Java version, use the `java` command with the `-version` option. This book uses Java 1.8 for all examples:

```
% java -version
java version "1.8.0_121"
Java(TM) SE Runtime Environment (build 1.8.0_121-b13)
Java HotSpot(TM) 64-Bit Server VM (build 25.121-b13, mixed mode)
```

To use Clojure REPL, first `unzip` the Clojure 1.8 release:

```
% unzip clojure-1.8.0.zip
Archive:  clojure-1.8.0.zip
  creating: clojure-1.8.0/
   ...
  inflating: clojure-1.8.0/clojure-1.8.0-slim.jar
  inflating: clojure-1.8.0/clojure-1.8.0.jar
  inflating: clojure-1.8.0/pom.xml
  inflating: clojure-1.8.0/build.xml
  inflating: clojure-1.8.0/readme.txt
  inflating: clojure-1.8.0/changes.md
  inflating: clojure-1.8.0/clojure.iml
  inflating: clojure-1.8.0/epl-v10.html
```

In the unzipped `clojure-1.8.0` folder, the `clojure-1.8.0.jar` JAR (https://en.wikipedia.org/wiki/JAR_(file_format)) is an executable JAR that contains the Clojure compiler. It is also used to start Clojure REPL using the `java` command:

```
% cd clojure-1.8.0
% java -jar clojure-1.8.0.jar
Clojure 1.8.0
user=> (+ 1 2 3)
6
user=>
```

The preceding method of starting the REPL with the Clojure JAR file works well until the last stable release of Clojure 1.8 at the time of writing this book. With Clojure 1.9 and onwards, it is recommended to use the Clojure `clj` tool (https://clojure.org/guides/deps_and_cli) or a build tool such as Leiningen (https://leiningen.org/) to set up a project and start REPL for the project with the required libraries.

repl.it (https://repl.it) is an online utility that allow you to access Clojure REPL online over the web browser.

Clojure build tools

Build tools are of prime importance for any programming language. They not only help to generate a deployable artifact for the application, but also manage the dependencies of the application throughout its development life cycle. Leiningen and Boot (`http://boot-clj.com/`) are two widely used build tools for Clojure. Since Clojure is a hosted language for JVM, Clojure build tools primarily generate JARs as deployable artifacts for all Clojure projects.

Leiningen

Leiningen is a build and project management tool that is written in Clojure and is widely used across Clojure projects. It describes a Clojure project using generic Clojure data structures. It integrates well with the Maven repository from the Java world and the Clojars (`https://clojars.org/`) repository of Clojure libraries, for dependency management and releases. Leiningen has built-in support for plugins to extend its functionality. It also provides an option to design application templates that can help create a Clojure application code layout with a single `lein` command. To separate project configuration from development, test, and production, it also has the concept of profiles, which can be used to change the project configuration at build time by using it with the `lein` command.

To set up lein, download the latest Lein script (`https://raw.githubusercontent.com/technomancy/leiningen/stable/bin/lein`) from the Leiningen GitHub repository (`https://github.com/technomancy/leiningen`), make it executable using the `chmod` command, and make sure that the script is available on your path, for example, by copying it to `~/bin` or `/usr/local/bin` in Linux. Once the lein script is available on your path, run it to download the latest self-install package and set up the environment. Lein downloads the executable JAR for Leiningen first time:

```
# Download the latest script (latest version)
% wget
https://raw.githubusercontent.com/technomancy/leiningen/stable/bin/lein

# Make it executable
% chmod a+x lein

# Run lein to setup
% lein
Downloading Leiningen ...
Leiningen is a tool for working with Clojure projects.
...
```

```
# Validate lein version
% lein version
Leiningen 2.8.0 on Java 1.8.0_121 Java HotSpot(TM) 64-Bit Server VM

# Downgrade to version 2.7.1, i.e. the version used in the book
% lein downgrade 2.7.1

# Validate lein version
% lein version
Leiningen 2.7.1 on Java 1.8.0_121 Java HotSpot(TM) 64-Bit Server VM
```

Note that the `lein` script always downloads the most recently released version. Once lein is set up, you can start REPL directly from the `lein` command:

```
% lein repl
nREPL server started on port 43952 on host 127.0.0.1 -
nrepl://127.0.0.1:43952
REPL-y 0.3.7, nREPL 0.2.12
Clojure 1.8.0
Java HotSpot(TM) 64-Bit Server VM 1.8.0_121-b13
 Docs: (doc function-name-here)
 (find-doc "part-of-name-here")
 Source: (source function-name-here)
 Javadoc: (javadoc java-object-or-class-here)
 Exit: Control+D or (exit) or (quit)
 Results: Stored in vars *1, *2, *3, an exception in *e

user=> (+ 1 2 3)
6
user=>
```

Boot

Boot is an alternative build system for Clojure that is gaining popularity. Boot treats build scripts as Clojure programs that can be extended using pods (`https://github.com/boot-clj/boot/wiki/Pods`). Pods also help to isolate classpaths for better dependency management and uses multiple Clojure runtimes. Instead of the profiles and plugins of Leiningen, Boot uses the common concept of tasks (`https://github.com/boot-clj/boot/wiki/Tasks`). Tasks are used across the Boot program to modify the build environment as per the context.

To set up Boot, download the latest `boot.sh` script (`https://github.com/boot-clj/boot-bin/releases/download/latest/boot.sh`) from the Boot GitHub repository (`https://github.com/boot-clj/boot`), make it executable using the `chmod` command, and make sure that the script is available on your path, for example, by copying it to `~/bin` or `/usr/local/bin` in Linux. Once the Boot script is available on your path, run it to set up the environment, as shown here:

```
# Download boot script
% curl -fsSLo boot
https://github.com/boot-clj/boot-bin/releases/download/latest/boot.sh

# Make it executable
% chmod 755 boot

# Run boot to setup
% boot
Downloading
https://github.com/boot-clj/boot/releases/download/2.7.2/boot.jar...
Running for the first time, BOOT_VERSION not set: updating to latest.
Retrieving maven-metadata.xml from https://repo.clojars.org/ (3k)
Retrieving boot-2.7.2.pom from https://repo.clojars.org/ (2k)
Retrieving boot-2.7.2.jar from https://repo.clojars.org/ (3k)
#http://boot-clj.com
#Sat Oct 21 19:43:24 IST 2017
BOOT_CLOJURE_NAME=org.clojure/clojure
BOOT_VERSION=2.7.2
BOOT_CLOJURE_VERSION=1.8.0
```

Once Boot is set up, you can start REPL directly from the `boot` command:

```
% boot repl
nREPL server started on port 33140 on host 127.0.0.1 -
nrepl://127.0.0.1:33140
REPL-y 0.3.7, nREPL 0.2.12
Clojure 1.8.0
Java HotSpot(TM) 64-Bit Server VM 1.8.0_121-b13
 Exit: Control+D or (exit) or (quit)
 Commands: (user/help)
 Docs: (doc function-name-here)
 (find-doc "part-of-name-here")
Find by Name: (find-name "part-of-name-here")
 Source: (source function-name-here)
 Javadoc: (javadoc java-object-or-class-here)
 Examples from clojuredocs.org: [clojuredocs or cdoc]
 (user/clojuredocs name-here)
 (user/clojuredocs "ns-here" "name-here")
boot.user=> (+ 1 2 3)
```

```
6
boot.user=>
```

 This book will focus on Leiningen as the build tool for the Clojure projects, but it is important to know that Leiningen is not the only build tool available for Clojure. Boot is also an option that can be used instead of Leiningen.

Clojure project

A Clojure project is a directory that contains source files, test files, resources, documentation, and project metadata. Source files are primarily from Clojure, but a project may contain Java source files as well. Leiningen has a default project template that can be used to quickly create a Clojure project structure using the lein new <project-name> command:

```
# Create a new project 'playground'
% lein new playground
Generating a project called playground based on the 'default' template.
The default template is intended for library projects, not applications.
To see other templates (app, plugin, etc), try `lein help new`.

# Show the 'playground' project directory structure
% tree playground
playground
├── CHANGELOG.md
├── doc
│   └── intro.md
├── LICENSE
├── project.clj
├── README.md
├── resources
├── src
│   └── playground
│       └── core.clj
└── test
    └── playground
        └── core_test.clj

6 directories, 7 files
```

Each Clojure project contains a project metadata file, `project.clj`, which defines all the project dependencies, profiles, and plugins that are required for the project. For example, the `project.clj` file of the `playground` project lists the project metadata and dependencies based on the default project template of Leiningen, as shown here:

```
(defproject playground "0.1.0-SNAPSHOT"
  :description "FIXME: write description"
  :url "http://example.com/FIXME"
  :license {:name "Eclipse Public License"
            :url "http://www.eclipse.org/legal/epl-v10.html"}
  :dependencies [[org.clojure/clojure "1.8.0"]])
```

The `defproject` is a Clojure macro that is defined by Leiningen and acts as a container for all project metadata directives. The default template omits the default configuration directives.

Configuring a project

A good project configuration must define separate profiles for development, test, and production. It should also have directives to test the implementation, check code quality, and generate test reports and documentation for the application. Each project configuration should also have the entry point into the application defined using the `:main` directive, which points to the namespace that contains the main function, as shown here:

```
(defproject playground "0.1.0-SNAPSHOT"
  :description "Playground Project"
  :url "http://example.com/playground"
  :license {:name "Eclipse Public License"
            :url "http://www.eclipse.org/legal/epl-v10.html"}
  :dependencies [[org.clojure/clojure "1.8.0"]]
  :main playground.core
  :profiles {:provided {:dependencies [[org.clojure/tools.reader "0.10.0"]
                                       [org.clojure/tools.nrepl "0.2.12"]]}
             :uberjar {:aot :all :omit-source true}
             :doc {:dependencies [[codox-theme-rdash "0.1.1"]]
                   :codox {:metadata {:doc/format :markdown}
                           :themes [:rdash]}}
             :dev {:resource-paths ["resources" "conf"]
                   :jvm-opts ["-Dconf=conf/conf.edn"]}
             :debug {:jvm-opts
                     ["-server"
                      (str "-agentlib:jdwp=transport=dt_socket,"
                           "server=y,address=8000,suspend=n")]}})
```

Project configuration should explicitly list source and test file locations using the *:source-paths* and *:test-paths* directive. If both Clojure and Java source code files are present in the project, then it is recommended to organize the source file under `src/clj` for Clojure and `src/jvm` for Java. Similarly, test files can be kept under `test/clj` and `test/jvm` for Clojure and Java, respectively. A reference `project.clj` file with the required project configuration is shown in the following code snippet:

```
(defproject playground "0.1.0-SNAPSHOT"
  ...
  :main playground.core
  :source-paths ["src/clj"]
  :java-source-paths ["src/jvm"]
  :test-paths ["test/clj" "test/jvm"]
  :resource-paths ["resources" "conf"]
  ...
)
```

Project resource files, such as startup, shutdown scripts, and more, can be kept in the `resources` directory and the project configuration files can be kept in the `conf` directory. Both the directories must be specified under the `:resource-paths` directive, as shown in the preceding snippet. To generate documentation and test reports, and check code quality, there are a number of third-party plugins available that can be added to the project configuration. For example, Codox (`https://github.com/weavejester/codox`) can be used to generate API documentation, Cloverage (`https://github.com/cloverage/cloverage`) can be used to test code coverage, and test2junit (`https://github.com/ruedigergad/test2junit`) can be used to generate test reports. Add these plugins in the configuration file, as shown here:

```
(defproject playground "0.1.0-SNAPSHOT"
  ...
  :resource-paths ["resources" "conf"]
  :plugins [[:lein-codox "0.10.3"]
            ;; Code Coverage
            [:lein-cloverage "1.0.9"]
            ;; Unit test docs
            [test2junit "1.2.2"]]
  :codox {:namespaces :all}
  :test2junit-output-dir "target/test-reports"
  :profiles {:provided {:dependencies [[org.clojure/tools.reader "0.10.0"]
                                        [org.clojure/tools.nrepl "0.2.12"]]}
             :uberjar {:aot :all :omit-source true}
             :doc {:dependencies [[codox-theme-rdash "0.1.1"]]
                   :codox {:metadata {:doc/format :markdown}
                           :themes [:rdash]}}
             :dev {:resource-paths ["resources" "conf"]
```

```
               :jvm-opts ["-Dconf=conf/conf.edn"]}
        :debug {:jvm-opts
                ["-server"
                 (str "-agentlib:jdwp=transport=dt_socket,"
                      "server=y,address=8000,suspend=n")]}})
```

Some of these plugins may also require extra Leiningen directives to be defined for them. Dependencies that are common across profiles must be listed under the :dependencies directive of the defproject macro, and the rest of the dependencies must be listed under the respective profiles, as shown in the preceding configuration.

The Leiningen GitHub repository has a sample.project.clj file (https://github.com/technomancy/leiningen/blob/master/sample.project.clj) that lists all supported project directives for a Clojure project that is managed by Leiningen. This file acts as detailed documentation for all the features of Leiningen.

Running a project

If the :main directive is defined in the project.clj file of the project, then the project can be run by directly calling the lein run command. lein run expects the namespace specified under :main directive to contain the Clojure main function. For example, the playground.core namespace must have a main function defined for lein run to work, as shown in the following implementation. Since the :source-paths parameter in the updated configuration of project.clj points to src/clj instead of the default src/, the core.clj source file, as shown in the following code, must reside within the src/clj/playground/ directory as per the namespace and configured source paths:

```
(ns playground.core
  (:gen-class))

(defn foo
  "I don't do a whole lot."
  [x]
  (println x "| Hello, World!"))

(defn -main
  [& args]
  (foo (or (first args) "Noname")))
```

If the main function is defined in the playground.core namespace, then it can be executed using lein run:

```
% lein run
Noname | Hello, World!

% lein run Clojure
Clojure | Hello, World!
```

Running tests

To run all the tests defined under the :test-paths directive, run the lein test command. Since the default template of Leiningen has only one test defined and it always fails, there will be a test failure reported, as shown in the following code snippet. Since the :test-paths parameter in the updated configuration of project.clj points to test/clj instead of the default test/, the generated core_test.clj test source file must reside within the test/clj/playground/ directory as per the namespace and configured test paths for tests to run, as shown here:

```
% lein test

lein test playground.core-test

lein test :only playground.core-test/a-test

FAIL in (a-test) (core_test.clj:7)
FIXME, I fail.
expected: (= 0 1)
  actual: (not (= 0 1))

Ran 1 tests containing 1 assertions.
1 failures, 0 errors.
Tests failed.
```

Generating reports

A good project deliverable must include test and coverage reports with associated API documentation. Based on the configured plugins under the plugins directive of project.clj, lein can be used to generate various reports as per the plugin documentation. The execution of each of the plugins using the lein command and their corresponding results are shown here:

```
% lein test2junit
Using test2junit version: 1.2.2
Running Tests...
```

```
Writing output to: target/test-reports
Creating default build.xml file.

Testing: playground.core-test

Ran 1 tests containing 1 assertions.
>1 failures, 0 errors.
Tests failed.
Tests failed.

% lein with-profiles +test cloverage
Loading namespaces: (playground.core)
Test namespaces: (playground.core-test)
Loaded playground.core .
Instrumented namespaces.

Testing playground.core-test

FAIL in (a-test) (core_test.clj:7)
FIXME, I fail.
expected: (= 0 1)
  actual: (not (= 0 1))

Ran 1 tests containing 1 assertions.
1 failures, 0 errors.
Ran tests.
Produced output in playground/target/coverage .
HTML: target/coverage/index.html
```

Namespace	% Forms	% Lines
playground.core	17.65	60.00
ALL FILES	17.65	60.00

```
Error encountered performing task 'cloverage' with profile(s):
'base,system,user,provided,dev,test'
Suppressed exit

% lein with-profiles +doc codox
Generated HTML docs in playground/target/doc
```

As a result of the execution of the commands shown in the preceding snippet, the output of `test2junit` is generated under the `target/test-reports/xml/playground.core-test.xml` file, which is a standard JUnit (`https://en.wikipedia.org/wiki/JUnit`) test report. Coverage reports are generated under `target/coverage/`, which contains an `index.html` file that can be viewed using a web browser to see a detailed report and review the instrumented code paths that were covered with the test cases. The documentation for the project is generated under the `target/doc` file, which contains the `index.html` file that can be viewed in a web browser to review the generated docs.

Generating artifacts

Clojure artifacts are generated as runnable JARs. To generate a runnable JAR, run the `lein uberjar` command, as shown in the following snippet. The artifact can be configured using the `uberjar` profile in `project.clj`:

```
% lein uberjar
Compiling playground.core
Created target/playground-0.1.0-SNAPSHOT.jar
Created target/playground-0.1.0-SNAPSHOT-standalone.jar

% java -jar target/playground-0.1.0-SNAPSHOT-standalone.jar
Noname | Hello, World!

% java -jar target/playground-0.1.0-SNAPSHOT-standalone.jar Clojure
Clojure | Hello, World!
```

Clojure IDE

An **integrated development environment** (IDE) is a software application that provides utilities for programmers to develop, build, and debug software applications. It consists of a code editor, build automation tool, and a debugger. Clojure has a growing number of IDEs available, out of which Emacs (`https://en.wikipedia.org/wiki/Emacs`) and Vim (`https://en.wikipedia.org/wiki/Vim_(text_editor)`) stand out. Although this book does not cover IDEs, wherever one is referred to, uses Emacs as the IDE. Both Emacs and Vim are text editors that need additional plugins to support Clojure. Emacs needs CIDER (`https://github.com/clojure-emacs/cider`), whereas Vim gets REPL support using Fireplace (`https://github.com/tpope/vim-fireplace`).

Some other Clojure IDEs that are widely used are:

- Eclipse (`https://www.eclipse.org/home/index.php`) with Counterclockwise (`http://doc.ccw-ide.org/`)
- Light Table (`http://lighttable.com/`)
- Sublime Text (`https://www.sublimetext.com/`) with SublimeREPL (`https://github.com/wuub/SublimeREPL`)
- Atom (`https://atom.io/`) with nrepl (`https://atom.io/packages/nrepl`)
- Cursive (`https://cursive-ide.com/`)

Summary

In this chapter, we focused on the development environment for the **Helping Hands** application. Since Clojure is our language of choice for implementation, we first looked at the history of Clojure and Lisp and understood why it is well suited for our use case. We also looked at the REPL environment and two build tools for Clojure—Leiningen and Boot. Further, we defined a reference Leiningen project configuration for our application and learned how to run an application and test it. We also learned how to generate documentation and reports, and how to create a deployable artifact. At the end, we briefly looked at the Clojure IDEs that can make our application development work easy.

In the next chapter, we will learn about REST specification. We will learn how to define REST APIs for microservices in the Helping Hands application that can help with direct messaging among the services.

5

REST APIs for Microservices

"Coming together is a beginning; keeping together is progress; working together is success."

- Henry Ford

One of the modes of interaction among microservices is direct messaging via APIs. REST APIs are one of the ways to make the direct messaging possible among microservices. REST APIs enable interoperability among microservices irrespective of the technology stack in which they are implemented. In this chapter, we will cover the following topics:

- The concept of REST
- How to define REST URIs with appropriate methods with status codes
- How to use REST-based HTTP URIs using utilities such as cURL
- REST APIs for the **Helping Hands** application

Introducing REST

REST stands for **representational state transfer**, and defines an architectural style for distributed hypermedia systems. It focuses on creating independent component implementations that are stateless and scale well. Applications that support REST do not store any information about the client state on the server side. Such applications require clients to maintain the state themselves and use the REST-style implementations, such as HTTP APIs exposed by the application, to transfer the state between them and the server. Clients who use the REST API may query the server for the latest state and represent the same state at the client side, thus keeping the client and server in sync.

The state of an application is defined by the state of the entities of the system. Entities can be related to the concept of **resources** in REST architecture. A resource is a key abstraction of information in REST. It is a conceptual mapping to a set of entities that is defined by the resource identifier. Any information that can be named or be the target of the REST resource identifier can be a resource. For example, a *consumer* is a resource for a *Service Consumer* service and an *order* is a resource for an *Order* service.

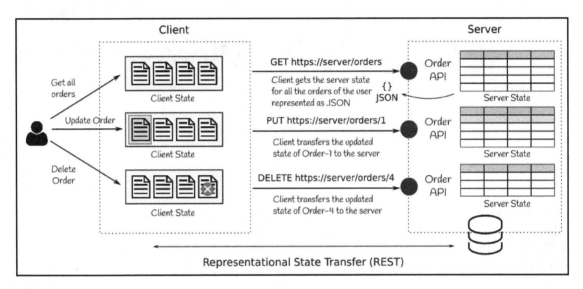

Resource identifiers in REST are defined as API endpoints that are mapped to HTTP URIs. The URIs point to one or more resources and allow the callers to perform operations on the resources, as shown in the preceding image. All the operations supported by REST are stateless; that is, none of the client state is persisted on the server side. The stateless nature of the REST APIs helps in creating services that scale horizontally without depending on shared state.

REST style is suited to microservices for direct communication and building synchronous APIs to get access to the entities. Each entity that is managed by a microservice can be directly mapped to the concept of a *resource* in REST.

The concept of REST was defined by Roy Fielding in 2000 as a part of his PhD dissertation on *Architectural Styles and the Design of Network-based Software Architectures* (`https://www.ics.uci.edu/~fielding/pubs/dissertation/fielding_dissertation_2up.pdf`). A RESTful system conforms to six guiding principles (`https://en.wikipedia.org/wiki/Representational_state_transfer#Architectural_constraints`) of client-server, statelessness, cacheability, layered system, code-on-demand, and uniform interface.

RESTful APIs

Web service APIs that conform to REST architecture is called RESTful APIs. Microservices mostly implement the HTTP-based RESTful APIs that are stateless and have a base URI and a media type (`https://en.wikipedia.org/wiki/Media_type`) for the representation of resources. It also supports predefined standard operations that are mapped to HTTP methods such as GET, POST, PUT, DELETE, and more.

For example, as shown in the following table, the *Order* service may define an API /orders to get access to the orders that it maintains. It can support a GET method to look up all the orders or get a specific order by specifying the order ID. It can also allow clients to create new orders by using the POST method or create an order with a specific ID by using the PUT method. Similarly, it can support the PUT method to update order details and the DELETE method to delete an order by specifying the order ID explicitly.

URI	HTTP method	Operation	Description
GET https://server/orders	GET	Read	Gets all the orders
GET https://server/orders/1	GET	Read	Gets the details of order with ID as 1
POST https://server/orders	POST	Create	Creates a new order and returns the ID
PUT https://server/orders/100	PUT	Create	Creates a new order with ID as 100
PUT https://server/orders/2	PUT	Update	Updates an existing order with ID as 2

| DELETE https://server/orders/1 | DELETE | Delete | Deletes an existing order with ID as 1 |

`GET`, `PUT`, `POST`, and `DELETE` are the most widely used HTTP methods for RESTful APIs. Other methods include `HEAD`, `OPTIONS`, `PATCH`, `TRACE`, and `CONNECT` (`https://en.wikipedia.org/wiki/Hypertext_Transfer_Protocol#Request_methods`). Each request that is sent to the URIs generates a response that may be HTML, JSON, XML, or any defined format. JSON is the preferred format for microservices that handle the core operations of the application. For example, the responses generated by the RESTful APIs of the *Order* service will contain a JSON object of order details or a JSON array of orders, where each order is represented as a JSON object with key-value pairs containing the order details.

Status codes

Status codes are important for clients to understand the outcome of the request and take required action on the response. Successful requests return a response with the required representation of resources, but failed requests generate a response representing the error instead. Status codes help clients to be well aware of the content of the response and take necessary action at the client side.

All microservices with RESTful APIs must support appropriate HTTP status codes (`https://en.wikipedia.org/wiki/List_of_HTTP_status_codes`) and send them to the client based on the outcome of the requested operation. Some of the status codes that must be implemented by all APIs of microservices are:

Status code	Usage
200 OK	Standard response code if the request was successful. A `GET` request must return the resource details in the response, and a `POST` request must return the outcome of the response.
201 Created	Sent when the request results in the creation of a resource. The response must contain the URI of the resource.
400 Bad Request	Client-side error response code if the request contains invalid or insufficient parameters. The response must include details of the issues with respect to request parameters for client to correct.
401 Unauthorized	Sent when authentication is required to access a resource and either client request is not authenticated or does not contain authentication/authorization tokens as expected by the server.

403 Forbidden	Sent when the client request is valid but it is not allowed to access the resource, possibly due to insufficient privileges.
404 Not Found	Sent when the requested resource is not found on the server.
405 Method Not Allowed	Sent when the requested method is not supported by the resource. For example, a resource may support only the GET method. In that case, sending a PUT request may result in a response with this error code.
500 Internal Server Error	Generic error response code sent by the server when the request fails with an unknown error that is not handled by the server and there is no other appropriate error message to send.

The preceding status codes must be implemented for the REST APIs. There are other status codes as well that may be used by the APIs. To review all the defined status codes, take a look at the HTTP status codes guide.

Naming conventions

REST APIs must be organized around resources of the system and must be easy to understand by just looking at the URIs. URIs must focus on one resource type at a time with operations mapped to HTTP request methods. They may have one or more related resources that can be further nested in the URI.

Good examples of URIs are /users, /consumers, /orders, and /services, not /getusers, /showorders, and more. A basic rule to define API URIs is to target nouns as resources and verbs as HTTP methods. For example, instead of creating a URI as /getusers, it is recommended to have the URI as /users with the HTTP method as GET. Similarly, instead of /showorders, the URI GET /orders must be created to provide all the orders in the response to the client. Guidelines for naming URIs are further explained in the following diagram:

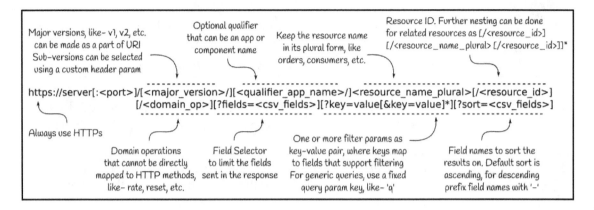

It is recommended to always use SSL (https://en.wikipedia.org/wiki/Transport_Layer_Security) by only using HTTPS-based URIs for all the APIs. The APIs must be versioned to upgrade them over time without breaking the integration with existing services. To specify the version of the API, a major version can be used as a prefix to all the API endpoints. Sub-versions must not be added to the URI. If required, they can be specified using a custom header parameter.

Versions can also be introduced via a media type. It is perfectly fine to include sub-versions as well with the media type. Versions may include breaking changes as well for the clients, but it is recommended to keep the changes as backward compatible as possible.

URIs may also contain application qualifiers that segment the API endpoints based on the target components or business operations. Each URI must be focused on a single resource type, and that name must be used in its plural form. To retrieve specific resources of the specified type, an ID must be appended to the URI. Here are some of the examples of URIs that follow the easy-to-understand naming convention:

URI	Description
GET https://server/v1/orders	Gets all the orders
GET https://server:9988/v1/orders	Gets all the orders
GET https://server/v1/tech/orders	Gets all the orders
GET https://server/v1/orders/7	Gets an order with ID 7
POST https://server/v1/orders	Creates a new order and returns the ID

`PUT https://server/v1/orders/17`	Updates the order ID 17, creates new if not present
`GET https://server/v1/orders/7/feedbacks`	Gets all feedbacks for order ID 7
`GET https://server/v1/orders/7/feedbacks/1`	Gets the feedback with ID 1 for order ID 7
`DELETE https://server/v1/orders/3`	Deletes the order with ID 3
`PUT https://server/v1/orders/7/rate`	Updates the rating for order ID 7
`GET https://server/v1/orders?fields=ts,id,name`	Gets all the orders with only ts, id and name field of the orders in the response
`GET https://server/v1/orders?status=open&sort=-ts,name`	Gets all the orders that have status as open, sorted by ts in descending order and name in ascending order

Using RESTful APIs via cURL

cURL is a command-line utility to transfer data using various protocols, including HTTP and HTTPS. cURL is widely used to try RESTful APIs using its command-line interface. For example, let's take a look at the APIs provided by MetaWeather (`https://www.metaweather.com/api/`) to query a location and get its weather information. Since it is a public API that maintains the weather information of well-known places, it allows only GET requests to get the details of the resources and does not allow creating or updating resources.

To get the weather of a location, the MetaWeather application requires the resource ID as defined by the system. To get the resource ID, MetaWeather provides a search API to look up the resources by a search query. The search API uses the GET method with the query as the URL parameter in the request and returns the JSON response with resources that match the query, as shown here:

```
% curl -XGET
"https://www.metaweather.com/api/location/search/?query=bangalore"
[{"title":"Bangalore","location_type":"City","woeid":2295420,"latt_long":"1
2.955800,77.620979"}]
```

The woeid field in the response is the resource ID required by the weather API that can be used to get the weather details of the queried location:

```
% curl -XGET "https://www.metaweather.com/api/location/2295420/"
{
 "title": "Bangalore",
 "location_type": "City",
 "woeid": 2295420,
 "latt_long": "12.955800,77.620979",
 "timezone": "Asia/Kolkata",
 "time": "2017-10-24T21:06:34.146240+05:30",
 "sun_rise": "2017-10-24T06:11:13.036505+05:30",
 "sun_set": "2017-10-24T17:56:02.483163+05:30",
 "timezone_name": "LMT",
 "parent": {
    "title": "India",
    "location_type": "Country",
    "woeid": 23424848,
    "latt_long": "21.786600,82.794762"
 },
 "consolidated_weather": [
    {
       "id": 6004071454474240,
       "weather_state_name": "Heavy Cloud",
       "weather_state_abbr": "hc",
       "wind_direction_compass": "NE",
       "created": "2017-10-24T15:10:08.268840Z",
       "applicable_date": "2017-10-24",
       "min_temp": 18.458000000000002,
       "max_temp": 29.392000000000003,
       "the_temp": 30.0,
       "wind_speed": 1.9876466767411649,
       "wind_direction": 51.745585344396069,
       "air_pressure": 969.60500000000002,
       "humidity": 63,
       "visibility": 11.150816730295077,
```

```
      "predictability": 71
    },
    ...
  ],
  "sources": [
    {
      "title": "BBC",
      "slug": "bbc",
      "url": "http://www.bbc.co.uk/weather/",
      "crawl_rate": 180
    },
    ...
  ]
}
```

The MetaWeather application APIs also support the OPTIONS method that can be used to find out the details of the API. For example, sending the request to the same search API with the OPTIONS HTTP method provides the required details in the response:

```
% curl -XOPTIONS
"https://www.metaweather.com/api/location/search/?query=bangalore"
{"name":"Location
Search","description":"","renders":["application/json"],"parses":["applicat
ion/json","application/x-www-form-urlencoded","multipart/form-data"]}
```

The MetaWeather application also responds with the appropriate status code and message in the response for an invalid resource ID:

```
% curl -v -XGET "https://www.metaweather.com/api/location/0/"
...
* Trying 172.217.26.179...
* Connected to www.metaweather.com (172.217.26.179) port 443 (#0)
...
* compression: NULL
* ALPN, server accepted to use http/1.1
> GET /api/location/0/ HTTP/1.1
> Host: www.metaweather.com
> User-Agent: curl/7.47.0
> Accept: */*
>
< HTTP/1.1 404 Not Found
< x-xss-protection: 1; mode=block
< Content-Language: en
< x-content-type-options: nosniff
< strict-transport-security: max-age=2592000; includeSubDomains
< Vary: Accept-Language, Cookie
< Allow: GET, HEAD, OPTIONS
```

```
< x-frame-options: DENY
< Content-Type: application/json
< X-Cloud-Trace-Context: 507eec2981a7028e50e596fcb651acb7;o=1
< Date: Tue, 24 Oct 2017 16:07:36 GMT
< Server: Google Frontend
< Content-Length: 23
<
* Connection #0 to host www.metaweather.com left intact
{"detail":"Not found."}
```

REST APIs for Helping Hands

The Helping Hands application has *Consumer* and *Provider* services that expose the REST APIs to manage consumers and providers for the application. Each service provider in the application can register one or more services that are managed by *Service* APIs. Apart from these services, there is an *Order* service that manages all the orders placed by the consumers for the service and served by the providers of the service. The Helping Hands application also provides an application-wide *Lookup* service that provides a single API to look up services and orders by vicinity. All APIs provided by the Helping Hands microservices also handle errors with appropriate error messages in the response and the corresponding status code.

Consumer and Provider APIs

The APIs provided by the *Consumer* and *Provider* services target the *consumers* and *providers* resources of the system, respectively:

URI	Method	Params	Description
/consumers	POST	**Details (JSON)**	**Creates a new consumer and returns the consumer ID**
/consumers/1	PUT	Details to be updated (JSON)	Updates the details of an existing consumer
/consumers	GET	Fields (CSV), sort (CSV), page	Gets all the consumers based on request params
/consumers/1	DELETE	-	Deletes the specified consumer
/providers	POST	Details (JSON)	Creates a new provider and returns the provider ID

URI	Method	Params	Description
/providers/1	PUT	Details to be updated (JSON)	Updates the details of an existing provider
/providers/1/star	PUT	-	Increments the stars for the provider by one
/providers	GET	Fields (CSV), sort (CSV), page	Gets all the providers based on request params
/providers/1	DELETE	-	Deletes the specified provider

Service and Order APIs

The APIs provided by the *Service* and *Order* services target the provider *services* and *orders* resources of the system, respectively:

URI	Method	Params	Description
/services	POST	Details (JSON)	Creates a new service and returns the service ID
/services/1	PUT	Details to be updated (JSON)	Updates the details of an existing service
/services/1/star	PUT	-	Increments the stars for the service by one
/services	GET	Fields (CSV), sort (CSV), page	Gets all the services based on request params
/services/1	DELETE	-	Deletes the specified service
/orders	POST	Details (JSON)	Creates a new order and returns the order ID
/orders/1	PUT	Details to be updated (JSON)	Updates the details of an existing order
/orders	GET	Fields (CSV), sort (CSV), page	Gets all the orders based on request params
/orders/1	DELETE	-	Deletes the specified order

APIs for authentication and authorization have been intentionally left out from the discussion, but these will be addressed in *Part-4* of this book.

Summary

In this chapter, we learned about the concept of REST and how to design RESTful APIs with an easy-to-understand naming convention. We also learned about various request methods and status codes, and when to use what. At the end, we revisited the Helping Hands application to list down the REST APIs that will be required for the application across microservices.

In the next chapter, we will take a look at a Clojure framework called Pedestal (`http://pedestal.io/`) that we will be using to design microservices for the Helping Hands application. Pedestal will also be used to expose REST APIs for various microservices operations.

6
Introduction to Pedestal

"A conceptual framework is a 'frame that works' to put those concepts into practice."

- Paul Hughes

Microservices are implemented using a particular technology stack, which serves a single-bounded context and provides services around it. The services exposed for the external world must be scalable and support direct messaging as well as asynchronous requests. Pedestal (`http://pedestal.io/`) is one such Clojure framework that fits in well to create reliable and scalable services for microservice-based applications. It also fits in well with the Clojure stack of the **Helping Hands** application. In this chapter, you will:

- Learn about the basic concepts of Pedestal
- Learn how to define Pedestal routes and interceptors
- Learn how to handle errors with Pedestal interceptors
- Learn how to publish operational metrics with Pedestal
- Learn how to use Server-sent Events and Web Sockets with Pedestal

Pedestal concepts

Pedestal is an API-first Clojure framework that provides a set of libraries to build reliable and highly concurrent services that are dynamic in nature. It is an extensible framework that is data-driven and implemented using protocols (`https://clojure.org/reference/protocols`) to reduce the coupling between its components. It favors data over functions and functions over macros. It allows for the creation of data-driven routes and handlers that can apply a different behavior at runtime based on incoming requests. This makes it possible to create highly flexible and dynamic services that are well suited for microservice-based applications. It also supports the building of scalable asynchronous services using **server-sent events** (**SSE**) and WebSockets:

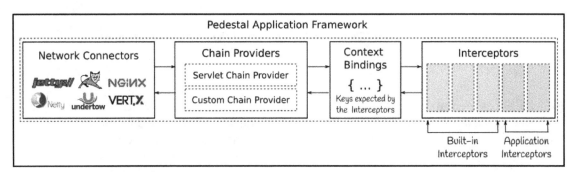

The Pedestal architecture is based on two main concepts, **Interceptors** and **Context Map**, and two secondary concepts, **Chain Providers** and **Network Connectors**. All the core logic of the Pedestal framework has been implemented as **Interceptors**, but the HTTP connection handler has been separated to create an interface for Chain Provider that sets up the initial Context Map and queue of **Interceptors** to start the execution. Pedestal includes a servlet chain provider out of the box that works with all the HTTP servers that work with servlets. It also sets up the required keys in the Context Map that are expected by the **Interceptors** as per the contract. Pedestal applications are not limited to just HTTP. Custom chain providers can be written to support other application protocols as well. They can also work with different transport protocols, such as reliable UDP based on the target chain provider and the underlying network connector.

 Pedestal initially had two separate parts—the Pedestal application and Pedestal server. Pedestal application was a ClojureScript-based frontend framework that has been discontinued. Now the focus is only on Pedestal server to build reliable services and APIs.

Interceptors

Pedestal interceptors are based on a software design pattern called **interceptor**. Interceptor is a service extension that registers events of interest with the framework and is invoked by the framework when those events occur within the control flow. Once the interceptor is invoked, it executes its functionality, and then the control flow returns to the framework. Most of Pedestal core logic is made up of one or more interceptors that can be composed together to build a chain of interceptors.

Interceptor in Pedestal is defined by a Clojure Map (`https://clojure.org/reference/data_structures#Maps`) that contains `:name`, `:enter`, `:leave`, and `:error` keys as shown in the following diagram. The `:name` key contains a namespaced keyword (`https://clojure.org/reference/namespaces`) for the interceptor and is optional. The `:enter` and `:leave` keys specify a Clojure function that takes a *Context Map* as input and returns a *Context Map* as output. Either the `:enter` or `:leave` key must be defined for the interceptor to be registered with the Pedestal framework. The function specified by the `:enter` key is called by the Pedestal framework when the data flows into the interceptor. The function specified by `:leave` is called when the response is being returned by the interceptor:

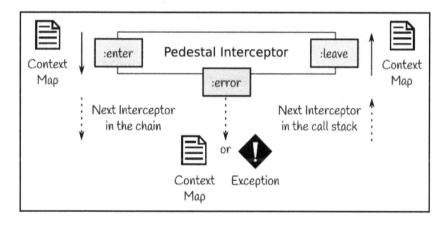

The function specified by :error is called when an exception event is triggered by the interceptor execution or if the execution fails with an error. To handle the exception event, the :error key specifies a Clojure function that takes two arguments—a **Context Map** and an ex-info (https://clojuredocs.org/clojure.core/ex-info) exception that was thrown by the interceptor. It either returns a **Context Map**, optionally, with the exception reattached for other interceptors to handle, or throws an exception for the Pedestal framework to handle.

The interceptor chain

Interceptors in Pedestal can be composed as an interceptor chain that follows the *Chain of Responsibility* (https://en.wikipedia.org/wiki/Chain-of-responsibility_pattern) design pattern. Each interceptor does exactly one job and when composed together as an interceptor chain, they achieve a bigger task consisting of one or more jobs.

The *Chain of Responsibility* pattern helps with navigating the composite structure of the interceptor chain. The control flow within the interceptor chain is controlled by a *Context Map*. Since a *Context Map* itself is passed as input to each interceptor, interceptors can optionally add, remove, or reorder interceptors in the chain. This is one of the reasons why most of the modules of a web framework, such as *Routing, Content Negotiation, Request Handlers*, and more, are also implemented as interceptors by Pedestal.

Interceptor functions for :enter and :leave must return **Context Map** as a value for the execution flow to continue with the next interceptor. If the functions return a nil (https://clojure.org/reference/data_structures#nil) value, an internal server error is reported by the Pedestal framework and the execution flow terminates. An interceptor may return a core.async (https://clojure.github.io/core.async/) channel instead of the **Context Map**. In that case, the channel is treated like a promise to deliver the **Context Map** in the future. Once the channel delivers the **Context Map**, the chain executor closes the channel:

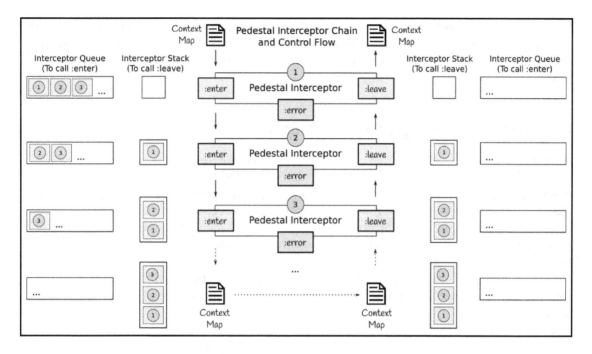

The chain executor calls each interceptor in the `core.async` library's go block (https://clojure.github.io/core.async/#clojure.core.async/go), so one interceptor may be called on a different thread than the next but all bindings are conveyed to each interceptor. In scenarios where the interceptor may take a long time to process the request or make an external API call, it is recommended to use a go block to send a channel as the return value and let Pedestal continue with the execution asynchronously. When Pedestal receives a channel as an output, it yields the interceptor thread and waits for a value to be produced by the channel. Only one value is consumed from the channel, and it must be a *Context Map*.

As shown in the preceding diagram, while executing the interceptor chain, all :enter functions are called in the order of interceptors listed in the chain. Once all the :enter functions of the interceptors are called, the resulting *Context Map* is sent through the :leave function of the interceptors but in reverse order. Since any of the interceptors in the chain can return asynchronously, Pedestal creates what it calls a virtual call stack of interceptors. It keeps a queue of interceptors for which it has to call the :enter function and also maintains a stack of interceptors for which the :enter function has been called, but the :leave function is pending. Keeping a stack allows Pedestal to call the :leave function in the reverse order of the :enter function calls of the interceptors in the chain. Both of these queues and stacks are kept in the *Context Map* and are accessible to the interceptors.

Since interceptors have access to the *Context Map*, they can change the execution plan for the rest of the request by modifying the sequence of interceptors in the chain. They can not only enqueue additional interceptors but can also terminate the request to skip all the remaining interceptors in the chain.

Importance of a Context Map

A context is just a *Clojure Map* (`https://clojure.org/reference/data_structures#Maps`) that is taken as input by the interceptor and also generated as an output. It contains all the values that control a Pedestal application, including interceptors, chains, execution stacks, queues, and context values that may be generated by interceptors or required by interceptors remaining in the interceptor chain. A *Context Map* also contains a sequence of predicate functions. If any one of the predicate function returns `true`, the chain is terminated. All the required functions and signal keys are also defined within the *Context Map* to enable async capabilities and facilitate the interaction between the platform and interceptors. The table shown here lists some of the keys that the interceptor chain keeps in the *Context Map*:

Key	Type	Description
`:bindings`	Map (var -> value)	Installed using with-bindings (`https://clojuredocs.org/clojure.core/with-bindings`) prior to execution
`:io.pedestal.interceptor.chain/error`	Exception	Most recent exception that triggered error handling
`:io.pedestal.interceptor.chain/execution-id`	Opaque	Unique ID for the execution
`:io.pedestal.interceptor.chain/queue`	Queue of interceptors	Interceptors to be executed next
`:io.pedestal.interceptor.chain/stack`	Stack of interceptors	Interceptors left to be executed
`:io.pedestal.interceptor.chain/terminators`	Collection of predicates	Checks for valid termination predicates after each `:enter` function

If the `:bindings` map is altered by an interceptor and returned in the output *Context Map*, then Pedestal will install the new bindings as thread local bindings prior to the execution of the next interceptor in the chain. The `:io.pedestal.interceptor.chain/queue` context key contains all the interceptors that are left to be executed. The first interceptor in the queue is the next one considered to be executed by calling the `:enter` function. This key must be used only for debugging purposes. To make any changes to the queue or execution flow, enqueue, `terminate`, or `terminate-when` (http://pedestal.io/api/pedestal.interceptor/io.pedestal.interceptor.chain.html#var-enqueue) in the interceptor chain must be called instead of changing the value of this key.

The termination predicates specified by the `:io.pedestal.interceptor.chain/terminators` keys are checked for a `true` predicate after each `:enter` function call. If there is a valid predicate found, Pedestal skips all other remaining interceptors' `:enter` functions and begins executing the `:leave` function of interceptors in the stack to terminate the execution flow.

The `:io.pedestal.interceptor.chain/stack` context key contains the interceptors for which the `:enter` function has already been called but the `:leave` function is pending. The interceptor at the top of the stack is executed first to make sure that the `:leave` function is called in the reverse order of `:enter` function calls.

In addition to the keys added by the interceptor chain, *Context Map* may contain keys that are added by other interceptors as well. For example, a servlet interceptor (http://pedestal.io/reference/servlet-interceptor), provided by Pedestal out of the box, adds servlet-specific keys to the *Context Map*, such as `:servlet-request`, `:servlet-response`, `:servlet-config`, and `:servlet`. When working with HTTP server, *Context Map* also has the `:request` and `:response` keys, which have request (http://pedestal.io/reference/request-map) and response (http://pedestal.io/reference/response-map) maps assigned to them, respectively.

 Pedestal extends beyond just HTTP services. You can extend services to Kafka-like (https://kafka.apache.org/) systems and also use different protocols such as SCTP, Reliable UDP, UDT, and more.
The `pedestal.service` Pedestal module is a collection of HTTP-specific interceptors.

Creating a Pedestal service

Pedestal provides a Leiningen (`https://leiningen.org/`) template named `pedestal-service` to create a new project with the required dependencies and directory layout for a Pedestal service. To create a new project using the template, use the `lein` command with the template name and a project name as shown here:

```
# Create a new project 'pedestal-play' with template 'pedestal-service'
% lein new pedestal-service pedestal-play
Retrieving pedestal-service/lein-template/0.5.3/lein-template-0.5.3.pom
from clojars
Retrieving pedestal-service/lein-template/0.5.3/lein-template-0.5.3.jar
from clojars
Generating a pedestal-service application called pedestal-play.
```

The `lein` command will create a new directory with the specified project name and add all the required dependencies to the `project.clj` file. It will also initialize the `server.clj` and `service.clj` files with the code template for a sample Pedestal service. The created project directory tree should look like the one shown here:

```
# Show the 'pedestal-play' project directory structure
% tree pedestal-play
pedestal-play
├── Capstanfile
├── config
│   └── logback.xml
├── Dockerfile
├── project.clj
├── README.md
├── src
│   └── pedestal_play
│       ├── server.clj
│       └── service.clj
└── test
    └── pedestal_play
        └── service_test.clj

5 directories, 8 files
```

To run the project, just use the `lein run` command and it will compile and start the sample service defined by the template at port `8080`. To test the service, open the `http://localhost:8080` URL and `http://localhost:8080/about` in a browser and observe the response. The first URL returns the response as **Hello World!**, whereas the second URL returns **Clojure 1.8.0 - served from /about**:

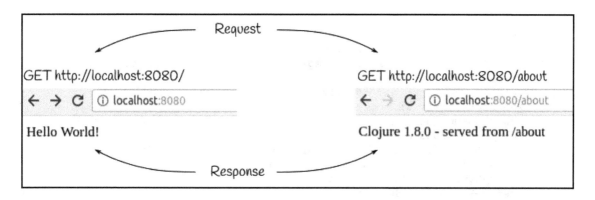

Both the endpoints can also be accessed from cURL as shown here:

```
% curl -v http://localhost:8080
* Rebuilt URL to: http://localhost:8080/
* Trying 127.0.0.1...
* Connected to localhost (127.0.0.1) port 8080 (#0)
> GET / HTTP/1.1
> Host: localhost:8080
> User-Agent: curl/7.47.0
> Accept: */*
>
< HTTP/1.1 200 OK
< Date: Fri, 03 Nov 2017 06:30:00 GMT
< Strict-Transport-Security: max-age=31536000; includeSubdomains
< X-Frame-Options: DENY
< X-Content-Type-Options: nosniff
< X-XSS-Protection: 1; mode=block
< X-Download-Options: noopen
< X-Permitted-Cross-Domain-Policies: none
< Content-Security-Policy: object-src 'none'; script-src 'unsafe-inline'
'unsafe-eval' 'strict-dynamic' https: http:;
< Content-Type: text/html;charset=utf-8
< Transfer-Encoding: chunked
<
* Connection #0 to host localhost left intact
Hello World!

% curl -v http://localhost:8080/about
* Trying 127.0.0.1...
* Connected to localhost (127.0.0.1) port 8080 (#0)
> GET /about HTTP/1.1
> Host: localhost:8080
> User-Agent: curl/7.47.0
> Accept: */*
```

```
>
< HTTP/1.1 200 OK
< Date: Fri, 03 Nov 2017 06:30:09 GMT
< Strict-Transport-Security: max-age=31536000; includeSubdomains
< X-Frame-Options: DENY
< X-Content-Type-Options: nosniff
< X-XSS-Protection: 1; mode=block
< X-Download-Options: noopen
< X-Permitted-Cross-Domain-Policies: none
< Content-Security-Policy: object-src 'none'; script-src 'unsafe-inline'
'unsafe-eval' 'strict-dynamic' https: http:;
< Content-Type: text/html;charset=utf-8
< Transfer-Encoding: chunked
<
* Connection #0 to host localhost left intact
Clojure 1.8.0 - served from /about
```

To run the application in dev mode, start a REPL session via CIDER (https://cider.readthedocs.io/en/latest/up_and_running/#launch-an-nrepl-server-and-client-from-emacs), and call the `pedestal-play.server/run-dev` function to start the server in dev mode.

Using interceptors and handlers

In the `pedestal-play` project, the `service.clj` source file defines two interceptors, `about-page` and `home-page`, which are used for the service. Additionally, it uses two HTTP-specific interceptors, `body-params` (http://pedestal.io/api/pedestal.service/io.pedestal.http.body-params.html#var-body-params) and `html-body` (http://pedestal.io/api/pedestal.service/io.pedestal.http.html#var-html-body), which are provided out of the box by the `pedestal.service` module. The `pedestal-play.service` namespace snippet is shown here with the interceptor declarations:

```
(ns pedestal-play.service
  (:require [io.pedestal.http :as http]
            [io.pedestal.http.route :as route]
            [io.pedestal.http.body-params :as body-params]
            [ring.util.response :as ring-resp]))

;; Used by GET /about
(defn about-page
  [request]
  (ring-resp/response (format "Clojure %s - served from %s"
                              (clojure-version)
                              (route/url-for ::about-page))))
```

```
;; Used by GET /
(defn home-page
  [request]
  (ring-resp/response "Hello World!"))

(def common-interceptors [(body-params/body-params) http/html-body])
```

. . .

Instead of taking a *Context Map* as input and returning the *Context Map*, the about-page and home-page interceptors take the request map (http://pedestal.io/reference/request-map) as an argument and return the response map (http://pedestal.io/reference/response-map). Such interceptors are called handlers and are treated as functions by the Pedestal framework. Handlers in the Pedestal framework do not have access to *Context Map*; therefore, they cannot change the sequence of interceptors in the chain and that is the reason they can only be used at the end of the interceptor chain to construct the response map. The response function, used by the home-page and about-page handlers, is a utility function provided by the Ring framework (https://github.com/ring-clojure/ring) to create a Ring response map with 200 status, no headers, and a given body content.

The body-params function returns an interceptor that parses the request body based on its MIME type (https://en.wikipedia.org/wiki/Media_type) and adds the relevant keys to the request map with the corresponding body parameters. For example, it will add a :form-params key with all the form parameters for the requests with the content type of application/x-www-form-urlencoded. The interceptor specified by the html-body var adds the Content-Type header parameter to the response with the type as text/html; charset=UTF-8. Since html-body acts on the response, the function for this interceptor is defined for the :leave key, whereas for body-params the function is defined for the :enter key of its interceptor map.

All the interceptors in Pedestal implement the IntoInterceptor protocol (http://pedestal.io/api/pedestal.interceptor/io.pedestal.interceptor.html#var-IntoInterceptor). Pedestal extends the IntoInterceptor protocol to a *Map, Function, List, Symbol,* or a *Var* and allows interceptors to be defined in any of these extended forms. The most common way of defining an interceptor is a Clojure Map (https://clojure.org/reference/data_structures#Maps) with :enter, :leave, and :error keys. It can be defined as a function, as well, to be considered a handler, such as the about-page and home-page of the pedestal-play project.

Creating routes

Interceptors in Pedestal are attached to routes that define the endpoints for clients to interact with the application. Pedestal provides three prominent ways of defining Routes (`http://pedestal.io/reference/routing-quick-reference#_routes`)—verbose, table, and terse. All three are defined as Clojure data structures with verbose being defined as a Map (`https://clojure.org/reference/data_structures#Maps`), table as a set (`https://clojure.org/reference/data_structures#Sets`), and terse as a vector (`https://clojure.org/reference/data_structures#Vectors`). These three formats are defined for convenience only. Pedestal internally converts all route definitions into the verbose form before processing them using the convenient function expand-routes (`http://pedestal.io/api/pedestal.route/io.pedestal.http.route.html#var-expand-routes`). The verbose syntax is a list of Maps with keywords that define a route. A list of keywords and their descriptions are shown in the following table:

Keyword	Sample value	Description
`:route-name`	`:pedestal-play.service/about-page`	Unique name for the route
`:app-name`	`:pedestal-play`	Optional name for the application
`:path`	`/about/:id`	Path URI
`:method`	`:get`	HTTP verb; can be `:get`, `:put`, `:post`, `:delete`, `:any`, and more
`:scheme`	`:http`	Optional, such as `:http` and `:https`
`:host`	`somehost.com`	Optional hostname
`:port`	`8080`	Port number
`:interceptors`	Vector of interceptors	Interceptor Maps with `:name`, `:enter`, `:leave`, and `:error` keys
`:query-constraints`	`{:name #".+" :search #"[0-9]+"}`	Constraints on query parameters, if any

Additionally, there are a few more keys derived from the `:path` parameter of verbose syntax, as follows:

Keyword	Sample value	Description
`:path-re`	`#"/\Qabout\E/([^/]+)"`	Regex used to match the path
`:path-parts`	`["about" :id]`	Parts of the Path URI
`:path-params`	`[:id]`	Path parameters
`:path-constraints`	`{:id "([^/]+)"}`	Constraints for path parameters, if any

The `pedestal.route` Pedestal module contains the implementation for both `Routes` and `Routers`. `Routers` are special interceptors that take `Routes` as input in verbose form and process the incoming requests to the `Routes` based on the implementation. `Routers` make sure that the requests are processed through the interceptors as per the interceptor chain. Any change in the interceptor chain by interceptors is handled by `Routers` efficiently.

In the `pedestal-play` project, the `service.clj` source file defines two routes, GET `/` and GET `/about`, which are bounded by the interceptor chain with `home-page` and `about-page` handlers at the end respectively, as shown in the following code:

```
;; Tabular Routes
(def routes #{["/" :get (conj common-interceptors `home-page)]
              ["/about" :get (conj common-interceptors `about-page)]})
```

The `:app-name`, `:host`, `:port`, and `:scheme` keys can be specified as maps that apply to all the routes specified in the list of routes, as shown in the following code:

```
(def routes #{{:app-name "Pedestal Play" :host "localhost" :port 8080
:scheme :http}
              ["/" :get (conj common-interceptors `home-page)]
              ["/about" :get (conj common-interceptors `about-page)]})
```

To see the verbose syntax for the routes, use the expand-routes (http://pedestal.io/api/pedestal.route/io.pedestal.http.route.html#var-expand-routes) function as shown in the following REPL session. The output of the expand-routes (http://pedestal.io/api/pedestal.route/io.pedestal.http.route.html#var-expand-routes) function is what is passed to the Pedestal router. The `:route-name` in the verbose format is derived from the name of the last interceptor in the chain or the symbol at the end of the chain that resolves to a function, such as `:pedestal-play.service/home-page`:

```
;; REPL
```

```
pedestal-play.server> (io.pedestal.http.route/expand-routes pedestal-
play.service/routes)
({:app-name "Pedestal Play",
  :route-name :pedestal-play.service/home-page,
  :scheme :http,
  :host "localhost",
  :port 8080,
  :path "/",
  :method :get,
  :path-re #"/\Q\E",
  :path-parts [""],
  :path-params [],
  :interceptors
  [{:name :io.pedestal.http.body-params/body-params,
    :enter #function[io.pedestal.interceptor.helpers/on-request/fn--9231],
    :leave nil,
    :error nil}
   {:name :io.pedestal.http/html-body,
    :enter nil,
    :leave #function[io.pedestal.interceptor.helpers/on-response/fn--9248],
    :error nil}
   {:name nil,
    :enter #function[io.pedestal.interceptor/eval157/fn--158/fn--159],
    :leave nil,
    :error nil}]}
 {:app-name "Pedestal Play",
  :route-name :pedestal-play.service/about-page,
  :scheme :http,
  :host "localhost",
  :port 8080,
  :path "/about",
  :method :get,
  :path-re #"/\Qabout\E",
  :path-parts ["about"],
  :path-params [],
  :interceptors
  [{:name :io.pedestal.http.body-params/body-params,
    :enter #function[io.pedestal.interceptor.helpers/on-request/fn--9231],
    :leave nil,
    :error nil}
   {:name :io.pedestal.http/html-body,
    :enter nil,
    :leave #function[io.pedestal.interceptor.helpers/on-response/fn--9248],
    :error nil}
   {:name nil,
    :enter #function[io.pedestal.interceptor/eval157/fn--158/fn--159],
    :leave nil,
    :error nil}]})
```

The same `Routes` can be defined in a terse syntax as well, using the vector (`https://clojure.org/reference/data_structures#Vectors`) of nested vectors. Each vector defines an application, optionally, with an application name, scheme, host, and port. Each application declaration has one or more nested vectors that define the routes. Each vector adds a path segment representing the hierarchical tree structure of routes, as shown in the following code:

```
(def routes
  `[["Pedestal Play" :http "localhost" 8080
    ["/" {:get home-page}
     ^:interceptors [(body-params/body-params) http/html-body]
     ["/about" {:get about-page}]]]])
```

Each route vector contains a path segment, such as /about, interceptor metadata map, constraints map, verb map, and child route vectors, if any. Interceptors defined in the interceptor metadata map are applied to every route defined in the verb map, and the verb key in the verb map contains the value of verb-specific handler functions or a list of interceptors.

Declaring routers

`Routers` are functions that are added as interceptors to the chain to analyze the requests based on the defined `Routes`. Pedestal creates a router based on the values of `:io.pedestal.http/routes` and `:io.pedestal.http/router` keys, as specified in the service map (`http://pedestal.io/reference/service-map`). The service map contains all the details for Pedestal to create a service including a router, routes, chain-provider properties, and more. It acts as a builder (`https://en.wikipedia.org/wiki/Builder_pattern`) for Pedestal services.

Pedestal provides three built-in routers that can be specified using the `:map-tree`, `:prefix-tree`, and `:linear-search` keywords. The `:map-tree` is the default router that has constant time complexity when applied to all routes that are static. It falls back to `prefix-tree` if any routes have path parameters or wildcards.

If the value of `:io.pedestal.http/router` is specified as a function then that function is used to construct a router. The function must take one argument, that is, the collection of routes in verbose format, and must return a router that satisfies router protocols (`http://pedestal.io/api/pedestal.route/io.pedestal.http.route.router.html#var-Router`).

Accessing request parameters

Servlet Chain Provider (`http://pedestal.io/api/pedestal.service/io.pedestal.http.impl.servlet-interceptor.html`) attaches a request map to the *Context Map* with the `:request` key before the first interceptor is invoked. The request map contains all the form, query, and URL parameters specified by the client of the API. These params are defined as maps of key-value pairs, where each key represents the parameter specified by the client. All the params are optional and are present only if they are specified by the client in the request. Here is a list of the keys that a request map may contain:

Key	Used for
`:path-params`	Present if any path parameters are specified and found by the *Router*
`:query-params`	Present if the query-params (`http://pedestal.io/api/pedestal.route/io.pedestal.http.route.html#var-query-params`) interceptor is used (default)
`:form-params`	Present if the body-params (`http://pedestal.io/api/pedestal.service/io.pedestal.http.body-params.html#var-body-params`) interceptor is used and the client sends the request with `application/x-www-form-urlencoded` as the content type
`:json-params`	Present if the body-params interceptor is used and the client sends the request with `application/json` as the content type
`:edn-params`	Present if the body-params interceptor is used and the client sends the request with `application/edn` as the content type
`:params`	Merged map of path, query, and request parameters

Apart from parameters, the request map also has these keys that are always present and can be used by interceptors in the chain:

Key	Type	Used for
`:async-supported?`	Boolean	True if this request supports asynchronous operations
`:body`	ServletInputStream	Body of the request
`:headers`	Map	Request headers sent by the client with all names converted to lower case
`:path-info`	String	Request path, below the context path; always present, at least /

:protocol	String	Name and version of the protocol with which the request was sent
:query-string	String	The part of the request's URL after the ? character
:remote-addr	String	IP Address of the client (or the last proxy to forward the request)
:request-method	Keyword	HTTP verb used, in lower case and in keyword form as determined by the method-param interceptor (default)
:server-name	String	Hostname of the server to which the request was sent
:server-port	Int	Port number to which the request was sent
:scheme	String	The name of the scheme used for the request, such as http, https, or ftp
:uri	String	Request URI from the protocol name up to the query string

To review the request map, add a new debug-page handler to the pedestal-play project and map it to the route /debug as shown in the following code snippet. The handler debug-page just returns the request map in the response with only the parameter keys of interest. It also converts it into a JSON string using the Cheshire (https://github.com/dakrone/cheshire) library:

```
(defn debug-page
  [request]
  (ring-resp/response
    (cheshire.core/generate-string
      (select-keys request
        [:params :path-params :query-params :form-params]))))

;; Common Interceptors used for all routes
(def common-interceptors [(body-params/body-params) http/html-body])

(def routes #{{:app-name "Pedestal Play" :host "localhost" :port 8080
:scheme :http}
                ["/" :get (conj common-interceptors `home-page)]
                ["/about" :get (conj common-interceptors `about-page)]
                ["/debug/:id" :post (conj common-interceptors `debug-page)]})
```

The cURL request to the `/debug` route now provides the entire request map that can be inspected for the `path`, `query`, and `form` params as shown in the following example:

```
curl -XPOST -d "formparam=1" "http://localhost:8080/debug/1?qparam=1"
{
  "params": {
    "qparam": "1",
    "formparam": "1"
  },
  "path-params": {
    "id": "1"
  },
  "query-params": {
    "qparam": "1"
  },
  "form-params": {
    "formparam": "1"
  }
}
```

Creating interceptors

A Pedestal interceptor can be defined as a map with the keys `:name`, `:enter`, `:leave`, and `:error`. For example, an interceptor `msg-play` can be defined for the `/hello` route of the `pedestal-play` project to change the query parameter `name` to upper case at the time of entry using the `:enter` function and appending a greeting at the time of exit using the `:leave` function. It is followed by the handler `hello-page` that reads the query parameters and adds a `Hello` greeting. Take a look at the following example:

```
;; Handler for /hello route
(defn hello-page
  [request]
  (ring-resp/response
    (let [resp (clojure.string/trim (get-in request [:query-params :name]))]
      (if (empty? resp) "Hello World!" (str "Hello " resp "!")))))


(def msg-play
  {:name ::msg-play
   :enter
   (fn [context]
       (update-in context [:request :query-params :name]
clojure.string/upper-case))
   :leave
```

```
    (fn [context] (update-in context [:response :body]
                              #(str % "Good to see you!")))})

;; Common Interceptors used for all routes
(def common-interceptors [(body-params/body-params) http/html-body])

(def routes #{{:app-name "Pedestal Play" :host "localhost" :port 8080
:scheme :http}
              ["/" :get (conj common-interceptors `home-page)]
              ["/about" :get (conj common-interceptors `about-page)]
              ["/debug/:id" :post (conj common-interceptors `debug-page)]
              ["/hello" :get
               (conj common-interceptors `msg-play `hello-page)]})
```

The cURL request to the /hello route with the name query parameter now provides the result as expected with both :enter and :leave events firing for the msg-play interceptor:

```
% curl "http://localhost:8080/hello?name=clojure"
Hello CLOJURE!Good to see you!
```

If the query parameter is not specified, it returns the Hello World greeting as per the implementation of the hello-page interceptor:

```
% curl "http://localhost:8080/hello?name="
Hello World!Good to see you!
```

Handling errors and exceptions

Interceptors might throw an exception due to an error in the implementation. For example, try calling the /hello route with no query parameter. It fails and throws an exception due to the usage of the upper-case function on a nil value of the :name parameter. The exception is thrown by the :enter function of the msg-play interceptor but there is no :error function defined for the interceptor to handle the exception. Such errors must be handled gracefully and errors must be reported to the caller using appropriate HTTP status codes. In this case, if the required parameter :name is not defined, then the route should return a response with a HTTP 400 Bad Request, along with a meaningful message for the caller.

Pedestal unifies error handling for both synchronous interceptors that return *Context Map*, and asynchronous interceptors that return a channel. It catches all exceptions thrown within an interceptor and binds it to the `:io.pedestal.interceptor.chain/error` key in the *Context Map*. Once the error is attached to the key, Pedestal starts looking for the next interceptor in the chain that has an `:error` function attached to it.

To handle the exception with the `/hello` route of the `pedestal-play` project, an `:error` function can be defined for the `msg-play` interceptor. The `:error` function can then catch any exception thrown by the interceptor and associate an appropriate response with the *Context Map*. Take a look at the following example:

```
(def msg-play
  {:name ::msg-play
   :enter
   (fn [context]
      (update-in context [:request :query-params :name]
                 clojure.string/upper-case))
   :leave
   (fn [context] (update-in context [:response :body]
                            #(str % "Good to see you!")))
   :error
   (fn [context ex-info]
      (assoc context :response {:status 400 :body "Invalid name!"}))})
```

The cURL request for the `/hello` route now provides an appropriate response with the correct status code and a message, as shown in the following example:

```
% curl -i "http://localhost:8080/hello"
HTTP/1.1 400 Bad Request
...

Invalid name!
```

The `:error` function receives two arguments, *Context Map* and an ex-info exception. It can either return a *Context Map* to catch the error or update the `:io.pedestal.interceptor.chain/error` key with the exception to look for a handler. It can also re-throw the exception or throw a new exception to signal something went wrong while handling the exception. In both cases, Pedestal will start looking for a handler of the exception. Pedestal keeps track of all the exceptions that were overridden by adding them in sequence to the key `:io.pedestal.interceptor.chain/suppressed` of *Context Map*.

Pedestal also provides an error-dispatch (`http://pedestal.io/api/`
`pedestal.interceptor/io.pedestal.interceptor.error.html#var-`
`error-dispatch`) macro to build error-handling (`http://pedestal.io/`
`reference/error-handling#_error_dispatch_interceptor`) interceptors
that use pattern matching to select a clause.

Logging

The Pedestal module `pedestal.log` contains components for logging and also reporting
runtime operational metrics. Pedestal uses Logback (`https://logback.qos.ch/`) for logging
and it can be configured by creating a `logback.xml` file in the project `config` directory.
Natively, logback-classic implements SLF4J (`https://www.slf4j.org/`), which is used by
Pedestal as well for logging. Pedestal implements each logging level—trace, debug, info,
warn, and error—as macros that take key-value pairs as parameters, printed using
the `pr` function (`https://clojuredocs.org/clojure.core/pr`). To log an exception via
Pedestal logger, the `:exception` key must be used with a `java.lang.Throwable` object as
a value assigned to it.

The default project template of Pedestal contains a `logback.xml` file in the `config`
directory along with the relevant dependencies added in the `project.clj` file for required
logger implementations. The default logging configuration of the `pedestal-play` project
logs the logback configuration in the console and also in the log file, as mentioned in the
`logback.xml` file. Take a look at the following example:

```
% lein run
18:53:30,595 |-INFO in ch.qos.logback.classic.LoggerContext[default] -
Could NOT find resource [logback.groovy]
18:53:30,595 |-INFO in ch.qos.logback.classic.LoggerContext[default] -
Could NOT find resource [logback-test.xml]
18:53:30,595 |-INFO in ch.qos.logback.classic.LoggerContext[default] -
Found resource [logback.xml] at [file:/pedestal-play/config/logback.xml]
...
18:53:30,686 |-INFO in ch.qos.logback.core.joran.action.AppenderAction -
About to instantiate appender of type
[ch.qos.logback.core.rolling.RollingFileAppender]
18:53:30,688 |-INFO in ch.qos.logback.core.joran.action.AppenderAction -
Naming appender as [FILE]
18:53:30,691 |-INFO in
ch.qos.logback.core.joran.action.NestedComplexPropertyIA - Assuming default
type [ch.qos.logback.classic.encoder.PatternLayoutEncoder] for [encoder]
property
18:53:30,711 |-INFO in
```

```
c.q.l.core.rolling.SizeAndTimeBasedRollingPolicy@2017577360 - Archive files
will be limited to [64 MB] each.
18:53:30,712 |-INFO in
c.q.l.core.rolling.SizeAndTimeBasedRollingPolicy@2017577360 - No
compression will be used
18:53:30,713 |-INFO in
c.q.l.core.rolling.SizeAndTimeBasedRollingPolicy@2017577360 - Will use the
pattern logs/pedestal-play-%d{yyyy-MM-dd}.%i.log for the active file
18:53:30,716 |-INFO in
ch.qos.logback.core.rolling.SizeAndTimeBasedFNATP@1e75bef1 - The date
pattern is 'yyyy-MM-dd' from file name pattern 'logs/pedestal-play-%d{yyyy-
MM-dd}.%i.log'.
18:53:30,716 |-INFO in
ch.qos.logback.core.rolling.SizeAndTimeBasedFNATP@1e75bef1 - Roll-over at
midnight.
18:53:30,719 |-INFO in
ch.qos.logback.core.rolling.SizeAndTimeBasedFNATP@1e75bef1 - Setting
initial period to Tue Nov 07 18:53:30 IST 2017
18:53:30,719 |-WARN in
ch.qos.logback.core.rolling.SizeAndTimeBasedFNATP@1e75bef1 -
SizeAndTimeBasedFNATP is deprecated. Use SizeAndTimeBasedRollingPolicy
instead
18:53:30,721 |-INFO in
ch.qos.logback.core.rolling.RollingFileAppender[FILE] - Active log file
name: logs/pedestal-play-2017-11-07.0.log
...
```

Once the server is started, the default Pedestal logger logs each route access request as an
INFO message in the log:

```
Creating your server...
INFO org.eclipse.jetty.server.Server - jetty-9.4.0.v20161208
INFO o.e.j.server.handler.ContextHandler - Started
o.e.j.s.ServletContextHandler@62765e11{/,null,AVAILABLE}
INFO o.e.jetty.server.AbstractConnector - Started
ServerConnector@58fef400{HTTP/1.1,[http/1.1, h2c]}{0.0.0.0:8080}
INFO org.eclipse.jetty.server.Server - Started @4829ms
INFO io.pedestal.http - {:msg "GET /hello", :line 80}
```

Pedestal's servlet interceptor (`http://pedestal.io/reference/servlet-interceptor`) provides a default error handler that logs the HTTP requests and also exceptions, if any. It also emits the exception stack trace in the response body in development mode. Pedestal's logging is backed by the `LoggerSource` protocol, which can be implemented for custom loggers.

Publishing operational metrics

Operational metrics are useful to understand the usage and performance of the application by observing its runtime state as reported by the metrics. Pedestal provides a logging component that uses the Metrics library (`http://metrics.dropwizard.io/3.2.3/`) to publish the metrics to JMX (`https://en.wikipedia.org/wiki/Java_Management_Extensions`) by default via `MetricRegistry` (`http://metrics.dropwizard.io/3.1.0/getting-started/#the-registry`). The protocol implemented by Pedestal metrics is `MetricRecorder`, which can be implemented for custom metrics implementation. By default, `MetricRecorder` provides four types of recorders as shown in the following table:

Metric recorder	Usage
Gauge	Used for the instantaneous measurement of a value
Counter	Used to increment/decrement a single numeric metric
Histogram	Used to measure the statistical distribution of values (min, max, mean, median, percentiles)
Meter	Used to measure the rate of a ticking metric

To count the number of requests received for each route of the `pedestal-play` project, a `counter` can be added and incremented every time the corresponding handler is called:

```
(ns pedestal-play.service
  (:require [io.pedestal.http :as http]
            [io.pedestal.http.route :as route]
            [io.pedestal.http.body-params :as body-params]
            [io.pedestal.log :as log]
            [ring.util.response :as ring-resp]))

(defn about-page
  [request]
  (log/counter ::about-hits 1)
  (ring-resp/response (format "Clojure %s - served from %s"
                              (clojure-version)
```

```
                              (route/url-for ::about-page))))

  (defn home-page
    [request]
    (log/counter ::home-hits 1)
    (ring-resp/response "Hello World!"))

  (defn debug-page
    [request]
    (log/counter ::debug-hits 1)
    (ring-resp/response
     (cheshire.core/generate-string
       (select-keys request [:params :path-params :query-params :form-
  params]))))

  (defn hello-page
    [request]
    (log/counter ::hello-hits 1)
    (ring-resp/response
     (let [resp (clojure.string/trim (get-in request [:query-params :name]))]
       (if (empty? resp) "Hello World!" (str "Hello " resp "!")))))
```

By default, the `counter` will be published via JMX and can be looked up using the JVM monitoring tool JConsole (`https://en.wikipedia.org/wiki/JConsole`). To publish the metrics to JMX, start the Pedestal application in REPL using `pedestal-play.server/run-dev` and access various routes defined for the `pedestal-play` application. Next, open JConsole and connect to the `clojure.main` process for metrics. It will start listing the route metrics under the `io.pedestal.metrics` MBean (`https://en.wikipedia.org/wiki/Java_Management_Extensions#Managed_beans`). Take a look at the following screenshot:

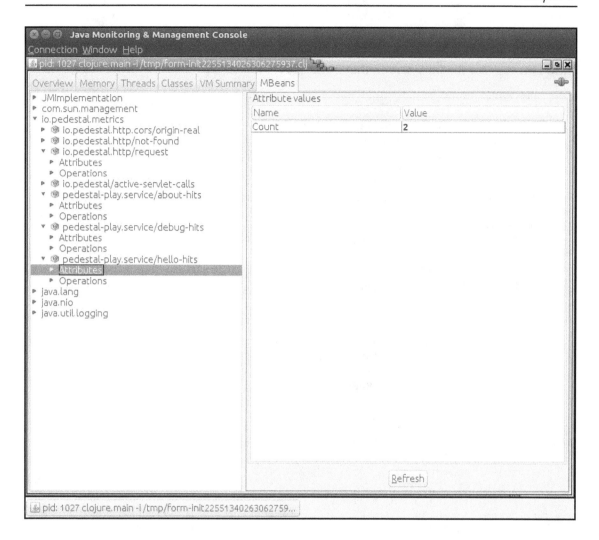

Using chain providers

Pedestal provides servlet interceptor as chain providers for HTTP-based web applications out of the box. It connects any servlet container to the interceptor chain. By default, the Pedestal application template uses the Jetty web server (https://www.eclipse.org/jetty/), but it also has support for chain providers that work with servers other than Jetty as well, such as Immutant (http://immutant.org/) and Tomcat (https://tomcat.apache.org/).

To start the application with the default server and chain provider, that is, for Jetty, run `lein run` within the `pedestal-play` application and observe the log messages. It shows the logs for the Jetty server, that is, the server in use:

```
Creating your server...

INFO org.eclipse.jetty.server.Server - jetty-9.4.0.v20161208
INFO o.e.j.server.handler.ContextHandler - Started
o.e.j.s.ServletContextHandler@62765e11{/,null,AVAILABLE}
INFO o.e.jetty.server.AbstractConnector - Started
ServerConnector@4789995a{HTTP/1.1,[http/1.1, h2c]}{0.0.0.0:8080}
INFO org.eclipse.jetty.server.Server - Started @4755ms

INFO io.pedestal.http - {:msg "GET /about", :line 80}
INFO io.pedestal.http - {:msg "GET /hello", :line 80}
```

To use a different chain-provider, say, `Immutant`, change the service map to use `Immutant` as the chain-provider. Take a look at the following code:

```
(def service {:env :prod
              ::http/routes routes
              ::http/resource-path "/public"
              ;; Either :jetty, :immutant or :tomcat
              ::http/type :immutant
              ::http/port 8080
              ...
              })
```

Also, change the `project.clj` file to use the `Immutant` implementation as follows:

```
(defproject pedestal-play "0.0.1-SNAPSHOT"
  :description "FIXME: write description"
  :url "http://example.com/FIXME"
  :license {:name "Eclipse Public License"
            :url "http://www.eclipse.org/legal/epl-v10.html"}
  :dependencies [[org.clojure/clojure "1.8.0"]
                 [io.pedestal/pedestal.service "0.5.3"]

                 ;; Remove this line and uncomment one of the next lines to
                 ;; use Immutant or Tomcat instead of Jetty:
                 ;;[io.pedestal/pedestal.jetty "0.5.3"]
                 [io.pedestal/pedestal.immutant "0.5.3"]
                 ;; [io.pedestal/pedestal.tomcat "0.5.3"]

                 [ch.qos.logback/logback-classic "1.1.8" :exclusions
[org.slf4j/slf4j-api]]
                 [org.slf4j/jul-to-slf4j "1.7.22"]
```

```
                        [org.slf4j/jcl-over-slf4j "1.7.22"]
                        [org.slf4j/log4j-over-slf4j "1.7.22"]]
    :min-lein-version "2.0.0"
    :resource-paths ["config", "resources"]
    ...
    :main ^{:skip-aot true} pedestal-play.server)
```

Now, the `lein run` logs show Undertow (`http://undertow.io/`) being used, that is, the web server used by `Immutant` libraries for the web. The routes and logging work exactly same as with the *Jetty* web server:

```
INFO org.xnio - XNIO version 3.4.0.Beta1
INFO org.xnio.nio - XNIO NIO Implementation Version 3.4.0.Beta1
WARN io.undertow.websockets.jsr - UT026010: Buffer pool was not set on
WebSocketDeploymentInfo, the default pool will be used
INFO org.projectodd.wunderboss.web.Web - Registered web context /

Creating your server...

INFO io.pedestal.http - {:msg "GET /about", :line 80}
INFO io.pedestal.http - {:msg "GET /hello", :line 80}
```

 Pedestal is not just limited to web applications. Interceptors in Pedestal can be used in message processing and data flow applications, as well, and are not limited to only request/reply-based web services.

Using server-sent events (SSE)

Server-sent events (SSE) (`https://www.w3.org/TR/eventsource/`) is a standard that enables efficient server-to-client streaming using a two-part implementation. The first part is the `EventSource` API that is implemented at the client side to initiate the SSE connection with the server, and the second part is the push protocol that defines the event stream data format that is used for the server-to-client communication.

The EventSource API of SSE is defined as a part of the HTML5 standard by W3C (https:/ /en.wikipedia.org/wiki/World_Wide_Web_Consortium) and is now supported by all the modern web browsers:

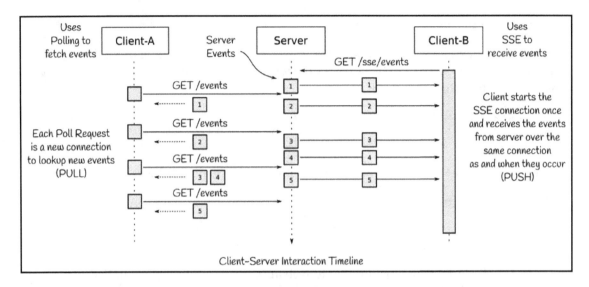

SSEs are primarily used to push real-time notifications, updates, and continuous data streams from server to client once an initial connection has been established by the client. Generally, the notifications and updates are pulled by the client by sending a request to the APIs or polling (https://en.wikipedia.org/wiki/Polling_(computer_science)) the server for updates. Polling requires a new connection to be established between the client and server for each request to pull the notifications and updates, as shown in the preceding diagram. SSE instead focuses on the push model in which the connection is established once by the client and is long-lived. All the notifications, updates, and data streams are pushed by the server over the same client connection. If a connection is lost, the client automatically reconnects with the server to keep the connection active. The flow between the server and the client is further illustrated in the preceding diagram for both polling and SSE modes of interaction.

The Pedestal service component includes support for SSE as well. It sends all its events as a part of a single response stream that is kept alive over time by sending events and/or periodic heartbeat data. If the response stream is closed or the connections is interrupted, the client can send a request to reopen it and continue to receive the events notifications from the server.

Creating interceptors for SSE

An interceptor for SSE can be created using the `start-event-stream` (http://pedestal.io/api/pedestal.service/io.pedestal.http.sse.html#var-start-event-stream) function provided by the Pedestal service component. It takes a function as input and returns an interceptor. The function expected by the `start-event-stream` function is called by Pedestal once the initial HTTP connection is established with the client; the HTTP response is prepared and Pedestal notifies the client that an SSE stream is starting. It takes a channel as input (https://clojure.github.io/core.async/), and *Context Map*. To send the events to the client, the function just publishes them on the channel provided as an argument to the function. In addition to the channel provided as an argument to the function, *Context Map* also contains a channel associated with the `:response-channel` key. This channel is directly connected with the response `OutputStream` and must not be used to send events to the client.

To create an interceptor for SSE in the `pedestal-play` project, define a function `sse-stream-ready` and pass it as an argument to the `start-event-stream`. The `start-event-stream` returns an interceptor that is assigned to a route `/events` that initiates SSE. The function `sse-stream-ready` reads a request parameter `counter` for the number of messages to be sent to the client and defaults to five. It publishes a Map on the channel `event-ch` with two keys, `:name` and `:data`, that contain a string value. It is recommended to use named events as they are helpful for clients to take appropriate action based on the name of the event. Once the required number of events are sent, it sends a `close` event and closes the channel. Once it closes the channel, Pedestal cleans up the connection. Take a look at the following code:

```
(ns pedestal-play.service
  (:require [io.pedestal.http :as http]
            [io.pedestal.http.sse :as sse]
            [io.pedestal.http.route :as route]
            [io.pedestal.http.body-params :as body-params]
            [io.pedestal.log :as log]
            [ring.util.response :as ring-resp]
            [clojure.core.async :as async]))


(defn sse-stream-ready
  "Starts sending counter events to client."
  [event-ch context]
  (let [count-num (Integer/parseInt
                    (or (-> (context :request)
                            :query-params :counter) "5"))]
    (loop [counter count-num]
```

```
(async/put!
 event-ch {:name "count"
           :data (str counter ", T: "
                      (.getId (Thread/currentThread)))})
(Thread/sleep 2000)
(if (> counter 1)
  (recur (dec counter))
  (do
    (async/put! event-ch {:name "close" :data "I am done!"})
    (async/close! event-ch))))))))

(def common-interceptors [(body-params/body-params) http/html-body])

(def routes #{{:host "localhost" :port 8080 :scheme :http}
              ["/" :get (conj common-interceptors `home-page)]
              ["/about" :get (conj common-interceptors `about-page)]
              ["/debug/:id" :post (conj common-interceptors `debug-page)]
              ["/hello" :get
               (conj common-interceptors `msg-play `hello-page)]
              ["/events" :get
               [(sse/start-event-stream sse-stream-ready)]]})
```

The route /events is defined under the routes of the pedestal-play application that are used to receive events over SSE. It has an interceptor assigned that is created by calling the start-event-stream function with the sse-stream-ready function that publishes the events. When a request reaches this interceptor, it pauses the interceptor execution and sends HTTP response headers to the client stating that an event stream is starting, and initiates a timed heartbeat to keep the connection alive. Once the connection is established, it calls the sse-stream-ready function with the channel and the current *Context Map*.

To try the SSE endpoint, run the pedestal-play application using lein run and use cURL to send the get request to the /events endpoint. Take a look at the following example:

```
% curl -i -XGET "http://localhost:8080/events"
HTTP/1.1 200 OK
Date: Wed, 08 Nov 2017 07:07:51 GMT
X-Frame-Options: DENY
X-XSS-Protection: 1; mode=block
X-Download-Options: noopen
Strict-Transport-Security: max-age=31536000; includeSubdomains
X-Permitted-Cross-Domain-Policies: none
Cache-Control: no-cache
X-Content-Type-Options: nosniff
Content-Security-Policy: object-src 'none'; script-src 'unsafe-inline'
'unsafe-eval' 'strict-dynamic' https: http:;
```

```
Content-Type: text/event-stream; charset=UTF-8
Connection: close

event: count
data: 5, T: 22

event: count
data: 4, T: 22

event: count
data: 3, T: 22

event: count
data: 2, T: 22

event: count
data: 1, T: 22

event: close
data: I am done!
```

By default, it sends five events, but that can be controlled using the request query parameter `counter`. Take a look at the following example:

```
% curl -XGET "http://localhost:8080/events?counter=2"
event: count
data: 2, T: 22

event: count
data: 1, T: 22

event: close
data: I am done!
```

The SSE interceptor sends a partial HTTP response to the client as a part of the connection initialization process itself, therefore, any downstream interceptors are not allowed to change the *Context Map* and the response map. They can only examine them.

> Pedestal supports the use of Last-Event-ID (https://www.w3.org/TR/eventsource/#last-event-id) as well, which allows the client to reconnect and resume from the point where it got disconnected. Based on the SSE spec (https://www.w3.org/TR/eventsource/), Pedestal supports assigning a string ID to the SSE stream that can be referred to by the client in the Last-Event-ID header to resume.

Using WebSockets

WebSockets is a communications protocol (`https://en.wikipedia.org/wiki/Communication_protocol`) that provides full-duplex (`https://en.wikipedia.org/wiki/Duplex_(telecommunications)#FULL-DUPLEX`) communication channels over a single TCP connection between client and server. It allows clients to send messages to the server and receive server events over the same TCP connection without polling. Compared to **Server-Sent Events (SSE)** (`https://www.w3.org/TR/eventsource/`), WebSockets support full-duplex communication between client and server instead of a one-way push. Also, SSEs are implemented over HTTP, which is an entirely different TCP protocol compared to WebSocket. Although both protocols are different, they both depend on the TCP layer.

 RFC 6455 (`https://tools.ietf.org/html/rfc6455`) states that WebSocket *is designed to work over HTTP ports 80 and 443 as well as to support HTTP proxies and intermediaries*, thus making it compatible with the HTTP protocol. To achieve compatibility, the WebSocket handshake uses the HTTP Upgrade header (`https://en.wikipedia.org/wiki/HTTP/1.1_Upgrade_header`) to change from the HTTP protocol to the WebSocket protocol.

Server-sent events are useful to send notifications or alerts from the server as and when they occur. If the application requires an interactive session between the client and the server, then WebSockets must be preferred.

Using WebSocket with Pedestal and Jetty

Pedestal provides out-of-the-box support for Jetty WebSockets as a part of its `pedestal.jetty` module. To create and register a WebSocket endpoint, Pedestal provides the `add-ws-endpoints` function that accepts a `ServletContextHandler` and a Map of WebSocket paths to the action Map. Based on the provided WebSocket paths, it produces the corresponding servlets and adds them to the context of the servlet container, that is, Jetty in this case. The servlet container then makes the WebSocket paths available for the clients to connect to using the WebSocket protocol. The WebSocket endpoints are communicated to the Jetty container using the `:context-configurator` key of the map assigned to the `::http/container-options` key of Pedestal's service map.

The `pedestal-play` project defines a `ws-paths` map that contains a single WebSocket path, `/chat`. The actions defined for the `/chat` path are `:on-connect`, `:on-text`, `:on-binary`, `:on-error`, and `:on-close`. The `start-ws-connection` function, provided by Pedestal, accepts a function of two arguments—the Jetty WebSocket session and its paired `core.async` channel—and returns a function that can be used as an `:on-connect` action handler. For other actions, the sample `pedestal-play` project just logs a message. Take a look at the following example:

```clojure
(ns pedestal-play.service
  (:require [io.pedestal.http :as http]
            [io.pedestal.http.sse :as sse]
            [io.pedestal.http.route :as route]
            [io.pedestal.http.body-params :as body-params]
            [io.pedestal.log :as log]
            [io.pedestal.http.jetty.websockets :as ws]
            [ring.util.response :as ring-resp]
            [clojure.core.async :as async]))

;; Atom to hold client sessions
(def ws-clients (atom {}))

(defn new-ws-client
  "Keeps track of all client sessions"
  [ws-session send-ch]
  (async/put! send-ch "Welcome!")
  (swap! ws-clients assoc ws-session send-ch))

(def ws-paths
  {"/chat" {:on-connect (ws/start-ws-connection new-ws-client)
            :on-text (fn [msg]
                       (log/info :msg (str "Client: " msg)))
            :on-binary (fn [payload offset length]
                         (log/info :msg "Binary Message!" :bytes payload))
            :on-error (fn [t]
                        (log/error :msg "WS Error happened" :exception t))
            :on-close (fn [num-code reason-text]
                        (log/info :msg "WS Closed:"
                                  :reason reason-text))}})

(def service {:env :prod
              ::http/routes routes
              ::http/resource-path "/public"
              ::http/type :jetty
              ::http/port 8080
              ;; Options to pass to the container (Jetty)
              ::http/container-options
```

```
{:h2c? true
 :h2? false
 :ssl? false
 :context-configurator #(ws/add-ws-endpoints % ws-paths)}})
```

In the `pedestal-play` example, the function provided to the `start-ws-connection` function is `new-ws-client`, a function that sends a `Welcome!` message to each new client and keeps track of client sessions. The `pedestal-play` example also defines a couple of utility methods, `send-and-close!` and `send-message-to-all!`, to send messages from the server side to the clients connected to the WebSocket. Take a look at the following example:

```
(defn send-and-close!
  "Utility function to send message to a client and close the connection"
  [message]
  (let [[ws-session send-ch] (first @ws-clients)]
    (async/put! send-ch message)
    (async/close! send-ch)
    (swap! ws-clients dissoc ws-session)
    (log/info :msg (str "Active Connections: " (count @ws-clients)))))

(defn send-message-to-all!
  "Utility function to send message to all clients"
  [message]
  (doseq [[^org.eclipse.jetty.websocket.api.Session session channel]
          @ws-clients]
    (when (.isOpen session)
      (async/put! channel message))))
```

To test the `/chat` WebSocket, start the `pedestal-play` application in REPL using the `pedestal-play.server/run-dev` function:

```
pedestal-play.server> (def srv (run-dev))

Creating your [DEV] server...
INFO org.eclipse.jetty.server.Server - jetty-9.4.0.v20161208
INFO o.e.j.server.handler.ContextHandler - Started
o.e.j.s.ServletContextHandler@15d129a1{/,null,AVAILABLE}
INFO o.e.jetty.server.AbstractConnector - Started
ServerConnector@766b5ac6{HTTP/1.1,[http/1.1, h2c]}{0.0.0.0:8080}
INFO org.eclipse.jetty.server.Server - Started @220932ms
#'pedestal-play.server/srv
pedestal-play.server>
```

Now, open the JavaScript console in a web browser and start the WebSocket session using the following commands:

```
// connects to the '/chat' endpoint with 'ws' protocol
w = new WebSocket("ws://localhost:8080/chat")

// log all the messages received from server on console
w.onmessage = function(e) { console.log(e.data); }

// message to be shown when server closes the connection
w.onclose = function(e) {
            console.log("The connection to the server has closed."); }

// send a message to server
w.send("Hello from the Client-1!");
```

Any message that is sent from the client is received by the server and logged on the REPL. Similarly, any message sent by the server using the function send-message-to-all! is broadcasted to all the active client connections. To close the WebSocket connection, call the send-and-close! function that will pick the first client connection, send a message, and close it. It also logs the number of active client connections as shown in the following code:

```
INFO pedestal-play.service - {:msg "Client: Hello from the Client-1!",
:line 113}
INFO pedestal-play.service - {:msg "Client: Hello from the Client-2!",
:line 113}
pedestal-play.server> (pedestal-play.service/send-message-to-all! "Hello
from Pedestal Server!")
nil
pedestal-play.server> (pedestal-play.service/send-and-close! "Goodbye from
Pedestal Server!")
INFO pedestal-play.service - {:msg "Active Connections: 1", :line 102}
nil
INFO pedestal-play.service - {:msg "WS Closed:", :reason nil, :line 119}
pedestal-play.server> (pedestal-play.service/send-and-close! "Goodbye from
Pedestal Server!")
INFO pedestal-play.service - {:msg "Active Connections: 0", :line 102}
nil
INFO pedestal-play.service - {:msg "WS Closed:", :reason nil, :line 119}
pedestal-play.server>
```

The following screenshot captures the WebSocket interactions among a REPL session and two browser clients, connected via a JavaScript console:

```
                 pedestal-play.server> (def srv (run-dev))

                 Creating your [DEV] server...
                 INFO  org.eclipse.jetty.server.Server - jetty-9.4.0.v20161208
                 INFO  o.e.j.server.handler.ContextHandler - Started o.e.j.s.ServletContextHandler@34031c40{/,null,AVAILABLE}
                 INFO  o.e.jetty.server.AbstractConnector - Started ServerConnector@601abc49{HTTP/1.1,[http/1.1, h2c]}{0.0.0.0:8080}
                 INFO  org.eclipse.jetty.server.Server - Started @1126504ms
                 #'pedestal-play.server/srv
                 INFO  pedestal-play.service - {:msg "Client: Hello from the Client-1!", :line 113}    ← Messages Received
                 INFO  pedestal-play.service - {:msg "Client: Hello from the Client-2!", :line 113}        from Client
                 pedestal-play.server> (pedestal-play.service/send-message-to-all! "Hello from Pedestal Server!")
Pedestal Server  nil
   (REPL)        pedestal-play.server> (pedestal-play.service/send-and-close! "Goodbye from Pedestal Server!")
                 INFO  pedestal-play.service - {:msg "Active Connections: 1", :line 102}          ← Messages Sent
                 nil                                                                                   to Client
                 INFO  pedestal-play.service - {:msg "WS Closed:", :reason nil, :line 119}
                 pedestal-play.server> (pedestal-play.service/send-and-close! "Goodbye from Pedestal Server!")
                 INFO  pedestal-play.service - {:msg "Active Connections: 0", :line 102}
                 nil
                 INFO  pedestal-play.service - {:msg "WS Closed:", :reason nil, :line 119}
                 pedestal-play.server> _

                 > w = new WebSocket("ws://localhost:8080/chat")
                 < ▶WebSocket {url: "ws://localhost:8080/chat", readyState: 0, bufferedAmount: 0, onopen: null, onerror: null, …}
                 > w.onmessage = function(e) { console.log(e.data); }
                 < f (e) { console.log(e.data); }
                 > w.onclose = function(e) { console.log("The connection to the server has closed."); }
WebSocket Client-1 < f (e) { console.log("The connection to the server has closed."); }
(JavaScript Console) > w.send("Hello from the Client-1!");    ← Message Sent
                 < undefined                                      to Server
                   Hello from Pedestal Server!              ← Messages Received
                   Goodbye from Pedestal Server!               from Server
                   The connection to the server has closed.
                 > |

                 > w = new WebSocket("ws://localhost:8080/chat")
                 < ▶WebSocket {url: "ws://localhost:8080/chat", readyState: 0, bufferedAmount: 0, onopen: null, onerror: null, …}
                 > w.onmessage = function(e) { console.log(e.data); }
                 < f (e) { console.log(e.data); }
                 > w.onclose = function(e) { console.log("The connection to the server has closed."); }
WebSocket Client-2 < f (e) { console.log("The connection to the server has closed."); }
(JavaScript Console) > w.send("Hello from the Client-2!");    ← Message Sent
                 < undefined                                      to Server
                   Hello from Pedestal Server!              ← Messages Received
                   Goodbye from Pedestal Server!               from Server
                   The connection to the server has closed.
                 > |
```

Summary

In this chapter, we learned about the concepts of the Pedestal framework and how to use them to create APIs. We also learned how to log useful information for debugging and monitoring the runtime state of the application using JMX metrics. We also looked at various web server plugins that can be used with Pedestal. Finally, we looked at how Pedestal can be used for SSEs and WebSockets for client-server interaction.

In the next chapter, we will take a look at a Datomic database that will be used for persistence by the microservices of the Helping Hands application. Datomic is written in Clojure and fits in well with the Helping Hands application, which requires transactions and temporal queries.

7

Achieving Immutability with Datomic

"Most of the biggest problems in software are problems of misconception."

- Rich Hickey

Microservices depend on the underlying database to reliably store and retrieve data. Often applications like **Helping Hands** need to store user transactions consistently along with user locations that may change over time. Instead of updating the user location permanently and losing the history of the changes, a good application must maintain the change in data so that it can be queried over time. Such requirements expect the data stored in the database to be immutable. Datomic (`http://www.datomic.com/`) is one such database that not only provides durable transactions but also has the concept of immutability built into its core so that users can query the state of the database over a period of time. Datomic is also written in Clojure, which is the technology stack of choice for the Helping Hands application. In this chapter, you will learn about the following:

- Datomic architecture and its data model
- How to store and retrieve data as facts with Datomic
- Datalog query language to retrieve facts
- How to query immutable facts with an example

Datomic architecture

Datomic is a distributed database that supports ACID (`http://docs.datomic.com/acid.html`) transactions and stores data as immutable facts. Datomic is focused on providing a robust transaction manager to keep the underlying data consistent, a data model to store immutable facts, and a query engine to help retrieve data as facts over time. Instead of having its own storage, it relies on an external storage service (`http://docs.datomic.com/storage.html`) to store the data on disk.

Datomic versus traditional database

A typical database is implemented as a monolithic application that contains the storage engine, query engine, and the transaction manager all packaged as a single application to which clients connect to store and retrieve data. **Datomic**, on the other hand, takes a radical approach of separating out the **Transaction Manager** (**Transactor**) as a separate process to handle all the transactions and commit the data to an underlying **Storage Service** that acts as a persistence store for all the data managed by **Datomic**. A high-level architecture of **Datomic** and its comparison with traditional databases is shown here:

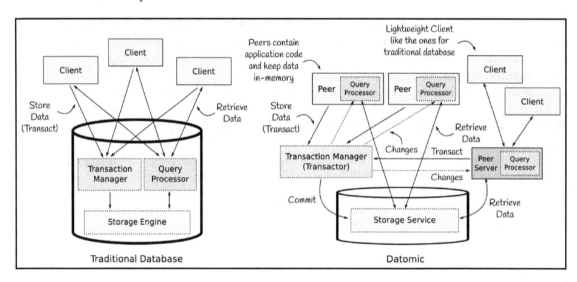

Clients of **Datomic** are called peers and have the application code and peer library (http://docs.datomic.com/integrating-peer-lib.html) that connect with the **Transactor** to store data consistently. Peers also query the underlying storage service for data and maintain a cache to reduce the load on the underlying storage service. Peers also receive updates from the **Transactor** as well and add to the cache. Peers in **Datomic** are thick clients that can be configured to cache (http://docs.datomic.com/caching.html) the data in-memory, or use external caching systems like Memcached (https://en.wikipedia.org/wiki/Memcached) to store the objects. The cache maintained by peers always contains immutable facts that are always valid.

Datomic also has a **Peer Server** that allows lightweight clients like that of traditional databases to connect to it directly to query the database. It acts as a central query processor for all the clients connected to it. Datomic provides a console (http://docs.datomic.com/console.html) as well, which has a graphical user interface to manage schema, examine transactions, and execute queries.

> Datomic is designed for transactional data and must be used to store user profiles, orders, inventory details, and more. It should not be used for high-throughput use cases such as those found in IoT (https://en.wikipedia.org/wiki/Internet_of_things), which requires a time-series database to store incoming data with high velocity.

Development model

Datomic provides two development models (http://docs.datomic.com/clients-and-peers.html)—**Peer** and **Client**. Both the models require a **Transactor** (http://docs.datomic.com/transactor.html) to be running to handle the transactions and store the data consistently. In the **Client** model, a **Peer Server** (http://docs.datomic.com/peer-server.html) is required in addition to the **Transactor** to coordinate the storage and query requests from the clients.

Both the development models and the participating components are shown in the following diagram:

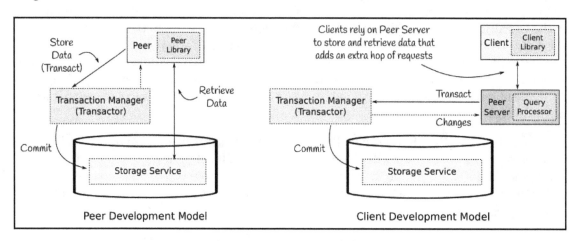

Clients are lightweight in the case of a client model as all the interaction with the **Transactor** and storage engine is handled by the **Peer Server** on behalf of the client, but it adds an additional hop of requests as all the requests are routed through **Peer Server** instead of directly connecting with the **Transactor** and the storage engine. Datomic provides a separate **Peer Library** and **Client Library** (http://docs.datomic.com/project-setup.html) for peer and client modes, respectively.

Data model

Datomic stores data as facts with each fact being a five-tuple (https://en.wikipedia.org/wiki/Tuple). These facts are called **Datoms**. Each datom consists of an **Entity ID, Attribute,** and **Value** that form the first three parts of the five-tuple. The fourth part defines the timestamp at which the fact was created and holds true. The fifth part consists of a boolean value that determines whether the defined datom is an addition or retraction of a fact. Multiple datoms of the same entity can be represented as an entity map with an attribute and value as key-value pairs. The **Entity ID** for the entity map is defined using the key **:db/id**:

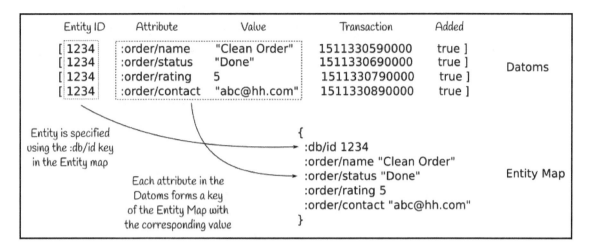

In the preceding example, there are four attributes—**order/name, :order/status, :order/rating**, and **:order/contact** defined for the order entity with the ID **1234**.

Schema

Each database in Datomic has an associated schema that defines all the attributes that can be associated with the entities. It also defines the type of value each attribute can contain. The attributes are themselves transacted as datoms, that is, they are also considered as entities with associated attributes that are defined by Datomic. The attributes supported by Datomic for schema definitions are as shown in the following table:

Attribute	Type	Description
`:db/ident`	Namespaced keyword	Unique name of an attribute in the form `<namespace>[.<nested-namespace>]/<name>`, such as `:order/name`. Namespaces are useful to prevent collisions but they can be omitted. `:db` is a restricted namespace used by Datomic internally.

:db/valueType	Keyword	Defines the type of value. Supported types are: • :db.type/keyword • :db.type/string • :db.type/boolean • :db.type/long • :db.type/bigint • :db.type/float • :db.type/double • :db.type/bigdec • :db.type/ref • :db.type/instant • :db.type/uuid • :db.type/uri • :db.type/bytes
:db/cardinality	Keyword	Specifies whether the attribute is single-valued or multi-valued. Possible cardinality types are: • :db.cardinality/one • :db.cardinality/many

Datomic also defines some optional schema (http://docs.datomic.com/schema.html) attributes such as :db/doc, :db/unique, :db/index, :db/fulltext, :db/isComponent, and :db/noHistory. The :db/ident, :db/valueType, and :db/cardinality attributes are mandatory.

Datomic also supports indexes (http://docs.datomic.com/indexes. html) that can be enabled for an attribute using the :db/index schema attribute. Internally, Datomic maintains four indexes that contain datoms ordered by *EAVT, AEVT, AVET*, and *VAET*, where *E* is entity, *A* is attribute, *V* is value, and *T* is transaction.

Using Datomic

Datomic can be downloaded freely from its Get Datomic (http://www.datomic.com/get-datomic.html) website. To start with Datomic, download the Datomic free edition that includes a memory database and embedded Datalog query engine. The free edition is also limited to two simultaneous peers and embedded storage that should be good enough to try out Datomic features and work with its data model.

Getting started with Datomic

To set up Datomic, download and extract the free edition's `datomic-free-x.x.xxxx.xx.zip` file. The free version of Datomic does not require any license key. For other versions, registration is mandatory to obtain a license key which must be added to transactor properties for Datomic to work. Datomic distribution contains two JARs, `datomic-free-x.x.xxxx.xx.jar` and `datomic-transactor-free-x.x.xxxx.xx.jar`. The `datomic-free` JAR file contains a peer library and `datomic-transactor` contains the implementation of the transactor. The distribution also contains a `bin` folder that has all the required scripts to start Datomic components as shown here:

```
datomic-free-0.9.5561.62
├──── bin
├──── CHANGES.md
├──── config
├──── COPYRIGHT
├──── datomic-free-0.9.5561.62.jar
├──── datomic-transactor-free-0.9.5561.62.jar
├──── lib
├──── LICENSE
├──── pom.xml
├──── README
├──── resources
├──── samples
└──── VERSION

5 directories, 8 files
```

To start with the free edition, create a new Clojure Leiningen project and add the `datomic-free` dependency. To build upon the `pedestal-play` project, add the dependencies to the existing project configuration file `project.clj` of project `pedestal-play` as shown here:

```
(defproject pedestal-play "0.0.1-SNAPSHOT"
  :description "FIXME: write description"
  :url "http://example.com/FIXME"
  :license {:name "Eclipse Public License"
            :url "http://www.eclipse.org/legal/epl-v10.html"}
  :dependencies [[org.clojure/clojure "1.8.0"]
                 [io.pedestal/pedestal.service "0.5.3"]
                 [frankiesardo/route-swagger "0.1.4"]

                 ;; Remove this line and uncomment one of the next lines to
                 ;; use Immutant or Tomcat instead of Jetty:
                 [io.pedestal/pedestal.jetty "0.5.3"]
```

```
;; [io.pedestal/pedestal.immutant "0.5.3"]
;; [io.pedestal/pedestal.tomcat "0.5.3"]

;; Datomic Free Edition
[com.datomic/datomic-free "0.9.5561.62"]

[ch.qos.logback/logback-classic "1.1.8"
 :exclusions [org.slf4j/slf4j-api]]
[org.slf4j/jul-to-slf4j "1.7.22"]
[org.slf4j/jcl-over-slf4j "1.7.22"]
[org.slf4j/log4j-over-slf4j "1.7.22"]]
:min-lein-version "2.0.0"
:resource-paths ["config", "resources"]
...
:main ^{:skip-aot true} pedestal-play.server)
```

The dependency of `com.datomic/datomic-free` will pull the required dependency from Clojars. Datomic distribution also provides a `bin/maven-install` script to install the JAR shipped in the distribution in the local Maven (`https://maven.apache.org/`) repository from where Leiningen can pull it for the project.

Now, start a REPL using `lein repl` or jack-in using the Emacs CIDER plugin to start using Datomic APIs. The namespace required to access the peer library is `datomic.api`. Include the namespace in a REPL session as shown here:

```
% lein repl
nREPL server started on port 33835 on host 127.0.0.1 -
nrepl://127.0.0.1:33835
REPL-y 0.3.7, nREPL 0.2.12
Clojure 1.8.0
Java HotSpot(TM) 64-Bit Server VM 1.8.0_121-b13
    Docs: (doc function-name-here)
          (find-doc "part-of-name-here")
  Source: (source function-name-here)
 Javadoc: (javadoc java-object-or-class-here)
    Exit: Control+D or (exit) or (quit)
 Results: Stored in vars *1, *2, *3, an exception in *e

pedestal-play.server=> (require '[datomic.api :as d])
nil
pedestal-play.server=>
```

 The Datomic free edition comes with in-memory storage. The data stored with the in-memory storage is only available for the lifetime of the application process when working with the Datomic free edition.

Connecting to a database

To connect to a database, first, define the database URI and create a database using
the `create-database` function of the `datomic.api` namespace. It takes as input a
database URI that defines the storage engine to be used, that is, mem for in-memory and the
database to be created, that is, `hhorder` for Helping Hands orders. It returns `true` if the
database is created successfully as shown here:

```
pedestal-play.server> (require '[datomic.api :as d])
nil
pedestal-play.server> (def dburi "datomic:mem://hhorder")
#'pedestal-play.server/dburi
pedestal-play.server> (d/create-database dburi)
true
pedestal-play.server>
```

Once the database is created, connect to it using the `connect` function provided by
the `datomic.api` namespace. It returns a `datomic.peer.LocalConnection` object that
can be used to transact with the database. Take a look at the following example:

```
pedestal-play.server> (def conn (d/connect dburi))
#'pedestal-play.server/conn
pedestal-play.server> conn
#object[datomic.peer.LocalConnection 0x299180eb
"datomic.peer.LocalConnection@299180eb"]
pedestal-play.server>
```

Transacting data

Datomic needs to know about the attributes to be used for the entities in the database
beforehand. Both attributes (schema) and facts (data) are transacted as datoms using
the `transact` function of the `datomic.api` namespace. Datoms can be transacted
individually or clubbed together as a part of single transaction by wrapping them in a
vector (https://clojure.org/reference/data_structures#Vectors). For example, all the
attributes for `hhorder` can be transacted using a single transaction by specifying all the
entity maps together within a vector and passing that vector as an argument to
the `transact` function as shown in the following example:

```
pedestal-play.server>
  (def result
    (d/transact conn [{:db/ident :order/name
                       :db/valueType :db.type/string
                       :db/cardinality :db.cardinality/one
```

```
                      :db/doc "Display Name of Order"
                      :db/index true}
                     {:db/ident :order/status
                      :db/valueType :db.type/string
                      :db/cardinality :db.cardinality/one
                      :db/doc "Order Status"}
                     {:db/ident :order/rating
                      :db/valueType :db.type/long
                      :db/cardinality :db.cardinality/one
                      :db/doc "Rating for the order"}
                     {:db/ident :order/contact
                      :db/valueType :db.type/string
                      :db/cardinality :db.cardinality/one
                      :db/doc "Contact Email Address"}]))
    #'pedestal-play.server/result
```

If the `:db/id` key is not defined as a part of the entity map, it is added by Datomic automatically. The `transact` function takes as parameter a Datomic connection and a vector of one or more datoms to transact. It returns a promise (https://en.wikipedia.org/wiki/Futures_and_promises) that can be dereferenced to see the transacted datoms, as well as the before and after state of the database. Take a look at the following example:

```
pedestal-play.server> (pprint @result)
{:db-before datomic.db.Db@6c5316fa,
 :db-after datomic.db.Db@351b51d3,
 :tx-data
 [#datom[13194139534312 50 #inst "2017-11-22T13:01:30.632-00:00"
13194139534312 true]
  #datom[63 10 :order/name 13194139534312 true]
  #datom[63 40 23 13194139534312 true]
  #datom[63 41 35 13194139534312 true]
  #datom[63 62 "Display Name of Order" 13194139534312 true]
  #datom[63 44 true 13194139534312 true]
  #datom[64 10 :order/status 13194139534312 true]
  #datom[64 40 23 13194139534312 true]
  #datom[64 41 35 13194139534312 true]
  #datom[64 62 "Order Status" 13194139534312 true]
  #datom[65 10 :order/rating 13194139534312 true]
  #datom[65 40 22 13194139534312 true]
  #datom[65 41 35 13194139534312 true]
  #datom[65 62 "Rating for the order" 13194139534312 true]
  #datom[66 10 :order/contact 13194139534312 true]
  #datom[66 40 23 13194139534312 true]
  #datom[66 41 35 13194139534312 true]
  #datom[66 62 "Contact Email Address" 13194139534312 true]
  #datom[0 13 65 13194139534312 true]
  #datom[0 13 64 13194139534312 true]
```

```
    #datom[0 13 66 13194139534312 true]
    #datom[0 13 63 13194139534312 true]],
  :tempids
  {-9223301668109598143 63,
   -9223301668109598142 64,
   -9223301668109598141 65,
   -9223301668109598140 66}}
```

Once the attributes are defined for the `hhorder` database, they can be associated with the entities. To add a new order, transact with the registered attributes as shown in the following example:

```
pedestal-play.server>
  (def order-result
    (d/transact conn [{:db/id 1
                        :order/name "Cleaning Order"
                        :order/status "Done"
                        :order/rating 5
                        :order/contact "abc@hh.com"}
                      {:db/id 2
                        :order/name "Gardening Order"
                        :order/status "Pending"
                        :order/rating 4
                        :order/contact "def@hh.com"}]))
  #'pedestal-play.server/order-result
```

For example, two orders with IDs 1 and 2 have been added to the `hhorder` database, which can now be queried via its `:db/id` or other defined attribute values.

Using Datalog to query

Datomic offers two ways to retrieve the data from the database—pull (`http://docs.datomic.com/pull.html`) and query (`http://docs.datomic.com/query.html`). The query method of retrieving facts from Datomic databases uses an extended form of Datalog (`https://en.wikipedia.org/wiki/Datalog`). To query the database, the `q` function of `datomic.api` needs to know the state of the database to run the query on. The current state of the database can be retrieved using the `db` function of `datomic.api`. Take a look at the following example:

```
pedestal-play.server> (d/q '[:find ?e ?n ?c ?s
                             :where [?e :order/rating 5]
                                    [?e :order/name ?n]
                                    [?e :order/contact ?c]
                                    [?e :order/status ?s]]
```

```
                          (d/db conn))
#{[1 "Cleaning Order" "abc@hh.com" "Done"]}
pedestal-play.server>
```

Each Datomic query must have either a :find and :where clause or a :find and :in clause present as a part of the query construct. A query, when given a set of clauses, scans through the database for all the facts that satisfy the given clauses and returns a list of facts. Datomic query grammar (http://docs.datomic.com/query.html#grammar) defines all the possible ways to query the database. Here are some of the examples to query the hhorder database:

```
;; Returns only the entity ID of the entities matching the clause
(d/q '[:find ?e
       :where [?e :order/rating 5]]
     (d/db conn))
#{[1]}

;; find all the entities with the three attributes and entity ID
(d/q '[:find ?e ?n ?c ?s
       :where [?e :order/name ?n]
              [?e :order/contact ?c]
              [?e :order/status ?s]]
     (d/db conn))
#{[1 "Cleaning Order" "abc@hh.com" "Done"] [2 "Gardening Order"
"def@hh.com" "Pending"]}

;; using 'or' clause
(d/q '[:find ?e ?n ?c ?s
       :where (or [?e :order/rating 4] [?e :order/rating 5])
              [?e :order/name ?n]
              [?e :order/contact ?c]
              [?e :order/status ?s]]
     (d/db conn))
#{[1 "Cleaning Order" "abc@hh.com" "Done"] [2 "Gardening Order"
"def@hh.com" "Pending"]}

;; using predicates
(d/q '[:find ?e ?n ?c ?s
       :where [?e :order/rating ?r]
              [?e :order/name ?n]
              [?e :order/contact ?c]
              [?e :order/status ?s]
              [(< ?r 5)]]
     (d/db conn))
#{[2 "Gardening Order" "def@hh.com" "Pending"]}
```

Achieving immutability

All the facts present in a Datomic database are immutable and are valid for any given timestamp. For example, the status of an order with :db/id 2 in the current state of the database is set as Pending. Take a look at the following example:

```
(d/q '[:find ?e ?s
       :where [?e :order/status ?s]]
     (d/db conn))
#{[1 "Done"] [2 "Pending"]}
```

Now, try to update the value of the :order/status attribute for order ID 2 to Done by transacting with its :db/id. Take a look at the following example:

```
;; update the status attribute to 'Done' for order ID '2'
(def status-result (d/transact conn [{:db/id 2 :order/status "Done"}]))
#'pedestal-play.server/status-result

;; query the latest state of database
(d/q '[:find ?e ?s :where [?e :order/status ?s]] (d/db conn))
#{[2 "Done"] [1 "Done"]}
```

After transacting, the status of the order ID 2 now shows the updated status in the current state of the database. Although the query shows that the status of order ID 2 is now Done, Datomic does not overwrite the value of the status for order ID 2 in-place. Instead, it adds a new datom with the recent transaction timestamp. Whenever the query is executed with the current state of the database, that is, using the db function of datomic.api, it always returns the facts with the most recent timestamp.

To retrieve the previous status of the order 2, use the state of the database before the transaction that updated the state. The return value of transact contains a :db-before key that can be used to run the same status query on the database state before the transaction. Take a look at the following example:

```
;; query the status on previous state
(d/q '[:find ?e ?s
       :where [?e :order/status ?s]]
     (@status-result :db-before))
#{[1 "Done"] [2 "Pending"]}
```

The result returns the previous status of order ID 2, that is, Pending. Immutability is one of the most powerful features of a Datomic database and is very useful to track the changes in the database.

Deleting a database

To delete an existing database, use the `delete-database` function of the `datomic.api` namespace. It takes as input the target database URI and returns `true` if the deletion succeeds as shown in the following example:

```
pedestal-play.server> (d/delete-database dburi)
true
```

 Datomic has a Day of Datomic (`http://www.datomic.com/training.html`) series that provides in-depth details about Datomic databases with detailed examples and tutorials to learn from.

Summary

In this chapter, we learned about Datomic architecture and how it is radically different from traditional databases. We learned about its data model and how it stores datoms. We also learned how to retrieve facts with Datomic APIs and its Datalog-based query engine. We also looked at its immutability constructs and how to query databases in current as well as historical states.

In the next part of this book, we will focus on the implementation of microservices for the Helping Hands application, which will use Pedestal as the base framework to design APIs and Datomic for persistence.

8

Building Microservices for Helping Hands

"It's not the ideas; it's design, implementation and hard work that make the difference."

- Michael Abrash

Identifying bounded context is the first step towards building a successful microservices-based architecture. Designing for scale and implementing them with the right technology stack is the next and the most crucial step in building a microservices-based application. This chapter brings together all the design decisions taken in the first part of the book (`Chapter 2`, *Microservices Architecture* and `Chapter 3`, *Microservices for Helping Hands Application*) and describes the steps to implement them using the Pedestal framework (`Chapter 6`, *Introduction to Pedestal*). In this chapter, you will learn how to:

- Implement Hexagonal design for microservices
- Create scalable microservices for Helping Hands using Pedestal
- Implement workflows for microservices using the Pedestal interceptor chain
- Implement the lookup service of Helping Hands to search for services and generate reports

Implementing Hexagonal Architecture

Hexagonal Architecture (`http://alistair.cockburn.us/Hexagonal+architecture`), as shown in the following diagram, aims to decouple the business logic from the persistence and the service layer. Clojure provides the concept of a protocol (`https://clojure.org/reference/protocols`) that can be used to define the interfaces, that act as ports of Hexagonal Architecture. These ports can then be implemented by the adapters, resulting in a decoupled implementation that can be swapped based on the requirement. Execution of these adapters can then be triggered via *Pedestal interceptors* based on the business logic.

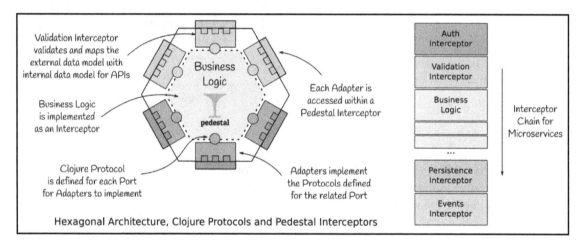

Hexagonal Architecture, Clojure Protocols and Pedestal Interceptors

Designing the interceptor chain and context

The interceptor chain must be defined for each microservice of the Helping Hands application separately. Each interceptor chain may consist of **interceptors** that authenticate the request, validate the data models, and apply the business logic. Interceptors can also be added to interact with the Persistence layer and to generate events as well. The list of probable interceptors that may be a part of Helping Hands services include:

- **Auth**: Used to authenticate and authorize requests received by the API endpoints exposed by the microservice.
- **Validation (data model)**: Used to validate the request parameters and map the external data model with the internal data model as expected by the business logic and underlying persistent store.

- **Business logic**: One or more interceptors to implement the business logic. These interceptors process the request parameters received by the API endpoints.
- **Persistence**: Persist the changes using one or more *adapters* that implement the *Port Protocol* defined for the microservice data model to be persisted.
- **Events**: Generate events asynchronously both for other microservices as well as for monitoring and reporting. These interceptors are added at the end of the chain to generate changelog events of the persistent store for other microservices to consume.

Pedestal context is a *Clojure map* that contains all the details related to the interceptor chain, request parameters, headers, and more. The same *context* m*ap* can also be used to share data with other interceptors in the chain. Instead of adding a key to the *context* m*ap* directly, it is recommended to keep a parent key, such as `tx-data`, that contains a m*ap* of keys that are related to the data being processed by the microservice. It may also contain the validated user details for other microservices to consume.

Creating a Pedestal project

To start with the implementation, create a project by the name of `helping-hands` and initialize it with a *Pedestal* template as discussed earlier in `Chapter 6`, *Introduction to Pedestal*. Once the project template is initialized, update the `project.clj` file and other configuration parameters as per the development environment setup of the *playground* application of `Chapter 4`, *Development Environment*. Once configured, the `project.clj` file should contain all the required dependencies and plugins, as shown here:

```
(defproject helping-hands "0.0.1-SNAPSHOT"
  :description "Helping Hands Application"
  :url
"https://www.packtpub.com/application-development/microservices-clojure"
  :license {:name "Eclipse Public License"
            :url "http://www.eclipse.org/legal/epl-v10.html"}
  :dependencies [[org.clojure/clojure "1.8.0"]
                 [io.pedestal/pedestal.service "0.5.3"]

                 ;; Remove this line and uncomment one of the next lines to
                 ;; use Immutant or Tomcat instead of Jetty:
                 [io.pedestal/pedestal.jetty "0.5.3"]
                 ;; [io.pedestal/pedestal.immutant "0.5.3"]
                 ;; [io.pedestal/pedestal.tomcat "0.5.3"]

                 [ch.qos.logback/logback-classic "1.1.8" :exclusions
[org.slf4j/slf4j-api]]
```

```
                    [org.slf4j/jul-to-slf4j "1.7.22"]
                    [org.slf4j/jcl-over-slf4j "1.7.22"]
                    [org.slf4j/log4j-over-slf4j "1.7.22"]]
  :min-lein-version "2.0.0"
  :source-paths ["src/clj"]
  :java-source-paths ["src/jvm"]
  :test-paths ["test/clj" "test/jvm"]
  :resource-paths ["config", "resources"]
  :plugins [[:lein-codox "0.10.3"]
            ;; Code Coverage
            [:lein-cloverage "1.0.9"]
            ;; Unit test docs
            [test2junit "1.2.2"]]
  :codox {:namespaces :all}
  :test2junit-output-dir "target/test-reports"
  ;; If you use HTTP/2 or ALPN, use the java-agent to pull in the correct
alpn-boot dependency
  ;; :java-agents [[org.mortbay.jetty.alpn/jetty-alpn-agent "2.0.5"]]
  :profiles {:provided {:dependencies [[org.clojure/tools.reader "0.10.0"]
                                       [org.clojure/tools.nrepl "0.2.12"]]}
             :dev {:aliases {"run-dev" ["trampoline" "run" "-m" "helping-
hands.server/run-dev"]}
                   :dependencies [[io.pedestal/pedestal.service-tools
"0.5.3"]]
                   :resource-paths ["config", "resources"]
                   :jvm-opts ["-Dconf=config/conf.edn"]}
             :uberjar {:aot [helping-hands.server]}
             :doc {:dependencies [[codox-theme-rdash "0.1.1"]]
                   :codox {:metadata {:doc/format :markdown}
                           :themes [:rdash]}}
             :debug {:jvm-opts
                     ["-server" (str "-agentlib:jdwp=transport=dt_socket,"
                                     "server=y,address=8000,suspend=n")]}}
  :main ^{:skip-aot true} helping-hands.server)
```

The project directory structure should contain the required files, as shown here:

```
.
├── Capstanfile
├── config
│   └── logback.xml
├── Dockerfile
├── project.clj
├── README.md
├── src
│   ├── clj
│   │   └── helping_hands
│   │       ├── core.clj
```

```
|      |              ├──── persistence.clj
|      |              ├──── server.clj
|      |              └──── service.clj
|      └──── jvm
└──── test
       ├──── clj
       |     └──── helping_hands
       |           ├──── core_test.clj
       |           └──── service_test.clj
       └──── jvm
```

```
9 directories, 11 files
```

Note the two new source files, `core.clj` and `persistence.clj`, that have been created manually and added to the project structure along with a `core_test.clj` file for test cases. This project acts as a template for each microservice that further extends the `service.clj` file with the implementation of routes and *direct messaging* endpoints. Initialization of the application happens in `core.clj` along with the implementation of interceptors and business logic. The persistence layer, along with its protocol, is defined in `persistence.clj`. The next step is to start defining the generic interceptors for Helping Hands microservices.

Defining generic interceptors

In addition to the business logic, each microservice needs to authenticate requests, validate incoming input parameters, map external data models to internal data models for business logic, and generate events for other microservices based on the action taken. All of these capabilities can also be implemented as a Pedestal interceptor for better flexibility and reduced maintenance overhead due to the separation of concern of each Pedestal interceptor.

Interceptor for Auth

Microservices that allow users to register services, lookup services, and create orders must integrate with the **Auth** service to make sure that the requests received by the service are genuine and the sender is authorized to perform the requested task. Instead of embedding Auth logic in all the microservices, it is recommended to separate it out as a microservice with which all other services can interact via direct messaging to authenticate the sender of the request.

The interaction with the Auth service can be embedded within a *Pedestal interceptor* that frontends the interceptor chain for all the secured APIs. This interceptor should capture the authentication and authorization details in the request and send them to the Auth service to validate. If the Auth service fails to validate the request, the interceptor should terminate the chain and return a HTTP 401 Unauthorized response, else it should add the sender profile details to the request and forward it to the next interceptor in the chain.

For example, auth is an interceptor that looks for a token in the request header. If it is present, it looks up the user details and populates them under the :user keyword of the Pedestal context map. If a token is not present in the header, it adds a HTTP 401 Unauthorized response with a message in the body and terminates the chain:

```
(ns helping-hands.service
  (:require [cheshire.core :as jp]
            [io.pedestal.http :as http]
            [io.pedestal.http.route :as route]
            [io.pedestal.http.body-params :as body-params]
            [io.pedestal.interceptor.chain :as chain]
            [ring.util.response :as ring-resp]))
...

(def auth
  {:name ::auth
   :enter
   (fn [context]
     (let [token (-> context :request :headers (get "token"))]
       (if-let [uid (and (not (nil? token)) (get-uid token))]
         (assoc-in context [:request :tx-data :user] uid)
         (chain/terminate
          (assoc context
                 :response {:status 401
                            :body "Auth token not found"})))))
   :error
   (fn [context ex-info]
     (assoc context
            :response {:status 500
                       :body (.getMessage ex-info)}))})

;; Tabular routes
(def routes #{["/" :get (conj common-interceptors `auth `home-page)]})
```

As of now, for simplicity, let's assume that the `get-uid` function just returns a response with `uid` as a field that has a fixed value, `hhuser`, that can be picked by interceptors, such as `home-page`, to construct the response further down the interceptor chain:

```
(ns helping-hands.service
  (:require [cheshire.core :as jp]
            [io.pedestal.http :as http]
            [io.pedestal.http.route :as route]
            [io.pedestal.http.body-params :as body-params]
            [io.pedestal.interceptor.chain :as chain]
            [ring.util.response :as ring-resp]))

...

(defn home-page
  [request]
  (ring-resp/response
   (if-let [uid (-> request :tx-data :user (get "uid"))]
     (jp/generate-string {:msg (str "Hello " uid "!")})
     (jp/generate-string {:msg (str "Hello World!")}))))

(defn- get-uid
  "TODO: Integrate with Auth Service"
  [token]
  (when (and (string? token) (not (empty? token)))
    ;; validate token
    {"uid" "hhuser"}))
```

Now, try to request the route / with and without a token. It will return the HTTP 200 OK response with the message containing the fixed user `hhuser`; whereas, without a token, it will return a HTTP 401 Unauthorized response. In the latter case, execution of the `home-page` interceptor is skipped entirely including both the `:enter` and `:leave` functions:

```
% curl -i -H "token: 1234" http://localhost:8080
HTTP/1.1 200 OK
...

{"msg":"Hello hhuser!"}

% curl -i http://localhost:8080
HTTP/1.1 401 Unauthorized
...

Auth token not found
```

The *Auth* service and related interceptor are explained in detail in *Part-4* of this book under `Chapter 11`, *Deploying and Monitoring Secured Microservices*.

Interceptor for the data model

Once the request is authenticated and authorized by the *Auth* interceptor, it should be validated against the **data model** of the microservice. This validation logic can also be implemented as a *Pedestal interceptor* that can review the input parameters specified with the request and make sure that it conforms to the data model. If the request parameters are valid, this interceptor should forward the request to the next interceptor in the chain with the required details, else it should terminate the chain and return a HTTP 400 Bad Request response.

The data model validation interceptor can also add additional details to the request. For example, if the request contains just the service ID, this interceptor can pull in the service details and service provider details and add it to the list of the parameters for the rest of the chain to process. It can also validate the presence and absence of the specified service ID.

For example, to create an order, a request must contain the service ID for which the order is to be created. The data model interceptor, in this case, can first validate that the request contains the service ID and if it does, it can validate the service ID with the external microservice that manages the *Service* database and pull in additional details:

```
(defn- get-service-details
  "TODO: Get the service details from external API"
  [sid]
  {"sid" sid, "name" "House Cleaning"})

(def data-validate
  {:name ::validate

   :enter
   (fn [context]
     (let [sid (-> context :request :form-params :sid)]
       (if-let [service (and (not (nil? sid)) (get-service-details sid))]
         (assoc-in context [:request :tx-data :service] service)
         (chain/terminate
          (assoc context
                 :response {:status 400
                            :body "Invalid Service ID"})))))

   :error
```

```
(fn [context ex-info]
  (assoc context
         :response {:status 500
                    :body (.getMessage ex-info)}))})

;; Tabular routes
(def routes #{["/" :post (conj common-interceptors `auth `data-validate
`home-page)]})
```

Now, the POST / endpoint uses both auth and data-validate interceptors to make sure that before the request hits the home-page interceptor, it has been authenticated and contains the required service details. The behavior of the endpoint is shown here using cURL requests:

```
% curl -i -XPOST http://localhost:8080
HTTP/1.1 401 Unauthorized
...

Auth token not found

% curl -i -XPOST -H "token: 1234" http://localhost:8080
HTTP/1.1 400 Bad Request
...

Invalid Service ID

% curl -i -XPOST -H "token: 1234" -d "sid=1" http://localhost:8080
HTTP/1.1 200 OK
...

{"msg":"Hello hhuser!"}
```

 Validation interceptors covered in this chapter use Clojure core conditional functions to achieve the desired validation. With the Clojure-1.9.0 release, it is recommended to move to Clojure spec (https://clojure.org/guides/spec) for all such validations.

Interceptor for events

Helping Hands microservices, such as *Service Provider* and *Service Consumer,* generate change log events for the *Lookup* service to pick up and update the local database for *Service Consumers* to look up. This requires certain events to be generated every time a change is pushed to the local database of the *Service Provider* and *Service Consumer* service. These events can be determined by an interceptor that is present in the chain right before the *Persistence interceptor* that persists the changes to the database. Apart from change-log events, each microservice may also publish events for monitoring and reporting. All these events can be generated by the same interceptor.

The events interceptor generates all the events required by other microservices and to monitor the entire application. Chapter 10, *Event Driven Patterns for Microservices*, and Chapter 11, *Deploying and Monitoring Secured Microservices,* talk about using external frameworks such as Kafka to publish and consume events for coordination and building an event-driven data pipeline for microservices.

Creating a microservice for Service Consumer

The *Service Consumer* microservice exposes APIs for end users to register as a consumer of the Helping Hands application. To look up registered services and place an order, the user of the application must be registered as a *Consumer.* As per the workflow of *Service Consumer* defined in Chapter 3, *Microservices for Helping Hands Application,* it requires the following APIs to create new consumers, get consumer profiles, and update consumer details:

URI	Description
GET /consumers/:id/?flds=name,address	Gets the details of the consumer with the specified :id if the :id is specified, else it gets the details of the authenticated consumer. Optionally, it accepts a CSV of fields to be returned in the response.
PUT /consumers/:id	Creates a new consumer with the specified ID.
POST /consumers	Creates a new consumer and returns the ID.

DELETE /consumers/:id	Deletes the consumer with the specified ID.

Adding routes

Pedestal routes are added for each of the identified APIs. The interceptor chain for each API consists of *Auth, Validation, Business Logic,* and *Event* interceptors that authorize the incoming requests, validate the required parameters, apply the business logic, and generate the relevant events, respectively, for other microservices and monitoring frameworks.

Since the interceptor chain of each route ends with a common `gen-events` interceptor, a `:route-name` must be defined for each route to make sure that they receive a unique name. If `:route-name` is not specified, *Pedestal* will try to assign the name of the last interceptor to each route and will fail with the *Route names are not unique* exception. Add the routes for the consumer service in the `service.clj` file, as shown in the following code snippet:

```
(ns helping-hands.consumer.service
  (:require [helping-hands.consumer.core :as core]
            [io.pedestal.http :as http]
            [io.pedestal.http.route :as route]
            [io.pedestal.http.body-params :as body-params]))

(def common-interceptors [(body-params/body-params) http/html-body])


;; Tabular routes
(def routes #{["/consumers/:id"
               :get (conj common-interceptors `auth `core/validate-id
                          `core/get-consumer `gen-events)
               :route-name :consumer-get]
              ["/consumers/:id"
               :put (conj common-interceptors `auth `core/validate-id
                          `core/upsert-consumer `gen-events)
               :route-name :consumer-put]
              ["/consumers"
               :post (conj common-interceptors `auth `core/validate
                           `core/create-consumer `gen-events)
               :route-name :consumer-post]
              ["/consumers/:id"
               :delete (conj common-interceptors `auth `core/validate-id
                             `core/delete-consumer `gen-events)
               :route-name :consumer-delete]})
```

Chapter 11, *Deploying and Monitoring Secured Microservices,* discusses the importance of events generated by the microservices for real-time monitoring and generating alerts.

Defining the Datomic schema

The *Service Consumer* microservice uses Datomic as the local database to store the consumer details. The schema for the consumer database consists of the following attributes:

:db/ident	:db/valueType	:db/cardinality	:db/index	:db/fulltext	:db/unique	:db/doc
:consumer/id	:db.type/string	:db.cardinality/one	true	false	:db.unique/identity	Unique consumer ID
:consumer/name	:db.type/string	:db.cardinality/one	true	true	-	Display name for the consumer
:consumer/address	:db.type/string	:db.cardinality/one	true	true	-	Consumer address
:consumer/mobile	:db.type/string	:db.cardinality/one	false	-	-	Mobile number
:consumer/email	:db.type/string	:db.cardinality/one	true	-	-	Email address
:consumer/geo	:db.type/string	:db.cardinality/one	false	-	-	CSV of latitude and longitude, specified in the format <lat>,<long>

Creating a persistence adapter

Persistence *protocol* for the *Consumer* service consists of upsert, entity, and delete functions that are implemented by each *adapter* of this port. *Adapters* implementing the persistence *protocol* are then used within the Pedestal interceptor to create, update, query, and delete *Consumer* details. The implementation of the protocol and corresponding record is shown in the following code snippet that must be added to the persistence.clj source file:

```
(ns helping-hands.consumer.persistence
  "Persistence Port and Adapter for Consumer Service"
  (:require [datomic.api :as d]))

;; --------------------------------------------------
;; Consumer Persistence Port for Adapters to Plug-in
;; --------------------------------------------------
(defprotocol ConsumerDB
  "Abstraction for consumer database"

  (upsert [this id name address mobile email geo]
    "Adds/Updates a consumer entity")
```

```
  (entity [this id flds]
    "Gets the specified consumer with all or requested fields")

  (delete [this id]
    "Deletes the specified consumer entity"))

;; -------------------------------------------------
;; Datomic Adapter Implementation for Consumer Port
;; -------------------------------------------------

(defn- get-entity-id
  [conn id]
  (-> (d/q '[:find ?e
             :in $ ?id
             :where [?e :consumer/id ?id]] (d/db conn) (str id))
      ffirst))

(defn- get-entity
  [conn id]
  (let [eid (get-entity-id conn id)]
    (->> (d/entity (d/db conn) eid) seq (into {}))))

(defrecord ConsumerDBDatomic [conn]
  ConsumerDB

  (upsert [this id name address mobile email geo]
    (d/transact conn
                (vector (into {} (filter (comp some? val)
                                         {:db/id id
                                          :consumer/id id
                                          :consumer/name name
                                          :consumer/address address
                                          :consumer/mobile mobile
                                          :consumer/email email
                                          :consumer/geo geo}))))))

  (entity [this id flds]
    (when-let [consumer (get-entity conn id)]
      (if (empty? flds)
        consumer
        (select-keys consumer (map keyword flds)))))

  (delete [this id]
    (when-let [eid (get-entity-id conn id)]
      (d/transact conn [[:db.fn/retractEntity eid]]))))
```

For example, the `ConsumerDB` protocol defines the port for the Persistence layer of the Consumer service that is implemented by the `ConsumerDBDatomic` record (`https://clojure.github.io/clojure/clojure.core-api.html#clojure.core/defrecord`) that acts as an adapter to manage the consumer database within the Datomic database. The `helping-hands.consumer.persistence` namespace also provides a `create-consumer-database` utility function to initialize the database and update the schema if the database is created for the first time, as shown here:

```
(defn create-consumer-database
  "Creates a consumer database and returns the connection"
  [d]
  ;; create and connect to the database
  (let [dburi (str "datomic:mem://" d)
        db (d/create-database dburi)
        conn (d/connect dburi)]
    ;; transact schema if database was created
    (when db
      (d/transact conn
                  [{:db/ident :consumer/id
                    :db/valueType :db.type/string
                    :db/cardinality :db.cardinality/one
                    :db/doc "Unique Consumer ID"
                    :db/unique :db.unique/identity
                    :db/index true}
                   {:db/ident :consumer/name
                    :db/valueType :db.type/string
                    :db/cardinality :db.cardinality/one
                    :db/doc "Display Name for the Consumer"
                    :db/index true
                    :db/fulltext true}
                   {:db/ident :consumer/address
                    :db/valueType :db.type/string
                    :db/cardinality :db.cardinality/one
                    :db/doc "Consumer Address"
                    :db/index true
                    :db/fulltext true}
                   {:db/ident :consumer/mobile
                    :db/valueType :db.type/string
                    :db/cardinality :db.cardinality/one
                    :db/doc "Consumer Mobile Number"
                    :db/index false}
                   {:db/ident :consumer/email
                    :db/valueType :db.type/string
                    :db/cardinality :db.cardinality/one
                    :db/doc "Consumer Email Address"
                    :db/index true}
```

```
                   {:db/ident :consumer/geo
                    :db/valueType :db.type/string
                    :db/cardinality :db.cardinality/one
                    :db/doc "Latitude,Longitude CSV"
                    :db/index false}]))
        (ConsumerDBDatomic. conn)))
```

The `create-consumer-database` function accepts a database name as input, such as `consumer`, and creates a Datomic database URI. The database URI prefix `datomic:mem://` signifies an in-memory database of Datomic that is used in this example. The `create-consumer-database` function tries to create a database and if it succeeds, it transacts the schema for the consumer database. It creates a connection to the database and returns it wrapped as a `ConsumerDBDatomic` record that can then be used to upsert consumers, retrieve them, and delete them based on the requirement.

Creating interceptors

The `helping-hands.consumer.core` namespace defines all the interceptors that are used for the routes of the *Consumer* microservice. Validation interceptors validate the input parameters and make sure that all the required fields are present in the request. They also prepare the input parameters for the business logic interceptors by creating a `:tx-data` key with all the required parameters.

Validation interceptors may also perform transformations, such as changing the CSV of the `flds` parameter to a vector of field names that is required as an input for the entity function defined by `ConsumerDB` protocol. They terminate the request with a HTTP 400 Bad Request status if the required parameters are not present. They also define the error handler to catch the exception in the chain and report them to the client with a HTTP 500 Internal Server Error status. The implementation of the validation interceptor is shown in the following code snippet:

```
(ns helping-hands.consumer.core
  "Initializes Helping Hands Consumer Service"
  (:require [cheshire.core :as jp]
            [clojure.string :as s]
            [helping-hands.consumer.persistence :as p]
            [io.pedestal.interceptor.chain :as chain])
  (:import [java.io IOException]
           [java.util UUID]))

;; delay the check for database and connection
;; till the first request to access @consumerdb
(def ^:private consumerdb
```

```
      (delay (p/create-consumer-database "consumer")))

;; -------------------------------
;; Validation Interceptors
;; -------------------------------

(defn- prepare-valid-context
  "Applies validation logic and returns the resulting context"
  [context]
  (let [params (merge (-> context :request :form-params)
                      (-> context :request :query-params)
                      (-> context :request :path-params))]
    (if (and (not (empty? params))
             ;; any one of mobile, email or address is present
             (or (params :id) (params :mobile) (params :email) (params
:address)))
        (let [flds (if-let [fl (:flds params)]
                     (map s/trim (s/split fl #","))
                     (vector))
              params (assoc params :flds flds)]
          (assoc context :tx-data params))
        (chain/terminate
         (assoc context
                :response {:status 400
                           :body (str "One of Address, email and "
                                      "mobile is mandatory")})))))

(def validate-id
  {:name ::validate-id

   :enter
   (fn [context]
     (if-let [id (or (-> context :request :form-params :id)
                     (-> context :request :query-params :id)
                     (-> context :request :path-params :id))]
       ;; validate and return a context with tx-data
       ;; or terminated interceptor chain
       (prepare-valid-context context)
       (chain/terminate
        (assoc context
               :response {:status 400
                          :body "Invalid Consumer ID"}))))

   :error
   (fn [context ex-info]
     (assoc context
            :response {:status 500
                       :body (.getMessage ex-info)}))})
```

```
(def validate
  {:name ::validate

   :enter
   (fn [context]
     (if-let [params (-> context :request :form-params)]
       ;; validate and return a context with tx-data
       ;; or terminated interceptor chain
       (prepare-valid-context context)
       (chain/terminate
         (assoc context
                :response {:status 400
                           :body "Invalid parameters"})))))

   :error
   (fn [context ex-info]
     (assoc context
            :response {:status 500
                       :body (.getMessage ex-info)}))})
```

The `helping-hands.consumer.core` namespace also defines the interceptors to get consumer details, perform `upsert` operations, create a consumer with a generated ID, and delete the consumer, as shown here:

```
;; --------------------------------
;; Business Logic Interceptors
;; --------------------------------

(def get-consumer
  {:name ::consumer-get

   :enter
   (fn [context]
     (let [tx-data (:tx-data context)
           entity (.entity @consumerdb (:id tx-data) (:flds tx-data))]
       (if (empty? entity)
         (assoc context :response {:status 404 :body "No such consumer"})
         (assoc context :response {:status 200
                                   :body (jp/generate-string entity)}))))

   :error
   (fn [context ex-info]
     (assoc context
            :response {:status 500
                       :body (.getMessage ex-info)}))})

(def upsert-consumer
```

```
{:name ::consumer-upsert

 :enter
 (fn [context]
   (let [tx-data (:tx-data context)
         id (:id tx-data)
         db (.upsert @consumerdb id (:name tx-data)
                     (:address tx-data) (:mobile tx-data)
                     (:email tx-data) (:geo tx-data))]
     (if (nil? @db)
       (throw (IOException.
               (str "Upsert failed for consumer: " id)))
       (assoc context
              :response {:status 200
                         :body (jp/generate-string
                                (.entity @consumerdb id []))}))))
 :error
 (fn [context ex-info]
   (assoc context
          :response {:status 500
                     :body (.getMessage ex-info)}))})

(def create-consumer
  {:name ::consumer-create

   :enter
   (fn [context]
     (let [tx-data (:tx-data context)
           ;; generate a random ID if it is not specified
           id (str (UUID/randomUUID))
           tx-data (if (:id tx-data) tx-data (assoc tx-data :id id))
           ;; create consumer
           db (.upsert @consumerdb id (:name tx-data)
                       (:address tx-data) (:mobile tx-data)
                       (:email tx-data) (:geo tx-data))]
       (if (nil? @db)
         (throw (IOException.
                 (str "Upsert failed for consumer: " id)))
         (assoc context
                :response {:status 200
                           :body (jp/generate-string
                                  (.entity @consumerdb id []))}))))

   :error
   (fn [context ex-info]
     (assoc context
            :response {:status 500
                       :body (.getMessage ex-info)}))})
```

```
(def delete-consumer
  {:name ::consumer-delete

  :enter
  (fn [context]
    (let [tx-data (:tx-data context)
          db (.delete @consumerdb (:id tx-data))]
      (if (nil? db)
        (assoc context :response {:status 404 :body "No such consumer"})
        (assoc context :response {:status 200 :body "Success"})))))
  :error
  (fn [context ex-info]
    (assoc context
            :response {:status 500
                       :body (.getMessage ex-info)}))})
```

Testing routes

The routes defined for the *Consumer* service allow users to create a new consumer, query for its properties, and delete it. As of now, for the *Auth interceptor*, assume that 123 is a valid token that is sent in the header of each request. To start with, create a consumer using the PUT /consumers/:id route with the ID set as 1, as shown here:

```
% curl -i -H "token: 123" -XPUT -d "name=ConsumerA"
http://localhost:8080/consumers/1
HTTP/1.1 200 OK
...

{"consumer/id":"1","consumer/name":"ConsumerA"}
```

It creates a new consumer and returns the consumer entity. To add a new field, use the same API with the same consumer ID and specify the new fields. It will do an upsert operation on the entity and add the new fields, as shown here:

```
curl -i -H "token: 123" -XPUT -d "email=user1@helpinghands.com"
http://localhost:8080/consumers/1
HTTP/1.1 200 OK
...

{"consumer/id":"1","consumer/name":"ConsumerA","consumer/email":"user1@help
inghands.com"}
```

To get the entity, use the `GET /consumers/:id` route. If the consumer ID is not found, it returns a HTTP 404 Not Found response:

```
% curl -i -H "token: 123" "http://localhost:8080/consumers/1"
HTTP/1.1 200 OK
...

{"consumer/id":"1","consumer/name":"ConsumerA","consumer/email":"user1@help
inghands.com"}

% curl -i -H "token: 123"
"http://localhost:8080/consumers/1?flds=consumer/name,consumer/email"
HTTP/1.1 200 OK
...

{"consumer/name":"ConsumerA","consumer/email":"user1@helpinghands.com"}

% curl -i -H "token: 123" "http://localhost:8080/consumers/2"
HTTP/1.1 404 Not Found
...

No such consumer
```

The `POST /consumers` route can also be used to create a consumer with a random ID:

```
% curl -i -H "token: 123" -XPOST -d
"name=ConsumerX&email=userx@helpinghands.com"
http://localhost:8080/consumers
HTTP/1.1 200 OK
...

{"consumer/id":"b46cdbbb-06a1-4375-9287-2230e3ad8ded","consumer/name":"Cons
umerX","consumer/email":"userx@helpinghands.com"}

% curl -i -H "token: 123"
"http://localhost:8080/consumers/b46cdbbb-06a1-4375-9287-2230e3ad8ded"
HTTP/1.1 200 OK
...

{"consumer/id":"b46cdbbb-06a1-4375-9287-2230e3ad8ded","consumer/name":"Cons
umerX","consumer/email":"userx@helpinghands.com"}
```

To delete a consumer, use the `DELETE /consumers/:id` route with an existing consumer ID:

```
% curl -i -H "token: 123" -XDELETE
"http://localhost:8080/consumers/b46cdbbb-06a1-4375-9287-2230e3ad8ded"
HTTP/1.1 200 OK
...

Success

% curl -i -H "token: 123"
"http://localhost:8080/consumers/b46cdbbb-06a1-4375-9287-2230e3ad8ded"
HTTP/1.1 404 Not Found
...

No such consumer
```

Creating a microservice for Service Provider

The *Service Provider* microservice exposes APIs for end users to register as a service provider of the Helping Hands application. *Service providers* can register one or more services with the Helping Hands application that they are willing to fulfill if an order is placed against it. As per the workflow of *Service Provider* defined in `Chapter 3`, *Microservices for Helping Hands Application,* the following APIs are required to create new providers, get provider profiles, and update provider details:

URI	Description
`GET /providers/:id/?flds=name,mobile`	Gets the details of the service provider with the specified `:id` if the `:id` is specified, else it gets the details of the authenticated user registered as a service provider. Optionally, it accepts a CSV of fields to be returned in the response.
`PUT /providers/:id`	Creates a new provider with the specified ID.
`POST /providers`	Creates a new provider and returns the ID.
`PUT /providers/:id/rate`	Adds to the latest ratings for the provider.
`DELETE /providers/:id`	Deletes the provider with the specified ID.

Adding routes

Routes for the *Service Provider* microservice are very similar to the *Consumer* service. The *Provider* service additionally provides a dedicated route to register a rating for the *Provider,* as shown here:

```
(def routes #{["/providers/:id"
               :get (conj common-interceptors `auth `core/validate-id
                          `core/get-provider `gen-events)
               :route-name :provider-get]
              ["/providers/:id"
               :put (conj common-interceptors `auth `core/validate-id
                          `core/upsert-provider `gen-events)
               :route-name :provider-put]
              ["/providers/:id/rate"
               :put (conj common-interceptors `auth `core/validate-id
                          `core/upsert-provider `gen-events)
               :route-name :provider-rate]
              ["/providers"
               :post (conj common-interceptors `auth `core/validate
                           `core/create-provider `gen-events)
               :route-name :provider-post]
              ["/providers/:id"
               :delete (conj common-interceptors `auth `core/validate-id
                             `core/delete-provider `gen-events)
               :route-name :provider-delete]})
```

Defining Datomic schema

The *Service Provider* microservice uses Datomic as the local database to store the provider details. The schema for the provider database consists of the following attributes:

:db/ident	:db/valueType	:db/cardinality	:db/index	:db/fulltext	:db/unique	:db/doc
:provider/id	:db.type/string	:db.cardinality/one	true	false	:db.unique/identity	Unique provider ID
:provider/name	:db.type/string	:db.cardinality/one	true	true	-	Display name for the provider
:provider/mobile	:db.type/string	:db.cardinality/one	false	-	-	Mobile number
:provider/since	:db.type/long	:db.cardinality/one	false	-	-	Active since in yyyy format

:provider/rating	:db.type/float	:db.cardinality/many	false	-	-	List of ratings received

Creating a persistence adapter

Persistence *protocol* consists of upsert, entity, and delete functions, similar to the *Consumer* service, that are defined in the persistence.clj source file, as follows:

```
(ns helping-hands.provider.persistence
  "Persistence Port and Adapter for Provider Service"
  (:require [datomic.api :as d]))

;; ---------------------------------------------------
;; Provider Persistence Port for Adapters to Plug-in
;; ---------------------------------------------------
(defprotocol ProviderDB
  "Abstraction for provider database"

  (upsert [this id name mobile since rating]
    "Adds/Updates a provider entity")

  (entity [this id flds]
    "Gets the specified provider with all or requested fields")

  (delete [this id]
    "Deletes the specified provider entity"))

;; ---------------------------------------------------
;; Datomic Adapter Implementation for Provider Port
;; ---------------------------------------------------

(defn- get-entity-id
  [conn id]
  (-> (d/q '[:find ?e
             :in $ ?id
             :where [?e :provider/id ?id]] (d/db conn) (str id))
      ffirst))

(defn- get-entity
  [conn id]
  (let [eid (get-entity-id conn id)]
    (->> (d/entity (d/db conn) eid) seq (into {}))))

(defrecord ProviderDBDatomic [conn]
  ProviderDB
```

```
  (upsert [this id name mobile since rating]
    (d/transact conn
                (vector (into {} (filter (comp some? val)
                                         {:db/id id
                                          :provider/id id
                                          :provider/name name
                                          :provider/mobile mobile
                                          :provider/since since
                                          :provider/rating rating})))))

  (entity [this id flds]
    (when-let [provider (get-entity conn id)]
      (if (empty? flds)
        provider
        (select-keys provider (map keyword flds)))))

  (delete [this id]
    (when-let [eid (get-entity-id conn id)]
      (d/transact conn [[:db.fn/retractEntity eid]]))))
```

The `helping-hands.provider.persistence` namespace also provides a `create-provider-database` utility function to initialize the database and update the schema if the database is created for the first time:

```
(defn create-provider-database
  "Creates a provider database and returns the connection"
  [d]
  ;; create and connect to the database
  (let [dburi (str "datomic:mem://" d)
        db (d/create-database dburi)
        conn (d/connect dburi)]
    ;; transact schema if database was created
    (when db
      (d/transact conn
                  [{:db/ident :provider/id
                    :db/valueType :db.type/string
                    :db/cardinality :db.cardinality/one
                    :db/doc "Unique Provider ID"
                    :db/unique :db.unique/identity
                    :db/index true}
                   {:db/ident :provider/name
                    :db/valueType :db.type/string
                    :db/cardinality :db.cardinality/one
                    :db/doc "Display Name for the Provider"
                    :db/index true
                    :db/fulltext true}
                   {:db/ident :provider/mobile
```

```
                  :db/valueType :db.type/string
                  :db/cardinality :db.cardinality/one
                  :db/doc "Provider Mobile Number"
                  :db/index false}
                 {:db/ident :provider/since
                  :db/valueType :db.type/long
                  :db/cardinality :db.cardinality/one
                  :db/doc "Provider Active Since EPOCH time"
                  :db/index false}
                 {:db/ident :provider/rating
                  :db/valueType :db.type/float
                  :db/cardinality :db.cardinality/many
                  :db/doc "List of ratings"
                  :db/index false}]))
        (ProviderDBDatomic. conn)))
```

Creating interceptors

The `helping-hands.provider.core` namespace defines all the interceptors that are used
for the routes of the *Provider* microservice. Validation interceptors validate the input
parameters and make sure that all the required fields are present in the request. Validation
interceptors for Provider routes work exactly in the same way as that of the
Consumer microservice routes. Additionally, they validate the datatype of the `rating`
and `since` fields to make sure that the business model gets the values in the format
expected by the Datomic database. The implementation of validation interceptors is shown
in the following code snippet:

```
(ns helping-hands.provider.core
  "Initializes Helping Hands Provider Service"
  (:require [cheshire.core :as jp]
            [clojure.string :as s]
            [helping-hands.provider.persistence :as p]
            [io.pedestal.interceptor.chain :as chain])
  (:import [java.io IOException]
           [java.util UUID]))

;; delay the check for database and connection
;; till the first request to access @providerdb
(def ^:private providerdb
  (delay (p/create-provider-database "provider")))


;; --------------------------------
;; Validation Interceptors
;; --------------------------------
```

```
(defn- validate-rating-ts
  "Validates the rating and timestamp"
  [context]
  (let [rating (-> context :request :form-params :rating)
        since_ts (-> context :request :form-params :since)]
    (try
      (let [context (if (not (nil? rating))
                      (assoc-in context [:request :form-params :rating]
                                (Float/parseFloat rating)) context)
            context (if (not (nil? since_ts))
                      (assoc-in context [:request :form-params :since]
                                (Long/parseLong since_ts)) context)]
        context)
      (catch Exception e nil))))

(defn- prepare-valid-context
  "Applies validation logic and returns the resulting context"
  [context]
  (let [params (merge (-> context :request :form-params)
                      (-> context :request :query-params)
                      (-> context :request :path-params))
        ctx (validate-rating-ts context)
        params (if (not (nil? ctx))
                 (assoc params
                        :rating (-> ctx :request :form-params :rating)
                        :since (-> ctx :request :form-params :since)))]
    (if (and (not (empty? params))
             (not (nil? ctx))
             ;; any one of id or mobile
             (or (params :id) (params :mobile)))
      (let [flds (if-let [fl (:flds params)]
                   (map s/trim (s/split fl #","))
                   (vector))
            params (assoc params :flds flds)]
        (assoc context :tx-data params))
      (chain/terminate
       (assoc context
              :response {:status 400
                         :body (str "ID, mobile is mandatory "
                                    "and rating, since must be a
number")})))))

(def validate-id
  {:name ::validate-id

   :enter
   (fn [context]
     (if-let [id (or (-> context :request :form-params :id)
```

```
                        (-> context :request :query-params :id)
                        (-> context :request :path-params :id))]
        ;; validate and return a context with tx-data
        ;; or terminated interceptor chain
        (prepare-valid-context context)
        (chain/terminate
         (assoc context
                :response {:status 400
                           :body "Invalid Provider ID"})))))

   :error
   (fn [context ex-info]
     (assoc context
            :response {:status 500
                       :body (.getMessage ex-info)}))})

(def validate
  {:name ::validate

   :enter
   (fn [context]
     (if-let [params (-> context :request :form-params)]
       ;; validate and return a context with tx-data
       ;; or terminated interceptor chain
       (prepare-valid-context context)
       (chain/terminate
        (assoc context
               :response {:status 400
                          :body "Invalid parameters"}))))

   :error
   (fn [context ex-info]
     (assoc context
            :response {:status 500
                       :body (.getMessage ex-info)}))})
```

Other interceptors, such as get-provider, upsert-provider, create-provider, and delete-provider, are similar to interceptors defined for the routes of the Consumer service, as shown here:

```
;; -------------------------------
;; Business Logic Interceptors
;; -------------------------------

(def get-provider
  {:name ::provider-get
```

```
    :enter
    (fn [context]
      (let [tx-data (:tx-data context)
            entity (.entity @providerdb (:id tx-data) (:flds tx-data))]
        (if (empty? entity)
          (assoc context :response {:status 404 :body "No such provider"})
          (assoc context :response {:status 200
                                     :body (jp/generate-string entity)})))))

    :error
    (fn [context ex-info]
      (assoc context
             :response {:status 500
                        :body (.getMessage ex-info)}))})

(def upsert-provider
  {:name ::provider-upsert

   :enter
   (fn [context]
     (let [tx-data (:tx-data context)
           id (:id tx-data)
           db (.upsert @providerdb id (:name tx-data)
                       (:mobile tx-data) (:since tx-data)
                       (:rating tx-data))]
       (if (nil? @db)
         (throw (IOException.
                  (str "Upsert failed for provider: " id)))
         (assoc context
                :response {:status 200
                           :body (jp/generate-string
                                   (.entity @providerdb id []))}))))
   :error
   (fn [context ex-info]
     (assoc context
            :response {:status 500
                       :body (.getMessage ex-info)}))})

(def create-provider
  {:name ::provider-create

   :enter
   (fn [context]
     (let [tx-data (:tx-data context)
           ;; generate a random ID if it is not specified
           id (str (UUID/randomUUID))
           tx-data (if (:id tx-data) tx-data (assoc tx-data :id id))
           ;; create provider
```

```
            db (.upsert @providerdb id (:name tx-data)
                         (:mobile tx-data) (:since tx-data)
                         (:rating tx-data))]
      (if (nil? @db)
        (throw (IOException.
                 (str "Upsert failed for provider: " id)))
        (assoc context
              :response {:status 200
                          :body (jp/generate-string
                                  (.entity @providerdb id []))})))))

  :error
  (fn [context ex-info]
    (assoc context
          :response {:status 500
                      :body (.getMessage ex-info)})))})
(def delete-provider
  {:name ::provider-delete

  :enter
  (fn [context]
    (let [tx-data (:tx-data context)
          db (.delete @providerdb (:id tx-data))]
      (if (nil? db)
        (assoc context :response {:status 404 :body "No such provider"})
        (assoc context :response {:status 200 :body "Success"}))))
  :error
  (fn [context ex-info]
    (assoc context
          :response {:status 500
                      :body (.getMessage ex-info)})))})
```

Testing routes

The routes defined for the *Provider* service allow users to create a new provider, query for its properties, and delete it. As of now, for the *Auth interceptor*, assume that 123 is a valid token that is sent in the header of each request. To start with, create a provider using the PUT /providers/:id route with ID set as 1:

```
% curl -i -H "token: 123" -XPUT -d "name=ProviderA"
http://localhost:8080/providers/1
HTTP/1.1 200 OK
...

{"provider/id":"1","provider/name":"ProviderA"}
```

To add a rating, use the PUT /providers/:id/rate route with the same ID as that of ProviderA:

```
% curl -i -H "token: 123" -XPUT -d "rating=5.0"
http://localhost:8080/providers/1/rate
HTTP/1.1 200 OK
...

{"provider/id":"1","provider/name":"ProviderA","provider/rating":[5.0]}
```

To get the provider, use the GET /providers/:id route. If the provider ID is not found, it returns a HTTP 404 Not Found response:

```
% curl -i -H "token: 123" "http://localhost:8080/providers/1"
HTTP/1.1 200 OK
...

{"provider/id":"1","provider/name":"ProviderA","provider/rating":[5.0]}

% curl -i -H "token: 123" "http://localhost:8080/providers/2"
HTTP/1.1 404 Not Found
...

No such provider
```

To delete a provider, use the DELETE /providers/:id route with an existing provider ID:

```
% curl -i -H "token: 123" -XDELETE "http://localhost:8080/providers/1"
HTTP/1.1 200 OK
...

Success

% curl -i -H "token: 123" "http://localhost:8080/providers/1"
HTTP/1.1 404 Not Found
...

No such provider
```

Creating a microservice for Services

The *Service* microservice manages the list of services offered by the *service providers* via the Helping Hands application. It exposes APIs for *service providers* to register *services* that are offered by them. As per the workflow of *Service,* defined in `Chapter 3`, *Microservices for Helping Hands Application,* the following APIs are required to create a new *service,* get *service* details, and update *service* details. Each *service* must already have the *service provider* registered with the Helping Hands application via the *Service Provider* microservice. Since only an existing *service provider* can register a *service,* the *service provider* ID is retrieved by the *Auth* token received with the request calling the *Service* API to create a new *service:*

URI	Description
`GET /services/:id/?flds=name,mobile`	Gets the details of the service with the specified `:id` if the `:id` is specified. Optionally, it accepts a CSV of fields to be returned in the response.
`PUT /services/:id`	Creates a new service with the specified ID.
`POST /services`	Creates a new service and returns the ID.
`PUT /services/:id/rate`	Adds to the latest ratings for the service.
`DELETE /services/:id`	Deletes the service with the specified ID.

Adding routes

Routes for *Service* are very similar to the *Provider* service. It also defines routes to create, modify, rate, and delete services. The route to create a *service* expects a provider ID as a mandatory parameter to make sure that each service is associated with a provider at the time of creation. Also, any change in provider ID using the `PUT /services/:id` route is validated against the *Provider* service to make sure that the specified *provider* exists and is registered with the Helping Hands application. The routes are shown in the following code snippet:

```
;; Tabular routes
(def routes #{["/services/:id"
               :get (conj common-interceptors `auth `core/validate-id-get
                          `core/get-service `gen-events)
               :route-name :service-get]
              ["/services/:id"
               :put (conj common-interceptors `auth `core/validate-id
                          `core/upsert-service `gen-events)
```

```
                         :route-name :service-put]
             ["/services/:id/rate"
             :put (conj common-interceptors `auth `core/validate-id
                           `core/upsert-service `gen-events)
             :route-name :service-rate]
             ["/services"
             :post (conj common-interceptors `auth `core/validate
                           `core/create-service `gen-events)
             :route-name :service-post]
             ["/services/:id"
             :delete (conj common-interceptors `auth `core/validate-id-get
                             `core/delete-service `gen-events)
             :route-name :service-delete]})
```

Defining a Datomic schema

The *Service* microservice uses Datomic as the local database to store the service details. Service maintains a provider ID as well. Although in the schema it is defined as type :db.type/string; if a common database is used for the provider and service then it is recommended to define the provider ID of type :db.type/ref to make better use of Datomic entity references. The schema for the service database consists of the following attributes:

:db/ident	:db/valueType	:db/cardinality	:db/index	:db/fulltext	:db/unique	:db/doc
:service/id	:db.type/string	:db.cardinality/one	true	false	:db.unique/identity	Unique service ID
:service/type	:db.type/string	:db.cardinality/one	true	true	-	Type of service
:service/provider	:db.type/string	:db.cardinality/one	false	-	-	Associated service provider ID
:service/area	:db.type/string	:db.cardinality/many	true	true	-	Service areas / locality
:service/cost	:db.type/float	:db.cardinality/one	false	-	-	Hourly cost
:service/rating	:db.type/float	:db.cardinality/many	false	-	-	List of ratings received
:service/status	:db.type/string	:db.cardinality/one	false	-	-	Status, one of #{"A","NA","D"} signifying *Available, Not ;Available,* and *Disabled*

There is also a *GeoLocation* field mentioned in the data model of the *Service* database in Chapter 3, *Microservices for Helping Hands Application*. This field is a derived field that is computed and stored by the *Lookup* service instead of being stored in the *Service* database. This field is used only for geolocation-based queries that the *Lookup* service will be handling.

Creating a persistence adapter

Persistence protocol `ServiceDB` consists of `upsert`, `entity`, and `delete` functions, similar to the *Provider* service, that are defined in the `persistence.clj` source file, as shown here:

```clojure
(ns helping-hands.service.persistence
  "Persistence Port and Adapter for Service"
  (:require [datomic.api :as d]))

;; ----------------------------------------------------
;; Service Persistence Port for Adapters to Plug-in
;; ----------------------------------------------------
(defprotocol ServiceDB
  "Abstraction for service database"

  (upsert [this id type provider area cost rating status]
    "Adds/Updates a service entity")

  (entity [this id flds]
    "Gets the specified service with all or requested fields")

  (delete [this id]
    "Deletes the specified service entity"))

;; ----------------------------------------------------
;; Datomic Adapter Implementation for Service Port
;; ----------------------------------------------------

(defn- get-entity-id
  [conn id]
  (-> (d/q '[:find ?e
             :in $ ?id
             :where [?e :service/id ?id]] (d/db conn) (str id))
      ffirst))

(defn- get-entity
  [conn id]
  (let [eid (get-entity-id conn id)]
    (->> (d/entity (d/db conn) eid) seq (into {}))))

(defrecord ServiceDBDatomic [conn]
  ServiceDB

  (upsert [this id type provider area cost rating status]
    (d/transact conn
                (vector (into {} (filter (comp some? val)
                                         {:db/id id
```

```
                                       :service/id id
                                       :service/type type
                                       :service/provider provider
                                       :service/area area
                                       :service/cost cost
                                       :service/rating rating
                                       :service/status status})))))

    (entity [this id flds]
      (when-let [service (get-entity conn id)]
        (if (empty? flds)
          service
          (select-keys service (map keyword flds)))))

    (delete [this id]
      (when-let [eid (get-entity-id conn id)]
        (d/transact conn [[:db.fn/retractEntity eid]])))))
```

The `helping-hands.service.persistence` namespace also provides a `create-service-database` utility function to initialize the database and update the schema if the database is created for the first time, as shown here:

```
(defn create-service-database
  "Creates a service database and returns the connection"
  [d]
  ;; create and connect to the database
  (let [dburi (str "datomic:mem://" d)
        db (d/create-database dburi)
        conn (d/connect dburi)]
    ;; transact schema if database was created
    (when db
      (d/transact conn
                  [{:db/ident :service/id
                    :db/valueType :db.type/string
                    :db/cardinality :db.cardinality/one
                    :db/doc "Unique Service ID"
                    :db/unique :db.unique/identity
                    :db/index true}
                   {:db/ident :service/type
                    :db/valueType :db.type/string
                    :db/cardinality :db.cardinality/one
                    :db/doc "Type of Service"
                    :db/index true
                    :db/fulltext true}
                   {:db/ident :service/provider
                    :db/valueType :db.type/string
                    :db/cardinality :db.cardinality/one
```

```
                :db/doc "Associated Service Provider ID"
                :db/index false}
             {:db/ident :service/area
                :db/valueType :db.type/string
                :db/cardinality :db.cardinality/many
                :db/doc "Service Areas / Locality"
                :db/index true
                :db/fulltext true}
             {:db/ident :service/cost
                :db/valueType :db.type/float
                :db/cardinality :db.cardinality/one
                :db/doc "Hourly Cost"
                :db/index false}
             {:db/ident :service/rating
                :db/valueType :db.type/float
                :db/cardinality :db.cardinality/many
                :db/doc "List of ratings"
                :db/index false}
             {:db/ident :service/status
                :db/valueType :db.type/string
                :db/cardinality :db.cardinality/one
                :db/doc "Status of Service (A/NA/D)"
                :db/index false}]))
       (ServiceDBDatomic. conn)))
```

Creating interceptors

The helping-hands.service.core namespace defines all the interceptors that are used
for the routes of the *Service* microservice. Since business model *interceptors* of *Service* are
exactly the same as those of the *Provider* service and depend only on the *Validation
interceptors*, let's focus only on the *interceptors* that validate the input parameters for *Service*
routes. The implementation of the validation interceptor is shown in the following code
snippet:

```
(ns helping-hands.service.core
  "Initializes Helping Hands Service Service"
  (:require [cheshire.core :as jp]
            [clojure.string :as s]
            [helping-hands.service.persistence :as p]
            [io.pedestal.interceptor.chain :as chain])
  (:import [java.io IOException]
           [java.util UUID]))

;; delay the check for database and connection
;; till the first request to access @servicedb
```

```
(def ^:private servicedb
  (delay (p/create-service-database "service")))

;; --------------------------------
;; Validation Interceptors
;; --------------------------------

(defn- validate-rating-cost
  "Validates the rating and cost"
  [context]
  (let [rating (-> context :request :form-params :rating)
        cost (-> context :request :form-params :cost)]
    (try
      (let [context (if (not (nil? rating))
                      (assoc-in context [:request :form-params :rating]
                                (Float/parseFloat rating)) context)
            context (if (not (nil? cost))
                      (assoc-in context [:request :form-params :cost]
                                (Float/parseFloat cost)) context)]
        context)
      (catch Exception e nil))))

(defn- prepare-valid-context
  "Applies validation logic and returns the resulting context"
  [context]
  (let [params (merge (-> context :request :form-params)
                      (-> context :request :query-params)
                      (-> context :request :path-params))
        ctx (validate-rating-cost context)
        params (if (not (nil? ctx))
                 (assoc params
                        :rating (-> ctx :request :form-params :rating)
                        :cost (-> ctx :request :form-params :cost)))]
    (if (and (not (empty? params))
             (not (nil? ctx))
             (params :id) (params :type) (params :provider)
             (params :area) (params :cost)
             (contains? #{"A" "NA" "D"} (params :type))
             (provider-exists? (params :provider)))
      (let [flds (if-let [fl (:flds params)]
                   (map s/trim (s/split fl #","))
                   (vector))
            params (assoc params :flds flds)]
        (assoc context :tx-data params))
      (chain/terminate
       (assoc context
              :response {:status 400
                         :body (str "ID, type, provider, area and cost is
```

```
mandatory "
                                    "and rating, cost must be a number with
type "
                                    "having one of values A, NA or
D")})))))

(def validate-id
  {:name ::validate-id

   :enter
   (fn [context]
     (if-let [id (or (-> context :request :form-params :id)
                     (-> context :request :query-params :id)
                     (-> context :request :path-params :id))]
       ;; validate and return a context with tx-data
       ;; or terminated interceptor chain
       (prepare-valid-context context)
       (chain/terminate
        (assoc context
               :response {:status 400
                          :body "Invalid Service ID"})))))

   :error
   (fn [context ex-info]
     (assoc context
            :response {:status 500
                       :body (.getMessage ex-info)}))})

(def validate-id-get
  {:name ::validate-id-get

   :enter
   (fn [context]
     (if-let [id (or (-> context :request :form-params :id)
                     (-> context :request :query-params :id)
                     (-> context :request :path-params :id))]
       ;; validate and return a context with tx-data
       ;; or terminated interceptor chain
       (let [params (merge (-> context :request :form-params)
                           (-> context :request :query-params)
                           (-> context :request :path-params))]
         (if (and (not (empty? params))
                  (params :id))
           (let [flds (if-let [fl (:flds params)]
                        (map s/trim (s/split fl #","))
                        (vector))
                 params (assoc params :flds flds)]
             (assoc context :tx-data params))
```

```
            (chain/terminate
             (assoc context
                    :response {:status 400
                               :body "Invalid Service ID"})))))
        (chain/terminate
         (assoc context
                :response {:status 400
                           :body "Invalid Service ID"}))))

    :error
    (fn [context ex-info]
      (assoc context
             :response {:status 500
                        :body (.getMessage ex-info)}))})

(def validate
  {:name ::validate

   :enter
   (fn [context]
     (if-let [params (-> context :request :form-params)]
       ;; validate and return a context with tx-data
       ;; or terminated interceptor chain
       (prepare-valid-context context)
       (chain/terminate
        (assoc context
               :response {:status 400
                          :body "Invalid parameters"})))))

   :error
   (fn [context ex-info]
     (assoc context
            :response {:status 500
                       :body (.getMessage ex-info)}))})
```

For *Service*, the validation rule also includes validating a given provider ID against an external *Provider Service* to make sure that the provider of the service is already registered. To do so, the validation *interceptor* of *Service* makes an external API call asynchronously via the `provider-exists?` function and passes *Pedestal context* to business logic *interceptors* only when it finds that the provider ID is valid.

`clj-http` (`https://github.com/dakrone/clj-http`) is a Clojure library that is widely used to create HTTP clients to make API calls to external services. To make a GET call to an external service like that of GET `/providers/:id`, see `clj-http` GET (`https://github.com/dakrone/clj-http#get`).

Testing routes

The routes defined for *Service* allow users to create a new service, query for its properties, and delete it. As of now, for *Auth interceptor*, assume that 123 is a valid token that is sent in the header of each request. Here are a sample of cURL requests to create, query, and delete a service offered by the Helping Hands application:

```
;; Create a new service with required parameters
% curl -i -H "token: 123" -XPUT -d
"type=A&provider=1&area=bangalore&cost=250"
http://localhost:8080/services/1
HTTP/1.1 200 OK
...

{"service/id":"1","service/type":"A","service/provider":"1","service/area":
["bangalore"],"service/cost":250.0}

;; Get service properties by ID
% curl -i -H "token: 123" http://localhost:8080/services/1
HTTP/1.1 200 OK
...

{"service/id":"1","service/type":"A","service/provider":"1","service/area":
["bangalore"],"service/cost":250.0}

;; Delete the service
% curl -i -H "token: 123" -XDELETE http://localhost:8080/services/1
HTTP/1.1 200 OK
...

Success

;; Validate service no longer exists
% curl -i -H "token: 123" http://localhost:8080/services/1
HTTP/1.1 404 Not Found
...

No such service
```

Creating a microservice for Order

The *Order Service* receives the request from *Service Consumers* to create a new order for the *service* provided by a particular *service provider*. It exposes the following APIs for *consumers* to create a new order, get order details, and get the list of orders placed by them. It also allows the *consumers* to rate the *Order* based on the quality of service received. To create a new *Order,* APIs expect a service ID and provider ID to be specified along with the required details such as time slot, and more. The *consumer* ID is picked from the *Auth* token that is received as a part of request headers. The IDs specified for *Service* and *Service Provider* must already be registered with the Helping Hands application via the *Service* and *Service Provider* microservices. Creation of an *Order* also makes sure that the requested *service* is offered within the vicinity of the *consumer* based on the geolocation of the *consumer* and *service* being requested:

URI	Description
`GET /orders/?flds=cost,status`	Gets all the orders placed by the authenticated consumer.
`GET /orders/:id/?flds=name,mobile`	Gets the details of the order with the specified `:id` and placed by the authenticated consumer. Optionally, it accepts a CSV of fields to be returned in the response.
`PUT /orders/:id`	Creates a new order with the specified ID for the authenticated consumer.
`POST /orders`	Creates a new order for the authenticated consumer and returns the ID.
`PUT /orders/:id/rate`	Adds to the latest ratings for the order. Consumer ID of the order must match the authenticated consumer ID.
`DELETE /orders/:id`	Deletes the order with the specified ID for the authenticated consumer. Consumer ID of the order must match the authenticated consumer ID.

Adding routes

The *Order Service* allows consumers to create new orders, modify them, rate, and delete them. It also allows an authenticated user to get all the orders placed by the authenticated user ID. The routes required for this service are shown in the following code snippet:

```
;; Tabular routes
(def routes #{["/orders/:id"
               :get (conj common-interceptors `auth `core/validate-id-get
                          `core/get-order `gen-events)
               :route-name :order-get]
              ["/orders"
               :get (conj common-interceptors `auth `core/validate-all-orders
                          `core/get-all-orders `gen-events)
               :route-name :order-get-all]
              ["/orders/:id"
               :put (conj common-interceptors `auth `core/validate-id
                          `core/upsert-order `gen-events)
               :route-name :order-put]
              ["/orders/:id/rate"
               :put (conj common-interceptors `auth `core/validate-id
                          `core/upsert-order `gen-events)
               :route-name :order-rate]
              ["/orders"
               :post (conj common-interceptors `auth `core/validate
                          `core/create-order `gen-events)
               :route-name :order-post]
              ["/orders/:id"
               :delete (conj common-interceptors `auth `core/validate-id-get
                          `core/delete-order `gen-events)
               :route-name :order-delete]})
```

Defining Datomic schema

The *Order* microservice uses Datomic as the local database to store the order details. The schema for the order database consists of the following attributes:

:db/ident	:db/valueType	:db/cardinality	:db/index	:db/fulltext	:db/unique	:db/doc
:order/id	:db.type/string	:db.cardinality/one	true	false	:db.unique/identity	Unique order ID
:order/service	:db.type/string	:db.cardinality/one	false	-	-	Associated service ID
:order/provider	:db.type/string	:db.cardinality/one	false	-	-	Associated service provider ID
:order/consumer	:db.type/string	:db.cardinality/one	false	-	-	Associated consumer ID
:order/cost	:db.type/float	:db.cardinality/one	false	-	-	Hourly cost

:order/start	:db.type/long	:db.cardinality/one	false	-	-	EPOCH start time for the Slot
:order/end	:db.type/long	:db.cardinality/one	false	-	-	EPOCH end time for the slot
:order/rating	:db.type/float	:db.cardinality/many	false	-	-	List of ratings received
:order/status	:db.type/string	:db.cardinality/one	false	-	-	Status, one of #{"O","I","D","C"} signifying Open, In Progress, Done, and Cancelled

Creating a persistence adapter

Persistence protocol `OrderDB` consists of `upsert`, `entity`, and `delete` functions, similar to the *Provider* service. Additionally, it defines an `orders` function that can list all the orders of the given authenticated consumer ID, as shown here:

```
(ns helping-hands.order.persistence
  "Persistence Port and Adapter for Order"
  (:require [datomic.api :as d]))

;; ----------------------------------------------------
;; Order Persistence Port for Adapters to Plug-in
;; ----------------------------------------------------
(defprotocol OrderDB
  "Abstraction for order database"

  (upsert [this id service provider consumer
           cost start end rating status]
    "Adds/Updates an order entity")

  (entity [this id flds]
    "Gets the specified order with all or requested fields")

  (orders [this uid flds]
    "Gets all the orders of the authenticated user with all or requested
fields")

  (delete [this id]
    "Deletes the specified order entity"))

;; ----------------------------------------------------
;; Datomic Adapter Implementation for Order Port
;; ----------------------------------------------------

(defn- get-entity-id
  [conn id]
```

```clojure
      (-> (d/q '[:find ?e
                 :in $ ?id
                 :where [?e :order/id ?id]] (d/db conn) (str id))
        ffirst))

(defn- get-entity
  [conn id]
  (let [eid (get-entity-id conn id)]
    (->> (d/entity (d/db conn) eid) seq (into {}))))

(defn- get-entity-uid
  [conn uid]
  (->> (d/q '[:find ?e
              :in $ ?id
              :where [?e :order/consumer ?id]] (d/db conn) (str uid))
       (into []) flatten))

(defn- get-all-entities
  [conn uid]
  (let [eids (get-entity-uid conn uid)]
    (map #(->> (d/entity (d/db conn) %) seq (into {})) eids)))

(defrecord OrderDBDatomic [conn]
  OrderDB

  (upsert [this id service provider consumer
           cost start end rating status]
    (d/transact conn
                (vector (into {} (filter (comp some? val)
                                         {:db/id id
                                          :order/id id
                                          :order/service service
                                          :order/provider provider
                                          :order/consumer consumer
                                          :order/cost cost
                                          :order/start start
                                          :order/end end
                                          :order/rating rating
                                          :order/status status})))))

  (entity [this id flds]
    (when-let [order (get-entity conn id)]
      (if (empty? flds)
        order
        (select-keys order (map keyword flds)))))

  (orders [this uid flds]
    (when-let [orders (get-all-entities conn uid)]
```

```
            (if (empty? flds)
              orders
              (map #(select-keys % (map keyword flds)) orders)))))

    (delete [this id]
      (when-let [eid (get-entity-id conn id)]
        (d/transact conn [[:db.fn/retractEntity eid]])))))
```

The get-all-entities function queries the Datomic database for all the orders that have :order/consumer set to the given consumer ID that is provided as a parameter to the endpoint that requests all the orders for the consumer. It also allows to pick only the specified fields across the orders. The helping-hands.order.persistence namespace also provides a create-order-database utility function to initialize the database and update the schema if the database is created for the first time, as shown here:

```
(defn create-order-database
  "Creates a order database and returns the connection"
  [d]
  ;; create and connect to the database
  (let [dburi (str "datomic:mem://" d)
        db (d/create-database dburi)
        conn (d/connect dburi)]
    ;; transact schema if database was created
    (when db
      (d/transact conn
                  [{:db/ident :order/id
                    :db/valueType :db.type/string
                    :db/cardinality :db.cardinality/one
                    :db/doc "Unique Order ID"
                    :db/unique :db.unique/identity
                    :db/index true}
                   {:db/ident :order/service
                    :db/valueType :db.type/string
                    :db/cardinality :db.cardinality/one
                    :db/doc "Associated Service ID"
                    :db/index false}
                   {:db/ident :order/provider
                    :db/valueType :db.type/string
                    :db/cardinality :db.cardinality/one
                    :db/doc "Associated Service Provider ID"
                    :db/index false}
                   {:db/ident :order/consumer
                    :db/valueType :db.type/string
                    :db/cardinality :db.cardinality/one
                    :db/doc "Associated Consumer ID"}
                   {:db/ident :order/cost
                    :db/valueType :db.type/float
```

```
                 :db/cardinality :db.cardinality/one
                 :db/doc "Hourly Cost"
                 :db/index false}
                {:db/ident :order/start
                 :db/valueType :db.type/long
                 :db/cardinality :db.cardinality/one
                 :db/doc "Start Time (EPOCH)"
                 :db/index false}
                {:db/ident :order/end
                 :db/valueType :db.type/long
                 :db/cardinality :db.cardinality/one
                 :db/doc "End Time (EPOCH)"
                 :db/index false}
                {:db/ident :order/rating
                 :db/valueType :db.type/float
                 :db/cardinality :db.cardinality/many
                 :db/doc "List of ratings"
                 :db/index false}
                {:db/ident :order/status
                 :db/valueType :db.type/string
                 :db/cardinality :db.cardinality/one
                 :db/doc "Status of Order (O/I/D/C)"
                 :db/index false}]))
     (OrderDBDatomic. conn)))
```

Creating interceptors

The `helping-hands.order.core` namespace defines all the interceptors that are used for the routes of the *Order* microservice. The *Auth* interceptor is the generic interceptor that reads the token and updates the user ID field `:uid` for the *Order* routes to get all the orders for an authenticated user. For simplicity of the implementation, the *Auth* interceptor assumes that the token passed in the header is set to the consumer ID.

The *validation* interceptor for *Order* routes validates both *service ID* and the *provider ID* of the order to make sure that both provider and service are registered with the Helping Hands application and the same provider provides the specified service. The `service-exists?`, `provider-exists?`, and `consumer-exists?` functions validate the service, provider, and consumer, respectively. Additionally, the validation interceptor checks for the right value of `status` and the value of `rating`, `cost`, `start`, and `end` to be of type number, as shown in the following code snippet. The implementation of these functions are same as that of the *Consumer, Order,* and *Service* microservices implementations explained earlier:

```
(defn- prepare-valid-context
  "Applies validation logic and returns the resulting context"
  [context]
  (let [params (merge (-> context :request :form-params)
                      (-> context :request :query-params)
                      (-> context :request :path-params))
        ctx (validate-rating-cost-ts context)
        params (if (not (nil? ctx))
                 (assoc params
                        :rating (-> ctx :request :form-params :rating)
                        :cost (-> ctx :request :form-params :cost)
                        :start (-> ctx :request :form-params :start)
                        :end (-> ctx :request :form-params :end)))]
    (if (and (not (empty? params))
             (not (nil? ctx))
             (params :id) (params :service) (params :provider)
             (params :consumer) (params :cost) (params :status)
             (contains? #{"O" "I" "D" "C"} (params :status))
             (service-exists? (params :service))
             (provider-exists? (params :provider))
             (consumer-exists? (params :consumer)))
      (let [flds (if-let [fl (:flds params)]
                   (map s/trim (s/split fl #","))
                   (vector))
            params (assoc params :flds flds)]
        (assoc context :tx-data params))
      (chain/terminate
       (assoc context
              :response {:status 400
                         :body (str "ID, service, provider, consumer, "
                                    "cost and status is mandatory.
start/end, "
                                    "rating and cost must be a number with
status "
                                    "having one of values O, I, D or
C")}))))))
```

```
(def validate-id
  {:name ::validate-id

   :enter
   (fn [context]
     (if-let [id (or (-> context :request :form-params :id)
                     (-> context :request :query-params :id)
                     (-> context :request :path-params :id))]
       ;; validate and return a context with tx-data
       ;; or terminated interceptor chain
       (prepare-valid-context context)
       (chain/terminate
        (assoc context
               :response {:status 400
                          :body "Invalid Order ID"}))))

   :error
   (fn [context ex-info]
     (assoc context
            :response {:status 500
                       :body (.getMessage ex-info)}))})

(def validate-id-get
  {:name ::validate-id-get

   :enter
   (fn [context]
     (if-let [id (or (-> context :request :form-params :id)
                     (-> context :request :query-params :id)
                     (-> context :request :path-params :id))]
       ;; validate and return a context with tx-data
       ;; or terminated interceptor chain
       (let [params (merge (-> context :request :form-params)
                           (-> context :request :query-params)
                           (-> context :request :path-params))]
         (if (and (not (empty? params))
                  (params :id))
           (let [flds (if-let [fl (:flds params)]
                        (map s/trim (s/split fl #","))
                        (vector))
                 params (assoc params :flds flds)]
             (assoc context :tx-data params))
           (chain/terminate
            (assoc context
                   :response {:status 400
                              :body "Invalid Order ID"}))))
       (chain/terminate
        (assoc context
```

```
                        :response {:status 400
                                   :body "Invalid Order ID"}))))

    :error
    (fn [context ex-info]
      (assoc context
             :response {:status 500
                        :body (.getMessage ex-info)})})})

  (def validate-all-orders
    {:name ::validate-all-orders

     :enter
     (fn [context]
       (if-let [params (-> context :tx-data)]
         ;;Get user ID from auth uid
         (assoc-in context [:tx-data :flds]
                   (if-let [fl (-> context :request :query-params :flds)]
                     (map s/trim (s/split fl #","))
                     (vector)))
         (chain/terminate
          (assoc context
                 :response {:status 400
                            :body "Invalid parameters"}))))

     :error
     (fn [context ex-info]
       (assoc context
              :response {:status 500
                         :body (.getMessage ex-info)})})})
```

The `validate-id-get` interceptor is used for the `GET /orders/:id` requests and validates only the order ID and the order fields parameter. Similarly, the `validate-all-orders` interceptor is used with the `GET /orders` route to get all the orders of the authenticated consumer. The implementation of interceptors for the business logic of the *Order* service is similar to that of the previous implementation of *Consumer, Provider,* and *Service.* Additionally, the *Order* service defines interceptors to get all orders of the authenticated consumer that use the `orders` function of the `OrderDB` protocol, as shown here:

```
(ns helping-hands.order.core
  "Initializes Helping Hands Order Service"
  (:require [cheshire.core :as jp]
            [clojure.string :as s]
            [helping-hands.order.persistence :as p]
            [io.pedestal.interceptor.chain :as chain]])
```

```
  (:import [java.io IOException]
           [java.util UUID]))

;; delay the check for database and connection
;; till the first request to access @orderdb
(def ^:private orderdb
  (delay (p/create-order-database "order")))

(def get-all-orders
  {:name ::order-get-all

   :enter
   (fn [context]
     (let [tx-data (:tx-data context)
           entity (.orders @orderdb (:uid tx-data) (:flds tx-data))]
       (if (empty? entity)
         (assoc context :response {:status 404 :body "No such orders"})
         (assoc context :response {:status 200
                                   :body (jp/generate-string entity)}))))

   :error
   (fn [context ex-info]
     (assoc context
            :response {:status 500
                       :body (.getMessage ex-info)}))})
```

Testing routes

To test the routes of the *Order* service, create one or more orders by the same *consumer ID* and try to query all the orders for the same consumer ID. For simplicity, the routes assume the value of the `token` specified in the header as the *consumer ID* for the `GET /orders` route. Here is a list of cURL requests to demonstrate the process of creating, querying, and deleting the orders:

```
;; Add an order for Consumer with ID 1
% curl -i -H "token: 1" -XPUT -d
"service=1&provider=1&consumer=1&cost=500&status=O"
http://localhost:8080/orders/1
HTTP/1.1 200 OK
...

{"order/id":"1","order/service":"1","order/provider":"1","order/consumer":"
1","order/cost":500.0,"order/status":"O"}

;; Add another order for Consumer with ID 1
```

```
% curl -i -H "token: 1" -XPUT -d
"service=2&provider=2&consumer=1&cost=250&status=O"
http://localhost:8080/orders/2
HTTP/1.1 200 OK
...

{"order/id":"2","order/service":"2","order/provider":"2","order/consumer":"
1","order/cost":250.0,"order/status":"O"}

;; Add an order for Consumer with ID 2
% curl -i -H "token: 2" -XPUT -d
"service=1&provider=1&consumer=2&cost=250&status=I"
http://localhost:8080/orders/3
HTTP/1.1 200 OK
...

{"order/id":"3","order/service":"1","order/provider":"1","order/consumer":"
2","order/cost":250.0,"order/status":"I"}

;; Get all orders of consumer with ID 1
% curl -i -H "token: 1" http://localhost:8080/orders
HTTP/1.1 200 OK
...

[{"order/id":"1","order/service":"1","order/provider":"1","order/consumer":
"1","order/cost":500.0,"order/status":"O"},{"order/id":"2","order/service":
"2","order/provider":"2","order/consumer":"1","order/cost":250.0,"order/sta
tus":"O"}]

;; Get all orders of consumer with ID 2
% curl -i -H "token: 2" http://localhost:8080/orders
HTTP/1.1 200 OK
...

[{"order/id":"3","order/service":"1","order/provider":"1","order/consumer":
"2","order/cost":250.0,"order/status":"I"}]

;; Get all orders of consumer with ID 1 with specific fields
% curl -i -H "token: 1"
"http://localhost:8080/orders?flds=order/service,order/status"
...

[{"order/service":"1","order/status":"O"},{"order/service":"2","order/statu
s":"O"}]

;; Delete order with ID 2
% curl -i -H "token: 123" -XDELETE http://localhost:8080/orders/2
HTTP/1.1 200 OK
```

```
...

Success

;; Make sure that Order with ID 2 no longer exists
curl -i -H "token: 123" -XDELETE http://localhost:8080/orders/2
HTTP/1.1 404 Not Found
...

No such order

;; Check orders for consumer with ID 1 does not list Order with ID 2 now
curl -i -H "token: 1"
"http://localhost:8080/orders?flds=order/service,order/status"
HTTP/1.1 200 OK
...

[{"order/service":"1","order/status":"O"}]%

;; Delete the order with ID 3 that was the only order for consumer with ID
2
% curl -i -H "token: 123" -XDELETE http://localhost:8080/orders/3
HTTP/1.1 200 OK
...

Success

;; Make sure there are no other orders left for consumer with ID 2
% curl -i -H "token: 2" http://localhost:8080/orders
HTTP/1.1 404 Not Found
...

No such orders
```

Creating a microservice for Lookup

The *Lookup* service is used to search for *services* by type, geolocation, and availability. It subscribes to the events generated by the *Consumer, Provider, Service,* and *Order* microservices as an *Observer* and keeps a denormalized dataset that is faster to query for required *Services*. The *Lookup* service also adds longitude and latitude for the *Services* and *Consumers* that is derived from their `address` and service `area` or `locality`. To get the longitude and latitude from the service area, it depends on an external API. The *Lookup* service provides the following APIs for *consumers* to search for a service and also filter the services by type, ratings, and providers:

URI	Description
`GET /lookup/?q=query`	Filters all the services based on the specified query.
`GET /lookup/?q=query&type=type`	Filters all the services of a given `type` based on the specified query.
`GET /lookup/geo/?tl=40.73,-74.1&br=40.01,-71.12`	Looks up the service by the given latitude-longitude set for top-left (`tl`) and bottom-right (`br`) bounding box points or within a radius of a pre-defined distance from the consumer location.
`GET /validate/:service/?tl=40.73,-74.1&br=40.01,-71.12`	Validates if the specified `:service` ID is within the bounding box region specified by the top-left (`tl`) and bottom right (`br`) bounding box points or within a radius of a pre-defined distance from the consumer location.

`GET /status`	Gets the current status of the events including the number of orders placed over time, trending order types, trending location, top preferred service providers, and more.
`GET /status/consumer/:id`	Gets the current status of the events with key data points for the specified consumer ID.
`GET /status/provider/:id`	Gets the current status of the events with key data points for the specified provider ID.
`GET /status/service/:type`	Gets the current status of the events with key data points for the specified type of services.

The *Lookup* service does not provide any APIs to update the data as it maintains only a denormalized view of events received from *Consumer, Provider, Service,* and *Order* services. If there are any changes required in the data, they must be done with the APIs exposed by their corresponding microservices that manage it. The *Lookup* service will then receive the change events and reflect the changes in its local database.

Defining the Elasticsearch index

The *Lookup* microservice uses **Elasticsearch** as the local database to store all the events that are denormalized across databases maintained by *Consumer, Provider, Service* and *Order* microservices. Elasticsearch provides sub-second response for the search queries and also supports geolocation-based queries. It also supports aggregation and analytics out of the box to generate various reports for the Helping Hands application. Here is a mapping for the Elasticsearch index that is required for the *Lookup* service:

Field	Type	Mapping	Analyzer	Description
oid	string	-	keyword	Order ID
cid	string	-	keyword	Used for consumer ID
pid	string	-	keyword	Used for service provider ID
sid	string	-	keyword	Used for service ID
stype	string	-	keyword	Used for service type
locality	string	-	standard	Used to store the locality of the order
geo	string (lat,long)	geo_point	-	Used for geolocation-based queries
cost	float	-	-	Used to store the total cost of the order
ts_start	date (yyyyMMDD'T'HH:mm:ss)	-	-	Start date-time of the order
ts_end	date (yyyyMMDD'T'HH:mm:ss)	-	-	End date-time of the order
rating	float	-	-	Rating given for the order
status	string	-	keyword	Status of the order, one of O, I, D, C

The events are stored into Elasticsearch with the preceding index schema in *Lookup* index. The events are received by the *Lookup Service* via the *Kafka* topic that it subscribes to. The details of *Kafka*, the concept of topics and how to subscribe to it for events, have been explained in `Chapter 10`, *Event-Driven Patterns for Microservices*. In this chapter, the focus will be on how to query the Elasticsearch index that has the fields as per the schema of the *Lookup* index.

Creating query interceptors

All the routes of the *Lookup* service are of type `:get` as they are used only to query the data. Since the data resides with Elasticsearch, the requests needs to be mapped to relevant Elasticsearch queries to get the required result. Interceptors to query Elasticsearch data read the required fields from the `:tx-data` field of the *Pedestal context* as set by the *validation interceptors*. The implementation of the validator that wraps the queries to Elasticsearch is the same as that of other services explained earlier.

Elasticsearch defines a Query DSL (`https://www.elastic.co/guide/en/elasticsearch/reference/current/query-dsl.html`) that must be used to query the data against the Elasticsearch index. The Query DSL is based on JSON and involves creating a *JSON* structure of *query clauses* that are wrapped within a query or a filter context (`https://www.elastic.co/guide/en/elasticsearch/reference/current/query-filter-context.html`). *Query clauses* may be of type *leaf query clauses* or *compound query clauses*.

Leaf query clauses look for a particular value in a particular field, as shown in the following code snippet of an Elasticsearch query. For example, querying for all the orders that have status open; that is, O. The term query (`https://www.elastic.co/guide/en/elasticsearch/reference/current/query-dsl-term-query.html`), used to get the open orders, queries only for exact matches. Since the `status` field of the `lookup` schema has the mapping defined as that of type `keyword`, it supports exact matches via the Keyword Analyzer (`https://www.elastic.co/guide/en/elasticsearch/reference/current/analysis-keyword-analyzer.html`) of Elasticsearch:

```
{
  "query": {
    "term": {
      "status": "O"
    }
  }
}
```

Compound query clauses are used to wrap one or more query clause that may be of type *leaf* or *compound,* as shown in the following code snippet. For example, querying for all the orders that have status done; that is, D, and have a rating of four or more than that. Elasticsearch provides a Bool Query (https://www.elastic.co/guide/en/elasticsearch/ reference/current/query-dsl-bool-query.html) to create Boolean combinations of one or more queries to form a *compound clause.* For status, it uses a term query and for rating it uses a range query (https://www.elastic.co/guide/en/elasticsearch/reference/ current/query-dsl-range-query.html) of Elasticsearch that are compounded by a must clause that makes both the conditions to be satisfied for an order to be returned as a response of this query:

```
{
  "query": {
    "bool": {
      "must":[
        {
          "term": {
            "status": "D"
          }
        },
        {
          "range": {
            "rating": {
              "gte": 4
            }
          }
        }
      ]
    }
  }
}
```

Elastisch is a Clojure client that can be used to create Elasticsearch indexes and query them. Elasticsearch also provides the Java REST Client (https:/ /www.elastic.co/guide/en/elasticsearch/client/java-rest/current/ index.html) and Java APIs (https://www.elastic.co/guide/en/ elasticsearch/client/java-api/current/index.html) that can also be used with Clojure.

Using geo queries

Geo queries (https://www.elastic.co/guide/en/elasticsearch/reference/current/geo-queries.html) of Elasticsearch allow finding the records using a bounding box, distance from a given geo point, or the records lying within the polygon made up of geo points specified as a bounding region. The Helping Hands application requires geo queries for two of its routes, GET /lookup/geo and GET /validate/:service.

The first route allows *consumers* to look up available services within the specified bounding box of a latitude and longitude pair that can be selected via a map by drawing a rectangle. Alternatively, *consumers* can also look up a service within, say, a 5km radius of their location specified by their geolocation. Similarly, the second route validates that the selected service ID :service lies within the allowed limits of a *consumer* geolocation boundary. Both the routes internally use either a bounding box query (https://www.elastic.co/guide/en/elasticsearch/reference/current/query-dsl-geo-bounding-box-query.html) or a distance query (https://www.elastic.co/guide/en/elasticsearch/reference/current/query-dsl-geo-distance-query.html) of Elasticsearch, as shown here:

```
{
    "query": {
        "bool": {
            "must": {
                "match_all": {}
            },
            "filter": {
                "geo_bounding_box": {
                    "geo.location": {
                        "top_left": {
                            "lat": 13.17,
                            "lon": 77.38
                        },
                        "bottom_right": {
                            "lat": 12.73,
                            "lon": 77.88
                        }
                    }
                }
            }
        }
    }
}


{
    "query": {
        "bool" : {
```

```
            "must" : {
                "match_all" : {}
            },
            "filter" : {
                "geo_distance" : {
                    "distance" : "5km",
                    "geo.location" : {
                        "lat" : 12.97,
                        "lon" : 77.59
                    }
                }
            }
        }
    }
}
```

Geo queries based on bounding-box and distance requires fields to have the geo_point (https://www.elastic.co/guide/en/elasticsearch/reference/current/geo-point.html) mapping defined. To lookup by defining a shape, fields must have geo_shape (https://www.elastic.co/guide/en/elasticsearch/reference/current/geo-shape.html) mapping defined.

Getting status with aggregation queries

Elasticsearch also supports aggregations (https://www.elastic.co/guide/en/elasticsearch/reference/current/search-aggregations.html) that provide aggregated results based on the given queries. Aggregations are useful for the Helping Hands application to get the status of the orders and generate analytics reports that can be used to understand the usage of the application.

For example, to take a look at the orders received every month, a *date histogram* aggregation can be created on the ts_start field:

```
{
   "aggs": {
     "monthly_orders": {
       "date_histogram": {
         "field": "ts_start",
         "interval": "month"
       }
     }
   }
}
```

Similarly, to get the stats on ratings received across orders so far, `stats` aggregation can be used on the `rating` field, as shown in the following example. *Stats* returns the count, min, max, avg, and sum of the values of the specified field; that is, `rating` in this case:

```
{
  "aggs": {
    "rating_stats": {
      "stats": {
        "field": "rating"
      }
    }
  }
}
```

To know the current status of the orders across the application, terms aggregation (https:/
/www.elastic.co/guide/en/elasticsearch/reference/current/search-aggregations-
bucket-terms-aggregation.html) can be used on the `status` field, as shown in the
following example. Terms aggregation returns the current count of all the order statuses
across the system to get a report of how many orders are open, in progress, done, or closed:

```
{
  "aggs": {
    "order_status": {
      "terms": {
        "field": "status"
      }
    }
  }
}
```

Elasticsearch is also used to build a monitoring system for the Helping Hands application. Such a monitoring system relies heavily on aggregation queries of Elasticsearch to build a dashboard to understand the runtime state of the system. The monitoring system for the Helping Hands application is described in *Part IV*, Chapter 11, *Deploying and Monitoring Secured Microservices*.

Creating a microservice for alerts

The *Alert* service is used to send *email* alerts and SMS. Alerts can be generated at various levels by other microservices. For example, successful creation of a *consumer, provider, service,* or an *order* may require an email to be sent to the relevant stakeholders. Similarly, alerts may be required whenever there is a change in the status of the *order* or a *rating* is received. The *Alert* service does not maintain a local database, it just generates events for each successful alert sent that can be tracked for monitoring purposes. The following table lists the endpoints for the *Alert* service:

URI	Params	Description
POST /alerts/email	to, cc, subject, body	Sends an alert via email to one or more recipients.
POST /alerts/sms	to, body	Sends an alert via SMS to one or more recipients.

Adding routes

Mostly, the *Alert* service will listen for events as an *Observer* and will not receive requests to send alerts via routes. If it is required to send alerts synchronously, the /alerts/email and /alerts/sms routes can be used, as defined in the following code snippet:

```
(def routes #{["/alerts/email"
               :post (conj common-interceptors `auth `core/validate
                           `core/send-email `gen-events)
               :route-name :alert-email]
              ["/alerts/sms"
               :post (conj common-interceptors `auth `core/validate
                           `core/send-sms `gen-events)
               :route-name :alert-sms]})
```

Creating an email interceptor using Postal

Postal (`https://github.com/drewr/postal`) is a Clojure library that allows sending email. It requires SMTP connection details and the message as a map containing the required details of `to`, `from`, `cc`, `subject`, and `body` to send as an email. Postal can be used within the *Pedestal interceptor* to send an email if the required fields are validated and present in the context, as shown here:

```clojure
(ns helping-hands.alert.core
  "Initializes Helping Hands Alert Service"
  (:require [cheshire.core :as jp]
            [clojure.string :as s]
            [postal.core :as postal]
            [helping-hands.alert.persistence :as p]
            [io.pedestal.interceptor.chain :as chain])
  (:import [java.io IOException]
           [java.util UUID]))

;; --------------------------------
;; Validation Interceptors
;; --------------------------------

(defn- prepare-valid-context
  "Applies validation logic and returns the resulting context"
  [context]
  (let [params (-> context :request :form-params)]
    (if (and (not (empty? params))
             (not (empty? (:to params)))
             (not (empty? (:body params))))
      (let [to-val (map s/trim (s/split (:to params) #","))]
        (assoc context :tx-data (assoc params :to to-val)))
      (chain/terminate
       (assoc context
              :response {:status 400
                         :body "Both to and body are required"})))))

(def validate
  {:name ::validate

   :enter
   (fn [context]
     (if-let [params (-> context :request :form-params)]
       ;; validate and return a context with tx-data
       ;; or terminated interceptor chain
       (prepare-valid-context context)
       (chain/terminate
```

```
            (assoc context
                  :response {:status 400
                             :body "Invalid parameters"}))))

      :error
      (fn [context ex-info]
        (assoc context
              :response {:status 500
                         :body (.getMessage ex-info)}))})

  ;; -------------------------------
  ;; Business Logic Interceptors
  ;; -------------------------------

  (def send-email
    {:name ::send-email

     :enter
     (fn [context]
       (let [tx-data (:tx-data context)
             msg (into {} (filter (comp some? val)
                                  {:from "admin@helpinghands.com"
                                   :to (:to tx-data)
                                   :cc (:cc tx-data)
                                   :subject (:subject tx-data)
                                   :body (:body tx-data)}))
             result (postal/send-message
                      {:host "smtp.gmail.com"
                       :port 465
                       :ssl true
                       :user "admin@helpinghands.com"
                       :pass "resetme"}
                      msg)]
         ;; send email
         (assoc context :response
               {:status 200
                :body (jp/generate-string result)}))))

     :error
     (fn [context ex-info]
       (assoc context
             :response {:status 500
                        :body (.getMessage ex-info)}))})
```

Postal depends on the underlying SMTP server to accept the credentials and allow third-party clients to send emails. Services such as Gmail may restrict third-party clients to use username and password.

 To send alerts, it is recommended to use external services such as Amazon SES, Amazon SNS, and more as they are reliable to use and follow a pay-per-use model.

Summary

In this chapter, we focused on the step-by-step implementation of Helping Hands microservices using the *Pedestal* framework. We learned how to implement *Hexagonal Architecture* using Clojure protocols (`https://clojure.org/reference/protocols`) and *Pedestal interceptors*. We also implemented the required microservices for the Helping Hands application in Pedestal. In the next chapter, we will learn how to configure our microservices and maintain the runtime state of the application that includes connection with persistent storage and message queues to store data and send events, respectively.

9
Configuring Microservices

"I can't change the direction of the wind, but I can adjust my sails to always reach my destination."

- Jimmy Dean

Microservices must be configurable to adapt to the environment in which they are deployed. They must support external configuration parameters that can be specified at runtime to configure them as per the environment in which they are deployed. Once the configuration parameters are defined, a microservice must be able to effectively propagate the configurations across its modules. These configuration parameters might then be used to initialize database connections or maintain other application states that must be shared across the modules of a microservice. All the modules must have access to the exact same state at runtime. This chapter provides effective solutions to build such configurable services that can manage their runtime states effectively. In this chapter, you will learn how to do the following:

- Apply configuration principles to build highly configurable services
- Use `Omniconf` for configuration
- Validate configuration at startup and register it for use at runtime
- Use a `mount` library to compose and manage application states

Configuration principles

All the application parameters that are related to the environment and affect the application state must be made configurable. For example, the connection string for a **Datomic** database that is used by **Helping Hands** services can be made configurable so that it can be updated externally to point to a specific instance of Datomic in production. Configuration parameters also make it possible to test the application in various environments. For example, if a Datomic connection string is made configurable for Helping Hands services, it can be used to test the services with an in-memory instance of Datomic in local development environments and later changed to point to the production instance of Datomic once they are deployed.

Defining configuration parameters

Applications must support multiple ways of defining the configuration parameters. Using command-line arguments is one of the most common ways of specifying the configuration parameters for the application. Environment variables and external configuration files can also be specified for applications to pick the configuration parameters at runtime. Since *Clojure* uses *JVM* as its runtime engine, applications built in *Clojure* can accept configuration parameters as *Java* properties as well.

Applications that accept configuration parameters from multiple sources must decide on the preference of various sources. For example, configuration parameters specified at the command line as Java properties can overwrite the values defined by the environment variables that in turn can override the default configuration defined in the configuration file.

Using configuration parameters

One option to provide access to configuration parameters is to load them at startup and pass them as arguments to the functions. In this case, every time a new configuration parameter is added, it may result in the change of the function signature that can affect all the functions dependent on it.

Configuration parameters must not be tied directly to the arguments of the function because configuration parameters that are loaded at startup time may not change throughout the life cycle of the service. Instead, configuration parameters can be read once at startup and kept as immutable constants that can be directly accessed by all the functions that require one or more configuration parameter.

Reading the configuration parameters from various sources and making them accessible does not guarantee the configuration will be correct unless they are used by the application. For example, if the application needs a port number as a configuration parameter, it must be verified as soon as it is read and must be a short positive number with a maximum value of 65535. If these checks are not performed at the time the configurations are read, they are going to result in runtime exceptions later during the application life cycle. Detecting such configuration issues at a later point in time is costly as the configuration needs to be updated and the application needs to be redeployed to pick up on the updated configuration.

Using Omniconf for configuration

Omniconf (https://github.com/grammarly/omniconf) is an open source configuration library for Clojure projects that can be used to configure microservices of the Helping Hands application (refer to Chapter 3, *Microservices for Helping Hands Application*, and Chapter 8, *Building Microservices for Helping Hands*). Omniconf not only allows the application to define the preference with respect to various configuration sources but also to verify them at startup. Internally, it keeps all the configuration parameters stored as an immutable constant that can be accessed as a regular Clojure data structure.

 Omniconf is one of the options for configuration management. Libraries, such as Environ (https://github.com/weavejester/environ), Config (https://github.com/yogthos/config), Aero (https://github.com/juxt/aero), and Fluorine (https://github.com/reborg/fluorine) can also be used for configuration management.

Enabling Omniconf

To enable an Omniconf library for an existing project, such as *Helping Hands Consumer Service*, add the Omniconf dependency to the project.clj file and add JVM opts, conf to the dev profile that points to the conf.edn Omniconf configuration file:

```
(defproject helping-hands-consumer "0.0.1-SNAPSHOT"
  :description "Helping Hands Consumer Application"
  :url
"https://www.packtpub.com/application-development/microservices-clojure"
  :license {:name "Eclipse Public License"
            :url "http://www.eclipse.org/legal/epl-v10.html"}
  :dependencies [[org.clojure/clojure "1.8.0"]
                 [io.pedestal/pedestal.service "0.5.3"]
```

```
                    [io.pedestal/pedestal.jetty "0.5.3"]
                    ;; Datomic Free Edition
                    [com.datomic/datomic-free "0.9.5561.62"]
                    ;; Omniconf
                    [com.grammarly/omniconf "0.2.7"]
                    [ch.qos.logback/logback-classic "1.1.8" :exclusions
     [org.slf4j/slf4j-api]]
                    [org.slf4j/jul-to-slf4j "1.7.22"]
                    [org.slf4j/jcl-over-slf4j "1.7.22"]
                    [org.slf4j/log4j-over-slf4j "1.7.22"]]
       ...
    :profiles {:provided {:dependencies [[org.clojure/tools.reader "0.10.0"]
                                         [org.clojure/tools.nrepl "0.2.12"]]}
              :dev {:aliases {"run-dev" ["trampoline" "run" "-m"
                                         "helping-hands.consumer.server/run-
     dev"]}
                    :dependencies [[io.pedestal/pedestal.service-tools
     "0.5.3"]]
                    :resource-paths ["config", "resources"]
                    :jvm-opts ["-Dconf=config/conf.edn"]}
              :uberjar {:aot [helping-hands.consumer.server]}
              :doc {:dependencies [[codox-theme-rdash "0.1.1"]]
                    :codox {:metadata {:doc/format :markdown}
                            :themes [:rdash]}}
              :debug {:jvm-opts
                      ["-server" (str "-agentlib:jdwp=transport=dt_socket,"
                                      "server=y,address=8000,suspend=n")]}}}
    :main ^{:skip-aot true} helping-hands.consumer.server)
```

Integrating with Helping Hands

The Helping Hands services that were implemented in the previous chapter used a fixed Datomic database URI, such as `datomic:mem://consumer`, for the consumer database managed by the consumer service. Instead of fixing the name of the database and Datomic URI, it must be made configurable so that it can be changed at the time of deployment. For example, consider a scenario where you wish to run two instances of *Consumer* service but with separate consumer databases. It will not be possible to do so if the Datomic database URI is hardcoded in the implementation and not made configurable.

`Omniconf` requires all the configuration parameters to be defined via
the `omniconf.core/define` function. For the *Consumer* service of the Helping Hands
application, add a new `helping-hands.consumer.config` namespace and initialize the
configuration as shown here:

```clojure
(ns helping-hands.consumer.config
  "Defines Configuration for the Service"
  (:require [omniconf.core :as cfg]))

(defn init-config
  "Initializes the configuration"
  [{:keys [cli-args quit-on-error] :as params
    :or {cli-args [] quit-on-error true}}]
  ;; define the configuration
  (cfg/define
    {:conf {:type :file
            :required true
            :verifier omniconf.core/verify-file-exists
            :description "MECBOT configuration file"}
     :datomic
     {:nested
      {:uri {:type :string
             :default "datomic:mem//consumer"
             :description "Datomic URI for Consumer Database"}}}})
  ;; like- :some-option => SOME_OPTION
  (cfg/populate-from-env quit-on-error)
  ;; load properties to pick -Dconf for the config file
  (cfg/populate-from-properties quit-on-error)
  ;; Configuration file specified as
  ;; Environment variable CONF or JVM Opt -Dconf
  (when-let [conf (cfg/get :conf)]
    (cfg/populate-from-file conf quit-on-error))
  ;; like- :some-option => (java -Dsome-option=...)
  ;; reload JVM args to overwrite configuration file params
  (cfg/populate-from-properties quit-on-error)
  ;; like- :some-option => -some-option
  (cfg/populate-from-cmd cli-args quit-on-error)
  ;; Verify the configuration
  (cfg/verify :quit-on-error quit-on-error))

(defn get-config
  "Gets the specified config param value"
  [& args]
  (apply cfg/get args))
```

In this example, there is a mandatory configuration parameter, `:conf`, defined to be of `:file` that must point to the `conf.edn` configuration file. There is also a verifier attached to it that validates the presence of the `conf.edn` file based on the defined location. Also, there is a `:datomic` configuration parameter defined that is nested and has a `:uri` parameter, defined as `string` type, with a default value of `datomic:mem://consumer` that points to an in-memory Datomic database.

After defining the configuration parameters, the implementation checks for the `conf` parameter value by first loading the JVM properties. The `-Dconf` JVM property points to the `conf.edn` file as defined in the `dev` profile of `project.clj`. The configuration parameters are read in the sequence of environment variables, properties file, and command line, each overwriting the values defined by the previous source as per the loading sequence.

A `get-config` utility method is also defined within the same namespace for other modules to look up the configuration parameters that are loaded by this namespace using `Omniconf`. To load the configuration at startup, call the `init-config` method at the application entry point, that is, `helping-hands.consumer.server`, as shown here:

```
(ns helping-hands.consumer.server
  (:gen-class) ; for -main method in uberjar
  (:require [io.pedestal.http :as server]
            [io.pedestal.http.route :as route]
            [helping-hands.consumer.config :as cfg]
            [helping-hands.consumer.service :as service]))

...

(defn run-dev
  "The entry-point for 'lein run-dev'"
  [& args]
  (println "\nCreating your [DEV] server...")
  ;; initialize configuration
  (cfg/init-config {:cli-args args :quit-on-error true})
  (-> service/service ;; start with production configuration
      ...
      ;; Wire up interceptor chains
      server/default-interceptors
      server/dev-interceptors
      server/create-server
      server/start))

(defn -main
  "The entry-point for 'lein run'"
  [& args]
  (println "\nCreating your server...")
```

```
;; initialize configuration
(cfg/init-config {:cli-args args :quit-on-error true})
(server/start runnable-service))
```

Now, if you try to run the *Consumer* service in dev mode at REPL, `Omniconf` will load the configuration, verify it, and make it available via the `helping-hands.consumer.config/get-config` method. Since we haven't created the `conf.edn` file in the specified `conf/` location, the verifier should fail at the initialization step itself, as shown here:

```
helping-hands.consumer.server> (def server (run-dev))

Creating your [DEV] server...
CompilerException java.io.FileNotFoundException: config/conf.edn (No such
file or directory), compiling:(form-init3431514182044937086.clj:118:44)
```

Add a `conf.edn` file under the `config` directory and define only the Datomic URI configuration, as shown here:

```
{:datomic {:uri "datomic:mem://consumer"}}
```

Now, the configuration is valid, as it finds the defined `conf.edn` file. In this case, as shown in the REPL session in the following code snippet, `Omniconf` will dump the loaded configuration that can then be verified to make sure all the configuration parameters are loaded as expected. Note that the required `:conf` parameter is not defined in the `conf.edn` file, but it is defined as the JVM property that is also read in the sequence:

```
;; start service in dev mode
helping-hands.consumer.server> (def server (run-dev))

Creating your [DEV] server...
Omniconf configuration:
 {:conf #object[java.io.File 0x27a8b5d3 "config/conf.edn"],
  :datomic {:uri "datomic:mem://consumer"}}

#'helping-hands.consumer.server/server

;; try looking up the configuration parameter
helping-hands.consumer.server> (helping-hands.consumer.config/get-config
:datomic)
{:uri "datomic:mem//consumer"}
helping-hands.consumer.server> (helping-hands.consumer.config/get-config
:datomic :uri)
"datomic:mem//consumer"
```

Now, try changing the Datomic URl parameter in the `config.edn` file to
`datomic:mem://consumer-sample`. It will overwrite the default value and can then be
used by the application using the `get-config` method as shown here:

```
helping-hands.consumer.server> (def server (run-dev))

Creating your [DEV] server...
Omniconf configuration:
 {:conf #object[java.io.File 0x60e62394 "config/conf.edn"],
 :datomic {:uri "datomic:mem://consumer-sample"}}

#'helping-hands.consumer.server/server
helping-hands.consumer.server> (helping-hands.consumer.config/get-config
:datomic)
{:uri "datomic:mem://consumer-sample"}
helping-hands.consumer.server> (helping-hands.consumer.config/get-config
:datomic :uri)
"datomic:mem://consumer-sample"
```

The persistence namespace of the *Consumer* service can now read the database URI directly
from the configuration instead of expecting it as an argument of the `create-consumer-`
`database` function:

```
(ns helping-hands.consumer.persistence
  "Persistence Port and Adapter for Consumer Service"
  (:require [datomic.api :as d]
            [helping-hands.consumer.config :as cfg]))


...


(defn create-consumer-database
  "Creates a consumer database and returns the connection"
  []
  ;; create and connect to the database
  (let [dburi (cfg/get-config [:datomic :uri])
        db (d/create-database dburi)
        conn (d/connect dburi)]
    ;; transact schema if database was created
    (when db
      (d/transact conn
                  [{:db/ident :consumer/id
                    :db/valueType :db.type/string
                    :db/cardinality :db.cardinality/one
                    :db/doc "Unique Consumer ID"
                    :db/unique :db.unique/identity
                    :db/index true}
                   ...
```

```
        ]))
(ConsumerDBDatomic. conn)))
```

Omniconf works with both the Leiningen and Boot build tools of Clojure. For more details and usage information of all the possible options, take a look at the example-lein (https://github.com/grammarly/omniconf/tree/master/example-lein) and example-boot (https://github.com/grammarly/omniconf/tree/master/example-boot) projects of Omniconf.

Managing application states with mount

Once the configuration parameters are defined using Omniconf, they are accessible across the namespaces as immutable data. The configuration parameters are often used to create stateful objects, such as database connections. For example, in the *Consumer* service project, Omniconf made it possible to create a consumer database by directly looking up the :datomic :uri configuration parameter within the create-consumer-database function.

The helping-hands.consumer.persistence/create-consumer-database function has a side effect of database being created and also a new connection being initialized to connect to the created database. This connection has a state that must be shared across other namespaces of the *Helping Hands Consumer service* that need access to the database. In the current implementation, the connection was initialized at the first call to the helping-hands.consumer.core/consumerdb as shown here:

```
(ns helping-hands.consumer.core
  "Initializes Helping Hands Consumer Service"
  (:require [cheshire.core :as jp]
            [clojure.string :as s]
            [helping-hands.consumer.persistence :as p]
            [io.pedestal.interceptor.chain :as chain])
  (:import [java.io IOException]
           [java.util UUID]))

;; delay the check for database and connection
;; till the first request to access @consumerdb
(def ^:private consumerdb
  (delay (p/create-consumer-database)))
```

Instead of creating a state using *delay*, the state management can be handled effectively using a library, such as `mount` (`https://github.com/tolitius/mount`). Creating application states using `mount` allows for the reloading of the entire application state using `start` and `stop` functions provided by the `mount.core` namespace. The `mount` library also helps with state composition by allowing the application to start only with specific states and at the same time swapping others with new values. It also supports runtime arguments.

 Component (`https://github.com/stuartsierra/component`) is another Clojure library that is widely used to manage the life cycle of stateful objects in a Clojure project. `mount` is an alternative to the `Component` library with key differences (`https://github.com/tolitius/mount/blob/master/doc/differences-from-component.md#differences-from-component`), one of them being Component's requirement of the entire app being built around its component object model.

Enabling mount

To enable the `mount` library for the *Helping Hands Consumer service* application, add a mount dependency to the `project.clj` file as shown in the following code snippet. Also, create a new `helping-hands.consumer.state` namespace that will be used to define the states using the `mount.core/defstate` function, which can be referred to by other namespaces of the project to get access to the current state of the defined object, such as the Datomic database connection:

```
(defproject helping-hands-consumer "0.0.1-SNAPSHOT"
  :description "Helping Hands Consumer Application"
  :url
"https://www.packtpub.com/application-development/microservices-clojure"
  :license {:name "Eclipse Public License"
            :url "http://www.eclipse.org/legal/epl-v10.html"}
  :dependencies [[org.clojure/clojure "1.8.0"]
                 [io.pedestal/pedestal.service "0.5.3"]
                 [io.pedestal/pedestal.jetty "0.5.3"]
                 ;; Datomic Free Edition
                 [com.datomic/datomic-free "0.9.5561.62"]
                 ;; Omniconf
                 [com.grammarly/omniconf "0.2.7"]
                 ;; Mount
                 [mount "0.1.11"]
                 ...
                 ]
  ...
  :main ^{:skip-aot true} helping-hands.consumer.server)
```

Integrating with Helping Hands

To integrate mount with the *Helping Hands Consumer service* project, create a state for a Datomic database connection within the helping-hands.consumer.state namespace, as shown here:

```
(ns helping-hands.consumer.state
  "Initializes State for Consumer Service"
  (:require [mount.core :refer [defstate] :as mount]
            [helping-hands.consumer.persistence :as p]))

(defstate consumerdb
  :start (p/create-consumer-database)
  :stop (.stop consumerdb))
```

The :start clause is called at the time of startup and :stop is called at shutdown. The function stop is defined for the ConsumerDB protocol, as shown in the following example under the helping-hands.consumer.persistence namespace:

```
(ns helping-hands.consumer.persistence
  "Persistence Port and Adapter for Consumer Service"
  (:require [datomic.api :as d]
            [helping-hands.consumer.config :as cfg]))

(defprotocol ConsumerDB
  "Abstraction for consumer database"

  (upsert [this id name address mobile email geo]
    "Adds/Updates a consumer entity")

  (entity [this id flds]
    "Gets the specified consumer with all or requested fields")

  (delete [this id]
    "Deletes the specified consumer entity")

  (close [this]
    "Closes the database"))

...

(defrecord ConsumerDBDatomic [conn]
  ConsumerDB

  ...
```

```
(close [this]
  (d/shutdown true)))
```

Next, add the startup and shutdown hooks for mount at the application entry point under the helping-hands.consumer.server namespace. The shutdown hook defined at the application entry point calls the :stop clause of mount that must clean up all the resources related to the stateful object, that is, the Datomic connection as shown in the following example:

```
(ns helping-hands.consumer.server
  (:gen-class) ; for -main method in uberjar
  (:require [io.pedestal.http :as server]
            [io.pedestal.http.route :as route]
            [mount.core :as mount]
            [helping-hands.consumer.config :as cfg]
            [helping-hands.consumer.service :as service]))

...

(defn run-dev
  "The entry-point for 'lein run-dev'"
  [& args]
  (println "\nCreating your [DEV] server...")
  ;; initialize configuration
  (cfg/init-config {:cli-args args :quit-on-error true})
  ;; initialize state
  (mount/start)
  ;; Add shutdown-hook
  (.addShutdownHook
   (Runtime/getRuntime)
   (Thread. mount/stop))
  (-> service/service ;; start with production configuration
      ...
      ;; Wire up interceptor chains
      server/default-interceptors
      server/dev-interceptors
      server/create-server
      server/start))

(defn -main
  "The entry-point for 'lein run'"
  [& args]
  (println "\nCreating your server...")
  ;; initialize configuration
  (cfg/init-config {:cli-args args :quit-on-error true})
  ;; initialize state
  (mount/start)
```

```clojure
;; Add shutdown-hook
(.addShutdownHook
 (Runtime/getRuntime)
 (Thread. mount/stop))
(server/start runnable-service))
```

Once `mount` is set up to initialize the state at startup; the defined state `consumerdb` can now be referred to across namespaces and used directly for the `helping-hands.consumer.core` namespace as shown here:

```clojure
(ns helping-hands.consumer.core
  "Initializes Helping Hands Consumer Service"
  (:require [cheshire.core :as jp]
            [clojure.string :as s]
            [helping-hands.consumer.persistence :as p]
            [io.pedestal.interceptor.chain :as chain]
            [helping-hands.consumer.state :refer [consumerdb]])
  (:import [java.io IOException]
           [java.util UUID]))

;; delay the check for database and connection
;; till the first request to access @consumerdb
;; NO LONGER REQUIRED DUE TO MOUNT
;;(def ^:private consumerdb
;; (delay (p/create-consumer-database)))

...

;; Use the referred stateful consumerdb directly in the interceptor
(def upsert-consumer
  {:name ::consumer-upsert

   :enter
   (fn [context]
     (let [tx-data (:tx-data context)
           id (:id tx-data)
           db (.upsert consumerdb id (:name tx-data)
                       (:address tx-data) (:mobile tx-data)
                       (:email tx-data) (:geo tx-data))]
       ...))
   :error ...})
```

Summary

In this chapter, we focused on how to build configurable applications that can adapt as per the requirements and dependencies at hand. We looked at an open source configuration utility called `Omniconf` that provides an effective way to define and validate configuration parameters for Clojure applications.

We also looked at how the runtime state of the application can be composed and shared among various namespaces of the Clojure application. We looked at an open source library called `mount` that helps applications to manage and compose their states at runtime without affecting the overall structure of the implementation.

In the next chapter, we will learn how to adopt event-driven architecture for Helping Hands microservices. We will also learn how to build data flows for the microservices of Helping Hands.

10

Event-Driven Patterns for Microservices

"The single biggest problem with communication is the illusion that it has taken place."

- George Bernard Shaw

Microservices address a single bounded context and are deployed independently on one or more physical machines that are distributed across a network. Although they are deployed in isolation, they need to interact with each other to accomplish application-level tasks that may cut across multiple bounded contexts. The choice of communication medium and method has a great impact on the performance and durability of the entire microservice-based architecture. Events are one of the methods of asynchronous communication among microservices to exchange data of interest. *Part-1* of the book explains the importance of the observer model and how a message broker (`https://en.wikipedia.org/wiki/Message_broker`) helps in sending and receiving events in a microservices architecture. In this chapter, you will:

- Learn about event-driven patterns for effective messaging among microservices
- Learn how to use Apache Kafka as a message broker for microservices
- Learn how to use Apache Kafka for **Event Sourcing**
- Learn how to integrate Apache Kafka with **Helping Hands** microservices

Implementing event-driven patterns

Event-driven patterns address the observer model of communication to send messages among microservices. The messages are sent and received through a message broker that acts as a connecting bridge between the sender and the receiver. In a microservices architecture, these messages may be generated as events as an outcome of the action taken by the microservice. Messages for which the source microservice does not expect a response from the target service can be published as events asynchronously, instead of sending them over a REST API for direct communication. Since it is not a direct communication, an event can be published once and consumed by more than one microservice that has subscribed to receive it. Moreover, the sender does not get blocked by the receiver for each event that is published.

Message brokers also help to build a resilient architecture for event-driven communication as receivers need not be available while the event is being produced and they can consume the messages at will. In case of failures, the receiver can be restarted and it can start consuming the events where it left off. During the downtime, the message broker itself acts as a queue and caches all the events that were not consumed by the receiver and makes it available to the receiver on demand.

Asynchronous communication via events also decouples the sender from the receiver that helps in scaling both the sides independently. This feature is of prime importance in a microservice-based architecture as it allows the microservices to be deployed independently of other microservices from which it consumes the events via a message-broker. Event-driven patterns are also used for asynchronous tasks such as storing audit logs to keep track of runtime state of the application and sending alerts.

 The observer model, along with various data management patterns, are explained in Chapter 2, *Microservices Architecture* of this book.

Event sourcing

Events can be used to advertise the changes in the state of the entities managed by a microservice. In such cases, events carry the updated state of the entity including the entity identifier and the values of the fields that have changed. It is also recommended to include a unique identifier and version number as well with each update event. Any interested microservice can then subscribe to these events via a message broker and receive the changes to update the state of the entity locally. The *Lookup Service* of the Helping Hands application is one such service that listens to all the state change events generated by the *consumer, provider,* and *order* microservices to keep an updated dataset for users to look up.

One of the main advantages of publishing all the state changes across microservices as immutable events is to make sure that the state of the entire microservice-based application can be rebuilt by just processing these events in the sequence in which they are published. Both the current state of the application as well as the state in the past can be reconstructed by processing these events in the exact same sequence. Ability to replay the events not only helps in rebuilding the state of the application, but also helps in auditing and debugging.

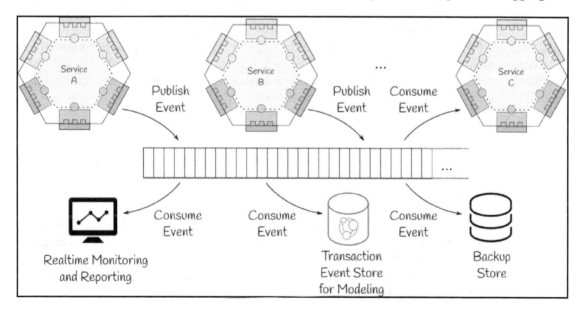

Message brokers, such as Apache Kafka (`https://kafka.apache.org/`), allow publishing messages decoupled from consuming them and effectively act as a storage system that maintains a durable log of published events. Such systems allow the events to be captured by multiple systems at the same time, as shown in the preceding diagram. For example, the events published by **Service A** and **Service B** can be consumed by **Service C**, but at the same time, these events can be backed-up in a backup store or captured in a transactional store for building machine learning models or captured for real-time monitoring and reporting of the application state in real time. Since the logs retained by the brokers are immutable and durable, applications that are developed in-future can also replay the events to build the temporal state of the application and work on it.

Using the CQRS pattern

The **Command Query Responsibility Segregation** (**CQRS**) pattern applies the command-query separation (`https://en.wikipedia.org/wiki/Command-query_separation`) principle by splitting the application into two parts, **query side** and **command side**. Query side is responsible for getting the data by only querying the state of the application, whereas command side is responsible for changing the state of the system by performing create, update, or delete operations on application data that may result in updation of one or more databases used by the application. Although the CQRS pattern is often used in conjunction with the event-sourcing pattern, it need not be tied to events and can be applied to any application with or without events. The CQRS pattern is recommended for applications that are not balanced with respect to read and write loads.

 CQS (`https://en.wikipedia.org/wiki/Command-query_separation`) principle was devised by Bertrand Meyer (`https://en.wikipedia.org/wiki/Bertrand_Meyer`), whereas CQRS term was first coined by Greg Young as part of CQRS documents (`https://cqrs.files.wordpress.com/2010/11/cqrs_documents.pdf`).

The CQRS pattern fits well with microservice-based architecture as the entire application is split into separate services, each having their own data model and publishing the changes in the state of their data model as events. But at the same time, it is also challenging to keep these separate models consistent. This is where sagas are useful, which support eventual consistency. The sagas pattern has been described in `Chapter 2`, *Microservices Architecture*.

For more details on the CQRS pattern and its usage, read the *CQRS* article by Martin Fowler (`https://martinfowler.com/bliki/CQRS.html`) and the *Clarified CQRS* article by Udi Dahan (`http://udidahan.com/2009/12/09/clarified-cqrs/`).

Introduction to Apache Kafka

Apache Kafka is a distributed streaming platform that allows applications to publish and subscribe to a stream of records. Apache Kafka is not just a message queue, it also allows applications to publish the events that are then stored by Kafka as an immutable log in a fault-tolerant way. It allows the producers and consumers of the events to scale horizontally without affecting each other. Since the events are logged in the same sequence as they are published within Kafka, it allows consumers to replay the log from and up to the desired point to reconstruct views of the application state.

Design principles

Kafka is run as a cluster of one or more servers that act as message brokers (`https://en.wikipedia.org/wiki/Message_broker`) in the system. Kafka categorizes the stream of records under topics that are used by producers and consumers to produce records and consume them, respectively. Each record consists of a key-value pair and a timestamp.

A typical Kafka cluster is shown in the following diagram along with the structure of a Kafka topic and its partitions. A **topic** is a core abstraction for a stream of records in Kafka. Producers publish the records to a topic that can have zero, one, or more *consumers* subscribed to it. Each topic consists of one or more *partitions* that are ordered, immutable sequence of records that is appended to a commit log and stored on a disk and replicated across servers for fault-tolerance and durability. Each record that is published on a topic gets assigned to a partition within which it is assigned a sequential identifier number that is called the **offset**. The offset uniquely identifies a record within the partition and is also used as a reference by consumers to track their state of consumption. Offsets allow consumers to reset themselves to an earlier state to either replay the records or fast-forward in time to skip the records. A Kafka cluster retains all the published records only for a configurable retention period. Post the configured retention period, the records are no longer available for consumers irrespective of whether they were consumed earlier or not:

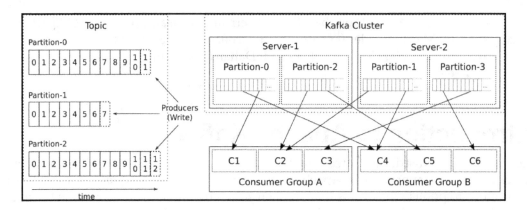

Kafka **producers** publish data to one or more topics and have the freedom to decide the partition for the published records. Kafka **consumers** always join with a consumer group label that is shared with one more consumer that may be present on one or more machines. The **Consumer Group** plays an important role in the way the Kafka cluster delivers the published records to the consumers. Each record published on a Kafka topic is delivered to only one consumer within a Consumer Group. For example, in the preceding diagram, there are two consumer groups—**Consumer Group A** and **Consumer Group B** and six consumers with three consumers in each group. Any record published on partitions 0, 1, 2, or 3 is sent to only one consumer within each group. For example, records published to **Partition-0** is sent to **C1** of **Consumer Group A** and **C2** of **Consumer Group B**. Kafka balances the flow of records across the consumers in the consumer groups.

 Apache Kafka provides total ordering over records only within a partition. Use cases that require total ordering over the records published on a topic must have the topic configured to have a single partition. This configuration also limits the throughput to only one consumer process per consumer group.

Getting Kafka

Apache Kafka is an open-source platform and can be downloaded from its download page (https://kafka.apache.org/downloads). For the examples in this book, download and extract the 1.0.0 release (https://www.apache.org/dyn/closer.cgi?path=/kafka/1.0.0/kafka_2.11-1.0.0.tgz) from one of the mirrors, as shown here:

```
# download Kafka 1.0.0 with Scala 2.11 (Recommended)
% wget
http://redrockdigimark.com/apachemirror/kafka/1.0.0/kafka_2.11-1.0.0.tgz
...
```

```
# extract Kafka distribution
% tar -xvf kafka_2.11-1.0.0.tgz
...
# switch to Kafka directory
% cd kafka_2.11-1.0.0
```

Apache Kafka Servers require Apache Zookeeper (`https://zookeeper.apache.org/`) for cluster coordination. Kafka distribution packages a single node Zookeeper instance for convenience; however, it is recommended to set up an external Zookeeper cluster for production deployments. Start a single node Zookeeper with the default properties file packaged with Kafka, as shown here:

```
# start Zookeeper
bin/zookeeper-server-start.sh config/zookeeper.properties
....
INFO binding to port 0.0.0.0/0.0.0.0:2181
(org.apache.zookeeper.server.NIOServerCnxnFactory)
```

Once the Zookeeper is started, either switch to a new terminal or put the Zookeeper process in the background to get the access to the same terminal. Next, start a Kafka server with the default properties file packaged with Kafka, as shown here:

```
# start Kafka Server
bin/kafka-server-start.sh config/server.properties
...
INFO Kafka version : 1.0.0 (org.apache.kafka.common.utils.AppInfoParser)
INFO Kafka commitId : aaa7af6d4a11b29d
(org.apache.kafka.common.utils.AppInfoParser)
INFO [KafkaServer id=0] started (kafka.server.KafkaServer)
```

The default `server.properties` file contains a fixed `broker.id` property that is set to `0` and the listeners configured to a default port of `9092` with `log.dir` pointing to `/tmp`. For a single Kafka server, these settings are fine, but to start multiple Kafka servers on the same machine, these properties must be changed for each server to avoid ID, port, and commit log directory clashes. Next, create a topic by the name of `test` with a single partition, as shown here:

```
# create a topic
% bin/kafka-topics.sh --create --zookeeper localhost:2181 --replication-
factor 1 --partitions 1 --topic test
Created topic "test".

# List and confirm that topic was created
% bin/kafka-topics.sh --list --zookeeper localhost:2181
test
```

The create topic command requires the address to the Zookeeper that is used by Kafka cluster. Since Zookeeper was started with default properties, it would have taken the 2181 port if that was free on the machine. Next, start a producer in a new terminal and publish some messages, as shown here:

```
# start a new producer to produce the messages on topic 'test'
% bin/kafka-console-producer.sh --broker-list localhost:9092 --topic test
>Hello Kafka!
>Hello Helping Hands!
>
```

The started producer connects to the Kafka server on port 9092; that is, the default port of Kafka server. The started producer is also configured to publish the messages on the test topic that was created earlier. Once the producer is started, publish the two messages, as shown in the preceding code snippet, and start a consumer for the same topic in a new terminal, as shown here:

```
# start a new consumer to consume the messages from test topic from the
beginning
% bin/kafka-console-consumer.sh --bootstrap-server localhost:9092 --topic
test --from-beginning
Hello Kafka!
Hello Helping Hands!
```

The consumer receives the published messages and prints them on the console. Now, go back to the producer terminal and publish one more message and verify that consumer receives only the new message, as shown here:

```
# publish a new message
% bin/kafka-console-producer.sh --broker-list localhost:9092 --topic test
>Hello Kafka!
>Hello Helping Hands!
>Kafka Works!
>
```

```
# validate the message on the consumer terminal
% bin/kafka-console-consumer.sh --bootstrap-server localhost:9092 --topic
test --from-beginning
Hello Kafka!
Hello Helping Hands!
Kafka Works!
```

Kafka Manager (https://github.com/yahoo/kafka-manager) is a useful tool that helps in managing one or more Kafka clusters using a single web-based interface.

Using Kafka as a messaging system

Kafka provides both queuing (http://en.wikipedia.org/wiki/Message_queue) and publish-subscribe (http://en.wikipedia.org/wiki/Publish-subscribe_pattern) constructs of a messaging system by the concept of a **Consumer Group**. The messages published on a topic partition are broadcasted to a consumer within each Consumer Group and within the Consumer Group, each consumer receives the messages from a different partition of a topic. Therefore, the number of consumers present in the Consumer Group must not be more than the number of partitions present in a topic. If they are more than the number of partitions, then they will be just sitting idle and will only get the message if one of the consumers fails within the group. For example, to demonstrate the messaging capabilities of Kafka, start one more consumer for the test topic, as shown here:

```
# start another consumer
% bin/kafka-console-consumer.sh --bootstrap-server localhost:9092 --topic test --from-beginning
```

Once the consumer is started, any other message that is sent from the producer process is received by both the consumers. This happens because both the consumers are a part of the different Consumer Group and as per design, Kafka will broadcast the published messages on a topic across consumer groups. Since current setup has only one consumer in the Consumer Group, both consumers receive the message. Next, stop both of the consumer processes and start them as a part of the same Consumer Group, as shown here:

```
# start first consumer
% bin/kafka-console-consumer.sh --bootstrap-server localhost:9092 --topic test --group test --from-beginning

# start second consumer
% bin/kafka-console-consumer.sh --bootstrap-server localhost:9092 --topic test --group test --from-beginning
```

Now, the messages published via producer are received by only one of the consumers as both the consumers are a part of the test group and the test topic has a default partition count of 1. Try terminating the first consumer process that is receiving the messages and send a new message from the producer. Notice that now, the message is being received by the second consumer that becomes active and starts consuming the messages from the topic partition where the terminated consumer left off.

Using Kafka as an event store

Apache Kafka is not just limited to a messaging system, it can also be used as a durable storage for immutable records and to build a streaming data pipeline on top of it. It is well suited for use cases such as website activity tracking, real-time monitoring, log aggregation, and processing streams of data. Any messages that are published on a Kafka topic are persisted on disk and replicated across Kafka servers based on the configuration for fault tolerance. Since Kafka guarantees the sequence of messages within a topic partition, it allows consumers to control their read position irrespective of other consumers of the same topic. The following example shows how the events published by a producer are made available to the consumers based on the topic and the associated Consumer Group:

```
# start producer for 'test' topic
% bin/kafka-console-producer.sh --broker-list localhost:9092 --topic test
>Hello Apache Kafka!
>Hello Kafka Event!
>

# start consumer in 'test' consumer group listening to 'test' topic
% bin/kafka-console-consumer.sh --bootstrap-server localhost:9092 --topic
test --group test --from-beginning
Hello Apache Kafka!
Hello Kafka Event!

# consume from beginning in a different consumer group
# since it is a different consumer group, it replay messages that were
# published earlier as well as they were not committed by any other
# consumer in consumer group 'test1'
% bin/kafka-console-consumer.sh --bootstrap-server localhost:9092 --topic
test --group test1 --from-beginning
Hello Kafka!
Hello Helping Hands!
Kafka Works!
Hello Apache Kafka!
Hello Kafka Event!

# starting a consumer without the 'from-beginning' flag
# waits for new messages only and does not replay previous messages
% bin/kafka-console-consumer.sh --bootstrap-server localhost:9092 --topic
test --group test1

# starting a consumer without the 'from-beginning' flag
# waits for new messages only and does not replay previous messages
# even for the new consumer group 'test2'
% bin/kafka-console-consumer.sh --bootstrap-server localhost:9092 --topic
test --group test2
```

Kafka consumers can decide the offset from where they wish to start consuming the messages. In the preceding example, the consumer was started with a `--from-beginning` flag that tells the consumer to start consuming from the first offset, and that is why every time the consumer is started with this flag in a new Consumer Group, it will replay the received messages in each Consumer Group from the beginning, as shown in the preceding example. The replay of messages and offset retention also depends on the retention period set using Kafka server properties.

 The Apache Kafka configuration (`https://kafka.apache.org/documentation/#configuration`) page provides a list of configuration parameters for Apache Kafka servers.

Using Kafka for Helping Hands

The Helping Hands application uses Apache Kafka to implement the observer model and send asynchronous events among microservices. It is also used as an event store to capture all the state change events generated from microservices that are consumed by the Lookup service to build a consolidated view to server lookup requests. The Alert microservice of the Helping Hands application also receives the alert events via the Kafka topic and sends an email asynchronously.

Apache Kafka includes five core APIs:

- The `Producer` API allows applications to publish streams of events to one or more topics
- The `Consumer` API allows applications to consume published events from one or more topics
- The `Streams` API allows transforming streams from input topics and publish the results to output topics
- The `Connect` API allows support for various input and output sources to capture and dump stream of events
- The `AdminClient` API allows topics and server management along with other Kafka management operations

To integrate Kafka with the Helping Hands application, the `Producer` and `Consumer` APIs will only be required to produce state change events and consume them. The required topics can be created externally using `kafka-topics.sh` script, as shown in the previous section. To include the producer and consumer client APIs, add the project dependency of `kafka-clients`, as shown in the following example, to the `project.clj` file of the corresponding microservice project:

```
(defproject helping-hands-alert "0.0.1-SNAPSHOT"
  :description "Helping Hands Alert Application"
  :url
"https://www.packtpub.com/application-development/microservices-clojure"
  :license {:name "Eclipse Public License"
            :url "http://www.eclipse.org/legal/epl-v10.html"}
  :dependencies [[org.clojure/clojure "1.8.0"]
                 [io.pedestal/pedestal.service "0.5.3"]
                 [io.pedestal/pedestal.jetty "0.5.3"]
                 ;; Datomic Free Edition
                 [com.datomic/datomic-free "0.9.5561.62"]
                 ;; Omniconf
                 [com.grammarly/omniconf "0.2.7"]
                 ;; Mount
                 [mount "0.1.11"]
                 ;; postal for email alerts
                 [com.draines/postal "2.0.2"]
                 ;; kafka clients
                 [org.apache.kafka/kafka-clients "1.0.0"]
                 ;; logger
                 [org.clojure/tools.logging "0.4.0"]
                 [ch.qos.logback/logback-classic "1.1.8" :exclusions
[org.slf4j/slf4j-api]]
                 [org.slf4j/jul-to-slf4j "1.7.22"]
                 [org.slf4j/jcl-over-slf4j "1.7.22"]
                 [org.slf4j/log4j-over-slf4j "1.7.22"]]
  :min-lein-version "2.0.0"
  :source-paths ["src/clj"]
  :java-source-paths ["src/jvm"]
  :test-paths ["test/clj" "test/jvm"]
  ...
  :main ^{:skip-aot true} helping-hands.alert.server)
```

Using Kafka APIs

Although Clojure has Kafka wrappers (`https://cwiki.apache.org/confluence/display/`
`KAFKA/Clients#Clients-Clojure`) available, this book focuses on using Apache Kafka Java
APIs directly instead of a Clojure wrapper. To create a Kafka consumer, import the required
Java APIs, as shown here:

```
(ns helping-hands.alert.channel
  "Initializes Helping Hands Alert Channel Consumer"
  (:require [cheshire.core :as jp]
            [clojure.string :as s]
            [clojure.tools.logging :as log]
            [helping-hands.alert.config :as conf]
            [postal.core :as postal])
  (:import [java.util Collections Properties]
           [org.apache.kafka.common.serialization
            LongDeserializer StringDeserializer]
           [org.apache.kafka.clients.consumer
            Consumer ConsumerConfig KafkaConsumer]))
```

Next, define a function `create-kafka-consumer` that initializes a Kafka consumer and
returns it, as shown here:

```
(defn create-kafka-consumer
  "Creates a new Kafka Consumer"
  []
  (let [props (doto (Properties.)
                (.putAll (conf/get-config [:kafka]))
                (.put ConsumerConfig/KEY_DESERIALIZER_CLASS_CONFIG
                      (.getName LongDeserializer))
                (.put ConsumerConfig/VALUE_DESERIALIZER_CLASS_CONFIG
                      (.getName StringDeserializer)))
        consumer (KafkaConsumer. props)
        _ (.subscribe consumer (Collections/singletonList
                                 (get (conf/get-config [:kafka]) "topic")))]
    consumer))
```

The Kafka consumer requires a set of configurations to connect to the Kafka server and start
consuming the published messages. This configuration can be retrieved via Omniconf
configuration, as discussed in the previous chapter. To set the required configuration
parameter, first, define the configuration parameter for Omniconf to pick, as shown here:

```
(cfg/define
  {:conf {:type :file
          :required true
          :verifier omniconf.core/verify-file-exists
```

```
              :description "MECBOT configuration file"}
      :kafka {:type :edn
              :default {"bootstrap.servers" "localhost:9092"
                        "group.id" "alerts"
                        "topic" "hh_alerts"}
              :description "Kafka Consumer Configuration"}})
```

The bootstrap.servers parameter can have more than one Kafka server defined as a comma-separated value with the format of host:port. As per the preceding configuration, it uses a single Kafka server to connect to that is running locally on port 9092. Also, it takes as input a group.id that specifies the Consumer Group for the consumer and a topic to which it subscribes for messages. Once the consumer is created, it can be used to listen for messages on the configured topic, as shown here:

```
(defn capture-records
  "Consume the records using given consumer"
  [consumer result]
  (while true
    (doseq [record (.poll consumer 1000)]
      (swap! result conj record))
    (Thread/sleep 5000)))
```

The capture-records function takes as input a consumer that is created by the create-kafka-consumer function, as defined earlier. This function is a sample function that also takes an atom (https://clojuredocs.org/clojure.core/atom) as a second parameter that just captures the received messages that can be referred to later. To take a look at the received messages, they can also be logged or passed onto a function as a parameter to take further action on it. Also, note that this function has a never-ending while loop, so this must be called on a thread other than the application execution thread to make sure that the application execution thread is not blocked. To test the function, use the REPL, as shown in the following example, that initializes the consumer that connects to the same Kafka server that was started at the command line using the kafka-server-start.sh script:

```
;; initialize the required namespaces
helping-hands.alert.server> (require '[helping-hands.alert.channel :as
channel])
nil
helping-hands.alert.server> (require '[helping-hands.alert.config :as
conf])
nil

;; initialize the configuration for Omniconf to pick
helping-hands.alert.server> (conf/init-config {:cli-args [] :quit-on-error
true})
Omniconf configuration:
```

```
{:conf #object[java.io.File 0x5fa5f9a0 "config/conf.edn"],
 :kafka
 {"bootstrap.servers" "localhost:9092",
  "group.id" "alerts",
  "topic" "hh_alerts"}}

nil

;; create a consumer
helping-hands.alert.server> (def consumer (channel/create-kafka-consumer))
#'helping-hands.alert.server/consumer

;; create an atom to collect the responses
helping-hands.alert.server> (def records (atom []))
#'helping-hands.alert.server/records

;; wait for records
helping-hands.alert.server> (channel/consume-records consumer records)
```

Once the consumer is listening for messages, on the terminal, start a new producer for the same hh_alerts topic that the consumer is listening to using the kafka-console-producer.sh script, as shown in the following example. Note that we didn't create the topic but it is still available. The reason is the default configuration of Kafka allows it to auto-create the topic if it does not exist. The other topic, __consumer_offsets, is used by Kafka to manage the committed offsets:

```
% bin/kafka-topics.sh --list --zookeeper localhost:2181
__consumer_offsets
hh_alerts
test

% bin/kafka-console-producer.sh --broker-list localhost:9092 --topic
hh_alerts
>Sample Alert
>Sample Alert1
```

Publish a couple of messages from the producer, as shown in the preceding example, and check the records atom in REPL. It should have received the messages as follows:

```
;; C-c-b in CIDER breaks the execution to give back the control to REPL

;; lookup the published messages
helping-hands.alert.server> (pprint (map #(.value %) @records))
("Sample Alert" "Sample Alert1")
nil
helping-hands.alert.server>
```

Initializing Kafka with Mount

In the previous implementation, the Kafka consumer was created by calling the `create-kafka-consumer` function. Instead of creating a consumer by calling the function at runtime, it can be created and managed using `Mount`, as discussed in the previous chapter. To use `Mount`, make sure that the Mount dependency is added to the `project.clj` file, as shown here:

```
(defproject helping-hands-alert "0.0.1-SNAPSHOT"
  :description "Helping Hands Alert Application"
  :url
"https://www.packtpub.com/application-development/microservices-clojure"
  :license {:name "Eclipse Public License"
            :url "http://www.eclipse.org/legal/epl-v10.html"}
  :dependencies [[org.clojure/clojure "1.8.0"]
                 [io.pedestal/pedestal.service "0.5.3"]
                 [io.pedestal/pedestal.jetty "0.5.3"]
                 ;; Datomic Free Edition
                 [com.datomic/datomic-free "0.9.5561.62"]
                 ;; Omniconf
                 [com.grammarly/omniconf "0.2.7"]
                 ;; Mount
                 [mount "0.1.11"]
                 ;; postal for email alerts
                 [com.draines/postal "2.0.2"]
                 ;; kafka clients
                 [org.apache.kafka/kafka-clients "1.0.0"]
                 ;; logger
                 [org.clojure/tools.logging "0.4.0"]
                 [ch.qos.logback/logback-classic "1.1.8" :exclusions
[org.slf4j/slf4j-api]]
                 [org.slf4j/jul-to-slf4j "1.7.22"]
                 [org.slf4j/jcl-over-slf4j "1.7.22"]
                 [org.slf4j/log4j-over-slf4j "1.7.22"]]
  :min-lein-version "2.0.0"
  :source-paths ["src/clj"]
  :java-source-paths ["src/jvm"]
  :test-paths ["test/clj" "test/jvm"]
  ...
  :main ^{:skip-aot true} helping-hands.alert.server)
```

Next, as shown in the following example, create a namespace and define the state of the Kafka consumer that creates a Kafka consumer to be used by the Alerts microservice and closes it when the service is shut down:

```
(ns helping-hands.alert.state
```

```
   "Initializes State for Alert Service"
   (:require [mount.core :refer [defstate] :as mount]
             [helping-hands.alert.channel :as c]))

(defstate alert-consumer
  :start (c/create-kafka-consumer)
  :stop (.close alert-consumer))
```

Next, add the startup and shutdown hooks for Mount at the application entry points, as shown in the following example for the Alerts microservice:

```
(ns helping-hands.alert.server
  (:gen-class) ; for -main method in uberjar
  (:require [io.pedestal.http :as server]
            [io.pedestal.http.route :as route]
            [mount.core :as mount]
            [helping-hands.alert.config :as cfg]
            [helping-hands.alert.service :as service]))

...

(defn run-dev
  "The entry-point for 'lein run-dev'"
  [& args]
  (println "\nCreating your [DEV] server...")
  ;; initialize configuration
  (cfg/init-config {:cli-args args :quit-on-error true})
  ;; initialize state
  (mount/start)
  ;; Add shutdown-hook
  (.addShutdownHook
   (Runtime/getRuntime)
   (Thread. mount/stop))
  (-> service/service ;; start with production configuration
      ...)
      ;; Wire up interceptor chains
      server/default-interceptors
      server/dev-interceptors
      server/create-server
      server/start))

(defn -main
  "The entry-point for 'lein run'"
  [& args]
  (println "\nCreating your server...")
  ;; initialize configuration
  (cfg/init-config {:cli-args args :quit-on-error true})
  ;; initialize state
```

```
(mount/start)
;; Add shutdown-hook
(.addShutdownHook
  (Runtime/getRuntime)
  (Thread. mount/stop))
(server/start runnable-service))
```

Note that Omniconf configuration is initialized before Mount is started to make sure that the consumer is able to pick the configuration parameters that are read by Omniconf. Once Mount is initialized, the `kafka-consumer` state can be used directly across the namespaces. For example, the following REPL session shows how to initialize the Alert service in *dev* mode and use the `kafka-consumer` state managed by Mount that is started with the *dev* instance of the service:

```
;; starts service in dev mode
;; also initializes Omniconf and
;; sets the Kafka consumer state
helping-hands.alert.server> (def server (run-dev))

Creating your [DEV] server...
Omniconf configuration:
 {:alert
 {:from "admin@helpinghands.com",
  :host "smtp.gmail.com",
  :port 465,
  :ssl true,
  :to "alerts@helpinghands.com",
  :user "admin@helpinghands.com",
  :creds <SECRET>},
 :conf #object[java.io.File 0x266875c9 "config/conf.edn"],
 :kafka
 {"bootstrap.servers" "localhost:9092",
  "group.id" "alerts",
  "topic" "hh_alerts"}}

#'helping-hands.alert.server/server

;; refer to the consumer state managed by mount
helping-hands.alert.server> (require '[helping-hands.alert.state :refer
[alert-consumer]])
nil

;; create a atom to capture records
helping-hands.alert.server> (def records (atom []))
#'helping-hands.alert.server/records

;; look for messages to capture
```

```
helping-hands.alert.server> (helping-hands.alert.channel/capture-records
alert-consumer records)
```

Now, publish a couple of messages from the command-line producer, as shown here:

```
% bin/kafka-console-producer.sh --broker-list localhost:9092 --topic
hh_alerts
>Hello
>Hi Mount!
>
```

The same messages are captured within the records atom, as shown in the following example. At the time of shutdown, Mount will stop the consumer and clean up the connection:

```
;; C-c-b in CIDER breaks the execution to give back the control to REPL

;; lookup the published messages
helping-hands.alert.server> (pprint (map #(.value %) @records))
("Hello" "Hi Mount!")
nil
helping-hands.alert.server>
```

Integrating the Alert Service with Kafka

The Alert microservice of the Helping Hands application receives the alert messages over the Kafka topic that is used to send the alert in an email. To send an email as soon as the message is received, it can be integrated within the loop that looks for a message published by the producer, as shown here:

```
(defn consume-records
  "Consume the records using given consumer"
  [consumer result]
  (while true
    (doseq [record (.poll consumer 1000)]
      (try
        (let [rmsg (jp/parse-string (.value record))
              msg (into {} (filter (comp some? val)
                                   {:from (conf/get-config [:alert :from])
                                    :to (get rmsg "to" (conf/get-config
[:alert :to]))
                                    :cc (rmsg "cc")
                                    :subject (rmsg "subject")
                                    :body (rmsg "body")}))
              result (postal/send-message
```

```
                        {:host (conf/get-config [:alert :host])
                         :port (conf/get-config [:alert :port])
                         :ssl (conf/get-config [:alert :ssl])
                         :user (conf/get-config [:alert :user])
                         :pass (conf/get-config [:alert :creds])}
                        msg)])
       (catch Exception e
          (log/error "Failed to send email" e)))
      (swap! result conj record))
    (Thread/sleep 5000)))
```

In the preceding function, once the message is received, it is parsed to get the JSON with the keys such as `to`, `cc`, `subject`, and `body` that are used to create an email and send it using the Postal library (`https://github.com/drewr/postal`) that was discussed in previous chapters. All the exceptions are caught and logged for review. In this case, the producer publishes a stringified JSON with the required keys, as shown here:

```
% bin/kafka-console-producer.sh --broker-list localhost:9092 --topic
hh_alerts
>{"to":"admin@helpinghands.com","subject":"Usage Alert","body":"Usage alert
exceeded threshold 100k req/sec"}
```

Using Avro for data transfer

The keys and values published on a Kafka topic must have associated SerDes (`https://en.wikipedia.org/wiki/SerDes`). The examples used in the previous section used `LongDeserializer` for keys and `StringDeserializer` for the Kafka Consumer. Similarly, the Kafka Producer for the corresponding consumer will use `LongSerializer` and `StringSerializer` to publish the key and value, respectively. Since microservices may be written in any programming language and may need to collaborate with other services over Kafka topics, the language-dependent SerDes is not a good option.

Avro (`https://avro.apache.org/`) is a data serialization format that is language agnostic and has support for most of the well-known programming languages (`https://cwiki.apache.org/confluence/display/AVRO/Supported+Languages`). Avro has its own declarative way of defining the schema (`https://avro.apache.org/docs/current/`) that can be mapped to the business model describing the entity. Once the schema is defined, the message is encoded against the schema at the producer end and then decoded at the consumer end using the same schema. As far as the schema is accessible to both producer and consumer, they can communicate via Avro messages irrespective of the programming language they are implemented in.

Avro Clojure library `abracad` (https://github.com/damballa/abracad) is a wrapper over Avro APIs that integrates well with the applications written in Clojure. To use `abracad`, include the dependency `[com.damballa/abracad "0.4.13"]` in the `project.clj` file. Once the dependencies are available, the SerDes for Avro can be defined as shown in the following example, and can be used instead of String SerDes by the Kafka producer and consumer:

```clojure
;; adopted from franzy-avro project
;; https://github.com/ymilky/franzy-avro
(deftype KafkaAvroSerializer [schema]
  Serializer
  (configure [_ _ _])
  (serialize [_ _ data]
    (when data
      (avro/binary-encoded schema data)))
  (close [_]))

(deftype KafkaAvroDeserializer [schema]
  Deserializer
  (configure [_ _ _])
  (deserialize [_ _ data]
    (when data
      (avro/decode schema data)))
  (close [_]))

(defn kafka-avro-serializer
  "Avro serializer for Apache Kafka. Use for serializing Kafka keys values.
  Values will be serialized according to the provided schema.
  If no schema is provided, a default EDN schema is assumed.
  See https://avro.apache.org/
  See https://github.com/damballa/abracad"
  [schema]
  (KafkaAvroSerializer. (or schema (aedn/new-schema))))

(defn kafka-avro-deserializer
  "Avro deserializer for Apache Kafka.
  Use for deserializing Kafka keys and values.
  If no schema is provided, a default EDN schema is assumed.
   See https://avro.apache.org/
   See https://github.com/damballa/abracad"
  [schema]
  (KafkaAvroDeserializer. (or schema (aedn/new-schema))))
```

Summary

In this chapter, we learned about the importance of event-driven patterns for microservices and how we can use Apache Kafka as a message broker to build a scalable and durable event-driven architecture. Event-driven architectures are scalable, but they are incredibly hard to debug for issues without being monitored in real time. In the next chapter, we will learn how to secure microservices and deploy them in production with a real-time monitoring system.

11

Deploying and Monitoring Secured Microservices

"The success of a production depends on the attention paid to detail."

- David O. Selznick

Microservices must be deployed in isolation and monitored for usage. Monitoring the current workload and processing time also helps to take a decision on when to scale them up or scale them down. Another important aspect of microservices-based architecture is security. One way to secure microservices is to allow each one of them to have their own authentication and authorization module. This approach soon becomes a problem, as each microservice is deployed in isolation, and it becomes incredibly hard to agree on common standards to authorize a user. Also, in this case, the ownership of users and their roles gets distributed across the services. This chapter addresses such issues and provides solutions to secure, monitor, and scale microservices-based applications. In this chapter, you will learn the following things:

- How to enable authentication and authorization for microservices
- How to use **JSON Web Token (JWT)** and **JSON Web Encryption (JWE)**
- How to create an authentication service that works with JSON Web Tokens
- How to capture audit logs and runtime metrics for real-time monitoring
- How to deploy microservices using Docker containers
- Why Kubernetes is useful for microservices-based deployments

Enabling authentication and authorization

Authentication is the process of identifying who the user is, whereas **authorization** is the process of verifying what the authenticated user has access to. The most common way of achieving authentication is by asking users to specify their username and password that can then be validated against the backend database of user credentials.

The passwords should never be stored in plaintext in the backend database. It is recommended to compute a one-way hash of the password and store that instead. To reset the password, the system can just generate a random password, store its hash, and share the random password in plaintext with the user. Alternatively, a unique URL can be sent to the user to reset the password through a form that can validate a user's identity via methods such as preset questions and answers and **one-time password** (OTP).

Authenticating the users is not enough for an application if the application has multiple security boundaries. For example, an application may require only certain users to send notification through the system and prevent all others. To do so, the application must create a security boundary for its resources that is often defined using roles that have one or more permissions that can be validated by the application before allowing access to its resources and features, such as notification. Roles and permissions are the key factors of authorization that allow an application to create multiple security boundaries for its resources.

Introducing Tokens and JWT

In a monolithic environment, authentication and authorization are handled within the same application using a module that validates the incoming requests for required authentication and authorization information, as shown in the following diagram; this module also allows the authorized users to define the roles and permissions and assign them to other users in the system to allow them access to the secured resources:

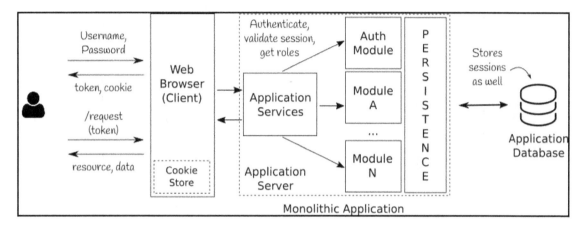

Monolithic applications may also maintain a session store against which each instance of the monolithic application can validate the incoming request and determine a valid session for the user. Often, such session information is stored in a cookie that is sent to the client as a token once the user is successfully authenticated. The cookie is then attached to each request by the client that can then be validated by the server for a valid session and associated roles to determine whether to allow or disallow access to the requested resource, as shown in the preceding diagram.

In a microservices-based application, each microservice is deployed in isolation and must not have the responsibility of maintaining a separate user database or session database. Moreover, there must be a standard way of authenticating and authorizing the users across microservices. It is recommended to separate out the authentication and authorization responsibility as a separate **Auth** service that can own the user database to authenticate and authorize users. This also helps in authenticating the user once via Auth service and then authorizing them to access the resources and related services through other microservices.

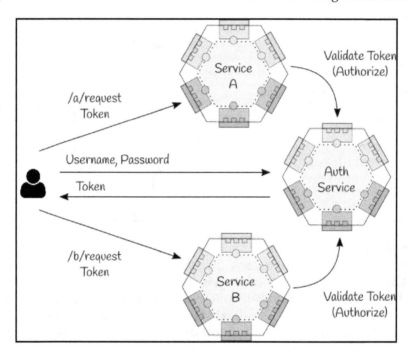

Since each microservice may use its own technology stack and have no prior knowledge of Auth service, there should be a common standard to validate the authenticated users across Microservices. **JSON Web Tokens (JWT)** is one such standard that consists of a header, payload, and signature that can be issued as a token to the user after successful authentication. Users can then send this token with each request to any microservice that can then validate it and grant access to the requested resources.

JWT can either have the content encrypted or secured using digital signature or message authentication codes. **JSON Web Signature (JWS)** represents the content secured with digital signatures or **Message Authentication Codes (MACs)**, whereas **JSON Web Encryption (JWE)** represents the encrypted content using JSON-based data structures. If the token is encrypted, it can only be read with a key that was used to encrypt the token. To read a JWE token, services must own the key that was used to encrypt the token. Instead of sharing the key across microservices, it is recommended to send the token to the Auth service directly to decrypt the token and authorize the request on behalf of the service. This may result in a performance bottleneck and single point of failure due to each service trying to get Auth service first for authorization. This can be prevented by caching the prevalidated tokens at each microservice level for a configurable amount of time that can be decided based on the expiry time of the token.

Expiry time is an important criteria while working with JWTs. JWTs with a very large expiry time must be avoided, as there is no way for the application to log out the user or invalidate the token. An issued token remains valid unless and until it expires. As far as the user owns a valid token, they are allowed to gain access to the services with the issued token. To prevent the issue of logout, one option is to let microservices always validate a token with the Auth service that maintains a cache of user authorization details that are kept in sync with the user's roles and permissions. Every time an Auth service receives a token, it can validate it against this cache, and if there is change in user roles or any other properties, it can invalidate the token that will force the user to request for a new token, and that token will now have the updated roles and the authorization details.

 For more details, refer to JWT RFC-7519 (`https://tools.ietf.org/html/rfc7519`), JWS RFC-7515 (`https://tools.ietf.org/html/rfc7515`), and JWE RFC-7516(`https://tools.ietf.org/search/rfc7516`).

Creating an Auth service for Helping Hands

The Auth service for Helping Hands can be built using the same pedestal project template as that of other microservices of Helping Hands. In this example, it uses JWE to create JWT tokens for the users. To start with, create a new project with the directory structure as shown in the following example; it contains a new namespace `helping-hands.auth.jwt` that contains the implementation related to JWT—the rest of the namespaces are used as described in the preceding chapters.

```
.
├── Capstanfile
├── config
```

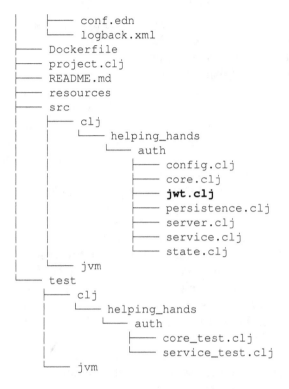

```
|      ├──── conf.edn
|      └──── logback.xml
├──── Dockerfile
├──── project.clj
├──── README.md
├──── resources
├──── src
|      ├──── clj
|      |      └──── helping_hands
|      |             └──── auth
|      |                    ├──── config.clj
|      |                    ├──── core.clj
|      |                    ├──── jwt.clj
|      |                    ├──── persistence.clj
|      |                    ├──── server.clj
|      |                    ├──── service.clj
|      |                    └──── state.clj
|      └──── jvm
└──── test
       ├──── clj
       |      └──── helping_hands
       |             └──── auth
       |                    ├──── core_test.clj
       |                    └──── service_test.clj
       └──── jvm
```

12 directories, 14 files

Using a Nimbus JOSE JWT library for Tokens

The Auth service project will additionally use a `Nimbus-JOSE-JWT` library (`https://bitbucket.org/connect2id/nimbus-jose-jwt/wiki/Home`) to create and validate JSON Web Tokens and a `permissions` (`https://github.com/tuhlmann/permissions`) library to authorize users against a set of roles and permissions. Add the `Nimbus-JOSE-JWT` and `permissions` library dependencies, as shown in the following `project.clj` file:

```
(defproject helping-hands-auth "0.0.1-SNAPSHOT"
  :description "Helping Hands Auth Service"
  :url
"https://www.packtpub.com/application-development/microservices-clojure"
  :license {:name "Eclipse Public License"
            :url "http://www.eclipse.org/legal/epl-v10.html"}
  :dependencies [[org.clojure/clojure "1.8.0"]
                 [io.pedestal/pedestal.service "0.5.3"]
                 [io.pedestal/pedestal.jetty "0.5.3"]
```

```
                    ;; Datomic Free Edition
                    [com.datomic/datomic-free "0.9.5561.62"]
                    ;; Omniconf
                    [com.grammarly/omniconf "0.2.7"]
                    ;; Mount
                    [mount "0.1.11"]
                    ;; nimbus-jose for JWT
                    [com.nimbusds/nimbus-jose-jwt "5.4"]
                    ;; used for roles and permissions
                    [agynamix/permissions "0.2.2-SNAPSHOT"]
                    ;; logger
                    [org.clojure/tools.logging "0.4.0"]
                    [ch.qos.logback/logback-classic "1.1.8"
                      :exclusions [org.slf4j/slf4j-api]]
                    [org.slf4j/jul-to-slf4j "1.7.22"]
                    [org.slf4j/jcl-over-slf4j "1.7.22"]
                    [org.slf4j/log4j-over-slf4j "1.7.22"]]
  :min-lein-version "2.0.0"
  :source-paths ["src/clj"]
  :java-source-paths ["src/jvm"]
  :test-paths ["test/clj" "test/jvm"]
  :resource-paths ["config", "resources"]
  :plugins [[:lein-codox "0.10.3"]
            ;; Code Coverage
            [:lein-cloverage "1.0.9"]
            ;; Unit test docs
            [test2junit "1.2.2"]]
  :codox {:namespaces :all}
  :test2junit-output-dir "target/test-reports"
  :profiles {:provided {:dependencies [[org.clojure/tools.reader "0.10.0"]
                                       [org.clojure/tools.nrepl "0.2.12"]]}
            :dev {:aliases
                  {"run-dev" ["trampoline" "run" "-m"
                              "helping-hands.auth.server/run-dev"]}
                  :dependencies
                    [[io.pedestal/pedestal.service-tools "0.5.3"]]
                  :resource-paths ["config", "resources"]
                  :jvm-opts ["-Dconf=config/conf.edn"]}
            :uberjar {:aot [helping-hands.auth.server]}
            :doc {:dependencies [[codox-theme-rdash "0.1.1"]]
                  :codox {:metadata {:doc/format :markdown}
                          :themes [:rdash]}}
            :debug {:jvm-opts
                    ["-server" (str "-agentlib:jdwp=transport=dt_socket,"
                                    "server=y,address=8000,suspend=n")]}}}
  :main ^{:skip-aot true} helping-hands.auth.server)
```

Creating a secret key for JSON Web Encryption

To start with the implementation of JWT with encrypted claims, first create a `get-secret` function to generate a secret key for encryption. Also, add a `get-secret-jwk` function that is used to create a JSON Web Key (`https://tools.ietf.org/html/rfc7517`) using the secret key generated by the `get-secret` function, as shown in the following code:

```clojure
(ns helping-hands.auth.jwt
  "JWT Implementation for Auth Service"
  (:require [cheshire.core :as jp])
  (:import [com.nimbusds.jose EncryptionMethod
            JWEAlgorithm JWSAlgorithm
            JWEDecrypter JWEEncrypter
            JWEHeader$Builder JWEObject Payload]
           [com.nimbusds.jose.crypto
            AESDecrypter AESEncrypter]
           [com.nimbusds.jose.jwk KeyOperation KeyUse
            OctetSequenceKey OctetSequenceKey$Builder]
           [com.nimbusds.jwt JWTClaimsSet JWTClaimsSet$Builder]
           [com.nimbusds.jwt.proc DefaultJWTClaimsVerifier]
           [com.nimbusds.jose.util Base64URL]
           [java.util Date]
           [javax.crypto KeyGenerator]
           [javax.crypto.spec SecretKeySpec]))

(def ^:cons khash-256 "SHA-256")

(defonce ^:private kgen-aes-128
  (let [keygen (KeyGenerator/getInstance "AES")
        _ (.init keygen 128)]
    keygen))

(defonce ^:private alg-a128kw
  (JWEAlgorithm/A128KW))

(defonce ^:private enc-a128cbc_hs256
  (EncryptionMethod/A128CBC_HS256))

(defn get-secret
  "Gets the secret key"
  ([] (get-secret kgen-aes-128))
  ([kgen]
   ;; must be created iff the key hasn't
   ;; been creaed earlier. Create once and
   ;; persist in an external database
   (.generateKey kgen)))
```

```
(defn get-secret-jwk
  "Generates a new JSON Web Key (JWK)"
  [{:keys [khash kgen alg] :as enc-impl} secret]
  ;; must be created iff the key hasn't
  ;; been creaed earlier. Create once and
  ;; persist in an external database
  (.. (OctetSequenceKey$Builder. secret)
      (keyIDFromThumbprint (or khash khash-256))
      (algorithm (or alg alg-a128kw))
      (keyUse (KeyUse/ENCRYPTION))
      (build)))
```

The preceding implementation shown generates a key using the **AES 128-bit** algorithm. The secret key generated by the `get-secret` function must be generated only once for the lifetime of the application. Therefore, it is recommended to store it in an external database that can be shared among the instances of the Auth service once it is scaled to more than one instance.

 `Nimbus-JOSE-JWT` also supports 256-bit algorithms. For 256-bit algorithms to work, JRE needs explicit *Java Cryptography Extension (JCE) Unlimited Strength Jurisdiction Policy Files* (`http://www.oracle.com/ technetwork/java/javase/downloads/jce8-download-2133166.html`).

The `get-secret-jwk` function takes the secret key as one of its input parameters and generates a JWK, as shown in the following REPL session; JWK consists of a Key Type (`kty`), Public Key Use (`use`), Key ID (`kid`), Key Value (`k`), and Algorithm (`alg`) parameters that are defined in JWK RFC-7517 (`https://tools.ietf.org/html/rfc7517`):

```
;; require the namespace
helping-hands.auth.server> (require '[helping-hands.auth.jwt :as jwt])
nil

;; create a secret key
helping-hands.auth.server> (def secret (jwt/get-secret))
#'helping-hands.auth.server/secret

;; create a JSON Web Key
helping-hands.auth.server> (def jwk (jwt/get-secret-jwk {} secret))
#'helping-hands.auth.server/jwk

;; dump the JSON object of JWK
helping-hands.auth.server> (.toJSONObject jwk)
{"kty" "oct", "use" "enc", "kid" "F5UNJYT4A-
GpngZwRMYfs8ZuCKsmRGt08Xo_dMQrY5w", "k" "CvTaCBfdEkAlXfuOnW7pnw", "alg"
"A128KW"}
```

Since JWK is just a representation of the secret key in a JSON format, the secret key can be retrieved from the JWK using a utility function, `enckey->secret`, as shown in the following implementation:

```
(defn enckey->secret
  "Converts JSON Web Key (JWK) to the secret key"
  [{:keys [k kid alg] :as enc-key}]
  (.. (OctetSequenceKey$Builder. k)
      (keyID kid)
      (algorithm (or alg alg-a128kw))
      (keyUse (KeyUse/ENCRYPTION))
      (build)
      (toSecretKey "AES"))))
```

The `enckey->secret` function takes Key ID (`kid`) and Key Value (`k`) as its input to create the secret key that is same as the one used to create the source JSON Web Key. The `alg` parameter is optional and falls back to the default AES-128 algorithm if it is not specified. The following REPL session shows how to create a secret key from JWK generated earlier and validate that it always generates the same JWK:

```
;; JSON Web Key (JWK) generated earlier
helping-hands.auth.server> (.toJSONObject jwk)
{"kty" "oct", "use" "enc", "kid" "F5UNJYT4A-
GpngZwRMYfs8ZuCKsmRGt08Xo_dMQrY5w", "k" "CvTaCBfdEkAlXfuOnW7pnw", "alg"
"A128KW"}

;; extract the secret key
helping-hands.auth.server> (def secret-extracted (jwt/enckey->secret {:k
(.getKeyValue jwk) :kid (.getKeyID jwk)}))
#'helping-hands.auth.server/secret-extracted

;; generate JSON Web Key that is exactly same as source
helping-hands.auth.server> (.toJSONObject (jwt/get-secret-jwk {} secret-
extracted))
{"kty" "oct", "use" "enc", "kid" "F5UNJYT4A-
GpngZwRMYfs8ZuCKsmRGt08Xo_dMQrY5w", "k" "CvTaCBfdEkAlXfuOnW7pnw", "alg"
"A128KW"}

helping-hands.auth.server> (.toJSONObject jwk)
{"kty" "oct", "use" "enc", "kid" "F5UNJYT4A-
GpngZwRMYfs8ZuCKsmRGt08Xo_dMQrY5w", "k" "CvTaCBfdEkAlXfuOnW7pnw", "alg"
"A128KW"}
```

Creating Tokens

The next step is to define the functions to create and read JWT. Since the JWT used for the Helping Hands application uses JWE to encrypt the claims, it is OK to add both user ID and roles information within the payload that can be later retrieved from a valid token to authorize the user.

The `create-token` and `read-token` functions shown in the following example provide a way to create a JSON Web Token and read an existing one, respectively. The `create-token` function uses a utility function—`create-payload`—to create the claim set and the payload of JWT. Claim sets that are relevant for the current example are `issueTime` that defines the epoch time of when this token was created, `expirationTime` that sets the time beyond which the token will be considered as expired, and `user` and `roles` custom claims that store the authenticated username and the roles assigned to the user at the time of issuing the token. For more details on the available claim set options, take a look at JWT RFC-7519 (`https://tools.ietf.org/html/rfc7519`).

```
(defn- create-payload
  "Creates a payload as JWT Claims"
  [{:keys [user roles] :as params}]
  (let [ts (System/currentTimeMillis)
        claims (.. (JWTClaimsSet$Builder.)
                   (issuer "Packt")
                   (subject "HelpingHands")
                   (audience "https://www.packtpub.com")
                   (issueTime (Date. ts))
                   (expirationTime (Date. (+ ts 120000)))
                   (claim "user" user)
                   (claim "roles" roles)
                   (build))]
    (.toJSONObject claims)))

(defn create-token
  "Creates a new token with the given payload"
  [{:keys [user roles alg enc] :as params} secret]
  (let [enckey (get-secret-jwk params secret)
        payload (create-payload {:user user :roles roles})
        passphrase (JWEObject.
                     (.. (JWEHeader$Builder.
                          (or alg alg-a128kw)
                          (or enc enc-a128cbc_hs256))
                         (build))
                     (Payload. payload))
        encrypter (AESEncrypter. enckey)
        _ (.encrypt passphrase encrypter)]
```

```
        (.serialize passphrase)))

(defn read-token
  "Decrypts the given token with the said algorithm
   Throws BadJWTException is token is invalid or expired"
  [token secret]
  (let [passphrase (JWEObject/parse token)
        decrypter (AESDecrypter. secret)
        _ (.decrypt passphrase decrypter)
        payload (.. passphrase getPayload toString)
        claims (JWTClaimsSet/parse payload)
        ;; throws exception if the token is invalid
        _ (.verify (DefaultJWTClaimsVerifier.) claims)]
    (jp/parse-string payload)))
```

The following REPL session shows the steps to create and read a token and later wait for it to get expired. Note the exception thrown by the library that can be captured to mark the event of token expiry:

```
;; generate a new token with the user and roles
helping-hands.auth.server> (def token (jwt/create-token {:user "hhuser"
:roles #{"hh/notify"}} secret))
#'helping-hands.auth.server/token

;; dump the compact serialization string
helping-hands.auth.server> token
"eyJlbmMiOiJBMTI4Q0JDLUhTMjU2IiwiYWxnIjoiQTEyOEtXIn0.FiAelEg_R8We8xEF2xRxcC
908BCoH1nRYvY3nV_jkqYO8JPp-QukBw.86-
JKq6cYFH2rtFBOXiA6A.Pxz3ZzBGKX2Cd_sjtYdEwKDltzKQiolWSvrjPbLLGL8NlShcWWEIqkd
7NL2WcXHukDa6zS4ANIWnee2hNWUraItqZFEY6N_RhXZVVXQvZJsqzeiueBxvxc1fj1LFUKsyR6
3oOwLd5ZIIT99ItrqaYPM88enMsjchsXYBJ_Tcb-
WR6R_KirmDBxCVjqFcg7OdWjjcKTP4FcUNIQU9G8fSnQ.pfLyW8ggXV8vQnidytJmMw"

;; read the token back
helping-hands.auth.server> (pprint (jwt/read-token token secret))
{"sub" "HelpingHands",
 "aud" "https://www.packtpub.com",
 "roles" ["hh/notify"],
 "iss" "Packt",
 "exp" 1515959756,
 "iat" 1515959636,
 "user" "hhuser"}
nil

;; wait for 2 mins (expiry time as per implementation)
;; token is now expired
helping-hands.auth.server> (pprint (jwt/read-token token secret))
```

```
BadJWTException Expired JWT
com.nimbusds.jwt.proc.DefaultJWTClaimsVerifier.<clinit>
(DefaultJWTClaimsVerifier.java:62)
```

Enabling users and roles for authorization

Ideally, the Auth service must be backed by a persistent store to keep the users, roles, and the secret key for the application. For the sake of simplicity of the example, create a sample in-memory database in the `helping-hands.auth.persistence` namespace, as follows:

```clojure
(ns helping-hands.auth.persistence
  "Persistence Implementation for Auth Service"
  (:require [agynamix.roles :as r]
            [cheshire.core :as jp])
  (:import [java.security MessageDigest]))

(defn get-hash
  "Creates a MD5 hash of the password"
  [creds]
  (.. (MessageDigest/getInstance "MD5")
      (digest (.getBytes creds "UTF-8"))))

(def userdb
  ;; Used ony for demonstration
  ;; TODO Persist in an external database
  (atom
   {:secret nil
    :roles {"hh/superadmin" "*"
            "hh/admin" "hh:*"
            "hh/notify" #{"hh:notify" "notify/alert"}
            "notify/alert" #{"notify:email" "notify:sms"}}
    :users {"hhuser" {:pwd (get-hash "hhuser")
                      :roles #{"hh/notify"}}
            "hhadmin" {:pwd (get-hash "hhadmin")
                       :roles #{"hh/admin"}}
            "superadmin" {:pwd (get-hash "superadmin")
                          :roles #{"hh/superadmin"}}}}))

(defn has-access?
  "Checks for relevant permission"
  [uid perms]
  (r/has-permission?
   (-> @userdb :users (get uid))
   :roles :permissions perms))

(defn init-db
```

```
"Initializes the roles for permission framework"
[]
(r/init-roles (:roles @userdb))
userdb)
```

`userdb` contains the sample in-memory database that consists of the `:secret` key that is initialized to nil and `:users` and `:roles` that contain information on the users and roles, respectively. Role definition follows the guidelines of the `permission` library and defines the roles and permissions as per the usage instructions (`https://github.com/tuhlmann/permissions#usage`) of the library. Roles have a slash, `/`, in their name and permissions have a colon, `:`, as defined in the preceding role definition. Role definitions are recursive, and one role can encapsulate both roles and permissions.

The `init-db` function is used to initialize the database and the role definitions. The `has-access?` is a utility function that can be used to validate whether a user contains a given set of permissions or not. The following REPL session describes the use of the `has-access?` function with an example:

```
;; require the persistence namespace
helping-hands.auth.server> (require '[helping-hands.auth.persistence :as
p])
nil

;; since there is no secret key define,
;; initialize the database with a secret-key
;; if it does not exist
helping-hands.auth.server> (let [db (p/init-db)]
                                 ;; if key does not exist, initialize one
                                 ;; and update the database with :secret key
                                 (if-not (:secret @db)
                                   (swap! db #(assoc % :secret (jwt/get-
secret)))) @db))
{:secret #object[javax.crypto.spec.SecretKeySpec 0xebc150b
"javax.crypto.spec.SecretKeySpec@17ce8"], :roles {"hh/superadmin" "*",
"hh/admin" "hh:*", "hh/notify" #{"notify/alert" "hh:notify"},
"notify/alert" #{"notify:email" "notify:sms"}}, :users {"hhuser" {:pwd
#object["[B" 0x1b46ced7 "[B@1b46ced7"], :roles #{"hh/notify"}}, "hhadmin"
{:pwd #object["[B" 0x7b9083e6 "[B@7b9083e6"], :roles #{"hh/admin"}},
"superadmin" {:pwd #object["[B" 0x64083ac1 "[B@64083ac1"], :roles
#{"hh/superadmin"}}}}

;; validate that `hhuser` has the ``hh:notify`` permission
helping-hands.auth.server> (p/has-access? "hhuser" #{"hh:notify"})
true

;; validate permissions that are not defined
```

```
helping-hands.auth.server> (p/has-access? "hhuser" #{"hh:admin"})
false

;; validate permissions that are obtained by other role references
helping-hands.auth.server> (p/has-access? "hhuser" #{"hh:notify"
"notify:email"})
true
```

The preceding example explicitly initializes the database at REPL and sets the secret key. Instead of explicitly initializing the database, it can be done at the startup itself using mount, as discussed in Chapter 9, *Configuring Microservices*. To allow mount to initialize the state of the database with the secret key and make it available for other namespaces, define the database state in the helping-hands.auth.state namespace, as follows:

```
(ns helping-hands.auth.state
  "Initializes State for Auth Service"
  (:require [mount.core :refer [defstate] :as mount]
            [helping-hands.auth.jwt :as jwt]
            [helping-hands.auth.persistence :as p]))

(defstate auth-db
  :start (let [db (p/init-db)]
           ;; if key does not exist, initialize one
           ;; and update the database with :secret key
           (if-not (:secret @db)
             (swap! db #(assoc % :secret (jwt/get-secret))) @db))
  :stop nil)
```

Next, enable the start and stop events by adding mount/start and mount/stop functions to the server startup functions in the helping-hands.auth.server namespace, as shown in the following example:

```
(ns helping-hands.auth.server
  (:gen-class) ; for -main method in uberjar
  (:require [io.pedestal.http :as server]
            [io.pedestal.http.route :as route]
            [mount.core :as mount]
            [helping-hands.auth.config :as cfg]
            [helping-hands.auth.service :as service]))

;; This is an adapted service map, that can be started and stopped
;; From the REPL you can call server/start and server/stop on this service
(defonce runnable-service (server/create-server service/service))

(defn run-dev
```

```
      "The entry-point for 'lein run-dev'"
      [& args]
      (println "\nCreating your [DEV] server...")
      ;; initialize configuration
      (cfg/init-config {:cli-args args :quit-on-error true})
      ;; initialize state
      (mount/start)
      ;; Add shutdown-hook
      (.addShutdownHook
        (Runtime/getRuntime)
        (Thread. mount/stop))
      (-> service/service ;; start with production configuration
          ...
          ;; Wire up interceptor chains
          server/default-interceptors
          server/dev-interceptors
          server/create-server
          server/start))

  (defn -main
    "The entry-point for 'lein run'"
    [& args]
    (println "\nCreating your server...")
    ;; initialize configuration
    (cfg/init-config {:cli-args args :quit-on-error true})
    ;; initialize state
    (mount/start)
    ;; Add shutdown-hook
    (.addShutdownHook
      (Runtime/getRuntime)
      (Thread. mount/stop))
    (server/start runnable-service))
```

Creating Auth APIs using Pedestal

The next step is to define APIs for the Auth service to authenticate and authorize users. Add the /tokens and /tokens/validate routes to the helping-hands.auth.service namespace, as follows:

```
(ns helping-hands.auth.service
  (:require [helping-hands.auth.core :as core]
            [cheshire.core :as jp]
            [io.pedestal.http :as http]
            [io.pedestal.http.route :as route]
            [io.pedestal.http.body-params :as body-params]
            [io.pedestal.interceptor.chain :as chain]
```

```
                     [ring.util.response :as ring-resp]))

;; Defines "/" and "/about" routes with their associated :get handlers.
;; The interceptors defined after the verb map (e.g., {:get home-page}
;; apply to / and its children (/about).
(def common-interceptors [(body-params/body-params) http/html-body])


;; Tabular routes
(def routes #{["/tokens"
               :get (conj common-interceptors
                          `core/validate `core/get-token)
               :route-name :token-get]
              ["/tokens/validate"
               :post (conj common-interceptors
                           `core/validate `core/validate-token)
               :route-name :token-validate]})

;; See http/default-interceptors for additional options you can configure
(def service {:env :prod
              ::http/routes routes
              ::http/resource-path "/public"
              ::http/type :jetty
              ::http/port 8080
              ;; Options to pass to the container (Jetty)
              ::http/container-options {:h2c? true
                                        :h2? false
                                        :ssl? false}})
```

The GET /tokens route looks for uid and pwd parameters or a valid authorization header to process the request. If the uid and pwd parameters are specified and they are valid, a JWT token is issued as part of the authorization header. If an existing JWT is specified as a part of the authorization header in the request, Auth service returns the username and the roles associated with it.

The POST /tokens/validate route expects a form parameter—perms—and a valid authorization header with JWT to authorize the user against the given permissions. This endpoint is used by other microservices of the Helping Hands application to authorize the user against the permissions required by the microservices to provide access to the resources that it manages. Since permissions and roles are defined as strings, administrators can initialize the Auth database with all the expected roles and permissions and assign them to users to allow or disallow access to services of the application.

The interceptors used for the routes defined in the preceding code snippet are implemented in the `helping-hands.auth.core` namespace, as shown in the following example; the `validate` interceptor prepares the `:tx-data` parameter with all the available request parameters and also validates the presence of either `uid` and `pwd` or an authorization header—if one of them does not exist, it returns a HTTP 400 Bad Request response:

```clojure
(ns helping-hands.auth.core
  "Initializes Helping Hands Auth Service"
  (:require [cheshire.core :as jp]
            [clojure.string :as s]
            [helping-hands.auth.jwt :as jwt]
            [helping-hands.auth.persistence :as p]
            [helping-hands.auth.state :refer [auth-db]]
            [io.pedestal.interceptor.chain :as chain])
  (:import [com.nimbusds.jwt.proc BadJWTException]
           [java.io IOException]
           [java.text ParseException]
           [java.util Arrays UUID]))

;; --------------------------------
;; Validation Interceptors
;; --------------------------------

(defn- prepare-valid-context
  "Applies validation logic and returns the resulting context"
  [context]
  (let [params (merge (-> context :request :form-params)
                      (-> context :request :query-params)
                      (-> context :request :headers)
                      (if-let [pparams (-> context :request :path-params)]
                        (if (empty? pparams) {} pparams)))]
    (if (or (and (params :uid) (params :pwd))
            (params "authorization"))
      (assoc context :tx-data params)
      (chain/terminate
        (assoc context
               :response {:status 400
                          :body "Invalid Creds/Token"})))))

(def validate
  {:name ::validate

   :enter
   (fn [context]
     (prepare-valid-context context))

   :error
```

```
(fn [context ex-info]
  (assoc context
         :response {:status 500
                    :body (.getMessage ex-info)})))})
```

The `get-token` interceptor looks for a valid `uid` and `pwd`, and issues a JWT if authentication is successful. If the `uid` and `pwd` are not present, it looks for a valid authorization header of a `Bearer` type and, if the token is valid, it returns the authenticated user ID and assigned roles that are associated with the user:

```
(defn- extract-token
  "Extracts user and roles map from the auth header"
  [auth]
  (select-keys
   (jwt/read-token
    (second (s/split auth #"\s+")) (auth-db :secret))
   ["user" "roles"]))

(def get-token
  {:name ::token-get

   :enter
   (fn [context]
     (let [tx-data (:tx-data context)
           uid (:uid tx-data)
           pwd (:pwd tx-data)
           auth (tx-data "authorization")]
       (cond

         (and uid pwd (Arrays/equals
                       (-> auth-db :users (get uid) :pwd)
                       (p/get-hash pwd)))
         (let [token (jwt/create-token
                      {:roles (-> auth-db :users (get uid) :roles)
                       :user uid} (auth-db :secret))]
           (assoc context :response
                  {:status 200
                   :headers {"authorization" (str "Bearer " token)}}))

         (and auth (= "Bearer" (-> (s/split auth #"\s+") first)))
         (try
           (assoc context :response
                  {:status 200
                   :body (jp/generate-string (extract-token auth))})
           (catch BadJWTException e
             (assoc context :response
                    {:status 401 :body "Token expired"})))
```

```
                    :else (assoc context :response {:status 401})))))
      :error
      (fn [context ex-info]
        (assoc context
               :response {:status 500
                          :body (.getMessage ex-info)})))})
```

The implementation of the `validate-token` interceptor shown in the following example authorizes the user associated with the JWT sent as an authorization header and a CSV of permissions specified as the `perms` form parameter:

```
(def validate-token
  {:name ::token-validate

   :enter
   (fn [context]
     (let [tx-data (:tx-data context)
           auth (tx-data "authorization")
           perms (if-let [p (tx-data :perms)]
                   (into #{} (map s/trim (s/split p #","))))]
       (if (and auth (= "Bearer" (-> (s/split auth #"\s+") first)))
         (try
           (if (p/has-access? ((extract-token auth) "user") perms)
             (assoc context :response {:status 200 :body "true"})
             (assoc context :response {:status 200 :body "false"}))
           (catch BadJWTException e
             (assoc context :response
                    {:status 401 :body "Token expired"}))
           (catch ParseException e
             (assoc context :response
                    {:status 401 :body "Invalid JWT"})))
         (assoc context :response {:status 401}))))

   :error
   (fn [context ex-info]
     (assoc context
            :response {:status 500
                       :body (.getMessage ex-info)}))})
```

To test the routes, start the Auth service using the `lein run` command or start it within a REPL as shown in the following example; as soon as the application is started, mount kicks in and initializes a secret key that is used to issue tokens and also read them for authorization:

```
helping-hands.auth.server> (def server (run-dev))

Creating your [DEV] server...
```

```
Omniconf configuration:
  {:conf #object[java.io.File 0x979c2d2 "config/conf.edn"]}

#'helping-hands.auth.server/server
helping-hands.auth.server>
```

Once the server is up and running, use cURL to try out various scenarios, as shown in the following example. If there are no authentication headers or valid credentials specified, the `validate` interceptor will kick in and mark it as a bad request, as follows:

```
% curl -i "http://localhost:8080/tokens"
HTTP/1.1 400 Bad Request
Date: Sun, 14 Jan 2018 20:49:48 GMT
...

Invalid Creds/Token

% curl -i -XPOST -d "perms=notify:email"
"http://localhost:8080/tokens/validate"
HTTP/1.1 400 Bad Request
Date: Sun, 14 Jan 2018 20:50:21 GMT
...

Invalid Creds/Token
```

If the specified credentials are invalid, it will throw a response with HTTP 401 Unauthorized status, as shown in the following example:

```
% curl -i "http://localhost:8080/tokens?uid=hhuser&pwd=hello"
HTTP/1.1 401 Unauthorized
Date: Sun, 14 Jan 2018 20:53:16 GMT
...

% curl -i -H "Authorization: Bearer abc" -XPOST -d "perms=notify:email"
"http://localhost:8080/tokens/validate"
HTTP/1.1 401 Unauthorized
Date: Sun, 14 Jan 2018 20:55:35 GMT
...

Invalid JWT
```

If the parameters are valid, endpoints work as expected, as shown for the `hhuser` user:

```
% curl -i "http://localhost:8080/tokens?uid=hhuser&pwd=hhuser"
HTTP/1.1 200 OK
Date: Sun, 14 Jan 2018 20:59:48 GMT
...
```

```
Authorization: Bearer
eyJlbmMiOiJBMTI4Q0JDLUhTMjU2IiwiYWxnIjoiQTEyOEtXIn0.YY_dMY8qoqfTHeZwGacsFY7
0tCaUvCjjPKYNFhuA2ppOD-
Deaj5zzw.BbK36SSYyuUeVVS9jpyIXw.6UNkLFMVF5Foj5qFX5vLdKcyOoU2G2eeVtHskSWBoZu
BnnAwI1NGrPc3PvQqKF4QkzlrbFfOYD2Vxd4YqYmj8Hcb1qVUQD1QgtYKiStIMujH--
ZRltPfy7m8VW1D31ToeqAYU1LLlXYSC1W3kSjZQiMFMU1LXkMqZVdmJyfQIL_SvizfWbYuZQPcy
DCxG5-XtVeG2r09vnvUybw8tKdafg.WML7xCZ-lZur1GXpNFNKrw
Transfer-Encoding: chunked

% curl -i -H "Authorization: Bearer
eyJlbmMiOiJBMTI4Q0JDLUhTMjU2IiwiYWxnIjoiQTEyOEtXIn0.YY_dMY8qoqfTHeZwGacsFY7
0tCaUvCjjPKYNFhuA2ppOD-
Deaj5zzw.BbK36SSYyuUeVVS9jpyIXw.6UNkLFMVF5Foj5qFX5vLdKcyOoU2G2eeVtHskSWBoZu
BnnAwI1NGrPc3PvQqKF4QkzlrbFfOYD2Vxd4YqYmj8Hcb1qVUQD1QgtYKiStIMujH--
ZRltPfy7m8VW1D31ToeqAYU1LLlXYSC1W3kSjZQiMFMU1LXkMqZVdmJyfQIL_SvizfWbYuZQPcy
DCxG5-XtVeG2r09vnvUybw8tKdafg.WML7xCZ-lZur1GXpNFNKrw"
"http://localhost:8080/tokens"
HTTP/1.1 200 OK
Date: Sun, 14 Jan 2018 21:00:11 GMT
...

{"user":"hhuser","roles":["hh/notify"]}

% curl -XPOST -i -H "Authorization: Bearer
eyJlbmMiOiJBMTI4Q0JDLUhTMjU2IiwiYWxnIjoiQTEyOEtXIn0.YY_dMY8qoqfTHeZwGacsFY7
0tCaUvCjjPKYNFhuA2ppOD-
Deaj5zzw.BbK36SSYyuUeVVS9jpyIXw.6UNkLFMVF5Foj5qFX5vLdKcyOoU2G2eeVtHskSWBoZu
BnnAwI1NGrPc3PvQqKF4QkzlrbFfOYD2Vxd4YqYmj8Hcb1qVUQD1QgtYKiStIMujH--
ZRltPfy7m8VW1D31ToeqAYU1LLlXYSC1W3kSjZQiMFMU1LXkMqZVdmJyfQIL_SvizfWbYuZQPcy
DCxG5-XtVeG2r09vnvUybw8tKdafg.WML7xCZ-lZur1GXpNFNKrw" -d
"perms=notify:email" "http://localhost:8080/tokens/validate"
HTTP/1.1 200 OK
Date: Sun, 14 Jan 2018 21:00:38 GMT
...

true%

% curl -XPOST -i -H "Authorization: Bearer
eyJlbmMiOiJBMTI4Q0JDLUhTMjU2IiwiYWxnIjoiQTEyOEtXIn0.YY_dMY8qoqfTHeZwGacsFY7
0tCaUvCjjPKYNFhuA2ppOD-
Deaj5zzw.BbK36SSYyuUeVVS9jpyIXw.6UNkLFMVF5Foj5qFX5vLdKcyOoU2G2eeVtHskSWBoZu
BnnAwI1NGrPc3PvQqKF4QkzlrbFfOYD2Vxd4YqYmj8Hcb1qVUQD1QgtYKiStIMujH--
ZRltPfy7m8VW1D31ToeqAYU1LLlXYSC1W3kSjZQiMFMU1LXkMqZVdmJyfQIL_SvizfWbYuZQPcy
DCxG5-XtVeG2r09vnvUybw8tKdafg.WML7xCZ-lZur1GXpNFNKrw" -d
"perms=notify:random" "http://localhost:8080/tokens/validate"
HTTP/1.1 200 OK
Date: Sun, 14 Jan 2018 21:00:49 GMT
...
```

```
false

% curl -XPOST -i -H "Authorization: Bearer
eyJlbmMiOiJBMTI4Q0JDLUhTMjU2IiwiYWxnIjoiQTEyOEtXIn0.YY_dMY8qoqfTHeZwGacsFY7
0tCaUvCjjPKYNFhuA2ppOD-
Deaj5zzw.BbK36SSYyuUeVVS9jpyIXw.6UNkLFMVF5Foj5qFX5vLdKcyOoU2G2eeVtHskSWBoZu
BnnAwI1NGrPc3PvQqKF4QkzlrbFfOYD2Vxd4YqYmj8Hcb1qVUQD1QgtYKiStIMujH--
ZRltPfy7m8VW1D31ToeqAYU1LLlXYSC1W3kSjZQiMFMU1LXkMqZVdmJyfQIL_SvizfWbYuZQPcy
DCxG5-XtVeG2r09vnvUybw8tKdafg.WML7xCZ-lZur1GXpNFNKrw" -d
"perms=notify:email" "http://localhost:8080/tokens/validate"
HTTP/1.1 401 Unauthorized
Date: Sun, 14 Jan 2018 21:03:55 GMT
...
```

Token expired

Auth service can be deployed in isolation and connected through the `auth` interceptor of rest of the services of the Helping Hands application to authorize the users. Users can obtain the token by calling the `/tokens` endpoint of Auth service directly and use the same token to authenticate and authorize themselves with other services.

 Buddy (`https://github.com/funcool/buddy`) is another Clojure library that has a Buddy Sign (`https://github.com/funcool/buddy-sign`) library that can also be used to generate JSON Web Tokens.

Monitoring microservices

A microservices-based application is highly flexible in terms of deployment and scaling. It consists of multiple services that may have one or more instances running on a cluster of machines across the network. In such a highly distributed and flexible environment, it is of utmost importance that each instance of a microservice is monitored in real time to get a clear view of the deployed services, their performance, and to capture issues of interest that must be reported as soon as they occur. Since each request to a microservice-based application may span out to one or more requests among microservices, there should be a mechanism to track the flow of requests and also locate the areas of bottleneck that can be addressed by performing a root cause analysis and often scaling the services further to meet the demand.

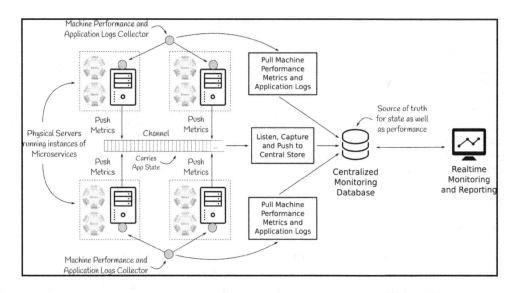

One of the ways to set up an effective monitoring system is to collect all the metrics across the services and machines and store them in a centralized repository, as shown in the preceding diagram. This centralized repository can then support the analysis of the captured metrics and help to generate alerts for the events of interest in real time. A centralized repository also helps in setting up the real-time view of the system to understand the behavior of each service and decide whether to scale it up or scale it down. To set up a centralized repository for the application, the metrics need to be either pulled from all the services and physical machines or pushed to the centralized repository by the services running on the physical machines. Both push and pull models are useful to set up an effective monitoring system that serves the source of truth for the state of the system as well as the performance of the environment that is crucial for effective utilization of the infrastructure used by the microservices-based application.

All the services must be responsible to push the metrics related to the state of the application to a common channel, such as **Apache Kafka** (https://kafka.apache.org/), on a common topic that can then be used to aggregate all the application-level metrics across the services and store them in a centralized repository. Application-level logs that are written to the file on the physical servers and the application-level metrics that are published via mediums such as JMX (http://www.oracle.com/technetwork/articles/java/javamanagement-140525.html) can be pulled by an external collector and later pushed to the centralized storage. To monitor the performance of the infrastructure, external collectors must also capture the stats of the physical machine, including CPU utilization, network throughput, disk I/O, and more, which can also be pushed to the central repository to get a holistic view of the resource utilization across the services of the application.

Using ELK Stack for monitoring

Elasticsearch (`https://www.elastic.co/products/elasticsearch`), Logstash (`https://www.elastic.co/products/logstash`), and Kibana (`https://www.elastic.co/products/kibana`), often referred to as ELK Stack or Elastic Stack (`https://www.elastic.co/elk-stack`), provide all the required components to set up a real-time monitoring infrastructure to capture, pull, and push the application and machine-level metrics into a centralized repository and build a monitoring dashboard for reporting and alerts. The following monitoring infrastructure diagram exhibits where each of the components of the ELK Stack fit in. Collectd (`https://collectd.org/`) and Apache Kafka (`https://kafka.apache.org/`) are not a part of ELK Stack, but ELK Stack provides seamless integration with these out of the box:

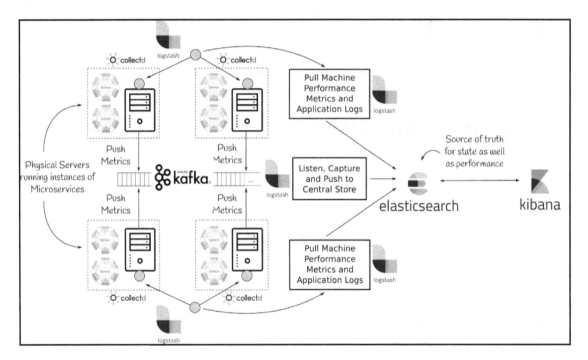

Collectd helps in capturing all the machine-level stats, including CPU, memory, disk, and network. The captured data can then be pulled through Logstash and pushed into Elasticsearch to analyze the overall performance and utilization of the infrastructure used by the services of the application. Logstash can also understand the standard set of application logs and pull the logged events from the log files generated on the machine and push it to the Elasticsearch cluster. Logstash also integrates well with Apache Kafka and can be used to capture the application state events published by the services and push them directly to Elasticsearch. Since Elasticsearch acts as a central repository for all the logs, events, and machine stats, Kibana can be used directly on top of Elasticsearch to analyze the stored metrics and build dashboards that are updated in real time as and when events arrive in Elasticsearch. Kibana can also be used to perform root cause analysis and generate alerts for the intended recipients.

 ELK Stack is useful for monitoring, but it is not the only option. Tools such as Prometheus (`https://prometheus.io/`) can also be used for monitoring. Prometheus supports a dimensional data model, flexible query language and efficient time series database with in-built alerting.

Setting up Elasticsearch

To set up Elasticsearch, download the latest version from the Elasticsearch download page (`https://www.elastic.co/downloads/elasticsearch`) and extract it, as shown in the following example; this book uses Elasticsearch 6.1.1, that can be downloaded from the release page of 6.1.1 (`https://www.elastic.co/downloads/past-releases/elasticsearch-6-1-1`):

```
# download elasticsearch 6.1.1 tar
% wget
https://artifacts.elastic.co/downloads/elasticsearch/elasticsearch-6.1.1.ta
r.gz
--
https://artifacts.elastic.co/downloads/elasticsearch/elasticsearch-6.1.1.ta
r.gz
Resolving artifacts.elastic.co (artifacts.elastic.co)... 184.73.156.41,
184.72.218.26, 54.235.82.130, ...
Connecting to artifacts.elastic.co
(artifacts.elastic.co)|184.73.156.41|:443... connected.
HTTP request sent, awaiting response... 200 OK
Length: 28462503 (27M) [application/x-gzip]
Saving to: 'elasticsearch-6.1.1.tar.gz'

elasticsearch-6.1.1.tar.gz 100%[===============================>] 27.14M
2.38MB/s in 21s
```

```
... (1.30 MB/s) - 'elasticsearch-6.1.1.tar.gz' saved [28462503/28462503]

# extract the downloaded tarball
% tar -xvf elasticsearch-6.1.1.tar.gz
...

# make sure that these directories are present
% tree -L 1 elasticsearch-6.1.1
elasticsearch-6.1.1
├── bin
├── config
├── lib
├── LICENSE.txt
├── modules
├── NOTICE.txt
├── plugins
└── README.textile

5 directories, 3 files
```

Although Elasticsearch will run straight out of the box with the `bin/elasticsearch` command, it is recommended to review the following important configurations and system settings for an effective Elasticsearch cluster. The settings marked as **ES Config** are generic for all Elasticsearch deployments, whereas the ones marked as **System Setting** are for the Linux operating system. The environment variable—`$ES_HOME`—refers to the extracted Elasticsearch installation folder, that is, `elasticsearch-6.1.1` for the command shown in the preceding code snippet.

Type	Config Location	Config Parameter	Value	Description
System Setting	`/etc/security/limits.conf`	`memlock`	unlimited	`<user> - memlock unlimited`
System Setting	`/etc/security/limits.conf`	`nofile`	65536	`<user> - nofile 65536`
System Setting	`/etc/sysctl.conf`	`vm.overcommit_memory`	1	`sudo sysctl vm.overcommit_memory=1`
System Setting	`/etc/sysctl.conf`	`vm.max_map_count`	262144	`sudo sysctl -w vm.max_map_count=262144`
System Setting	`/etc/fstab`	`Comment swap config`	-	`sudo swapoff -a`
ES JVM Options	`$ES_HOME/config/jvm.options`	`-Xms and -Xmx`	8g, 16g, and so on	Alternatively, set `ES_JAVA_OPTS` with these settings
ES Config	`$ES_HOME/config/elasticsearch.yml`	`cluster.name`	`<name>`	Name of the cluster for other nodes to join
ES Config	`$ES_HOME/config/elasticsearch.yml`	`node.name`	`<name>`	Node name to identify the node from ES interface. Good to have as hostname
ES Config	`$ES_HOME/config/elasticsearch.yml`	`path.data`	One or more `<path to keep indexes>`	One or more paths where ES keeps the data
ES Config	`$ES_HOME/config/elasticsearch.yml`	`path.logs`	`<path to log directory>`	Path where ES will keep the logs
ES Config	`$ES_HOME/config/elasticsearch.yml`	`bootstrap.memory_lock`	true	Disable swapping
ES Config	`$ES_HOME/config/elasticsearch.yml`	`network.host`	`<ip_address>`	IP address to bind to

ES Config	$ES_HOME/config/elasticsearch.yml	discovery.zen.ping.unicast.hosts	One or more `<ip>:<port>`	Seed list of other nodes in the cluster that are likely to be live and contactable
ES Config	$ES_HOME/config/elasticsearch.yml	discovery.zen.minimum_master_nodes	`<number of nodes>`	To avoid a split brain, this setting should be set to a quorum of master-eligible nodes, that is, (master_eligible_nodes / 2) + 1

Note that some of the system settings shown in the preceding table may require a system restart for them to take into effect. Also, settings like that of swap space must be done only if Elasticsearch is the only component running on the host operating system. Once all the settings are in place, each Elasticsearch node can be started using the following command; each node will join the cluster if they have the same cluster name and are a part of unicast hosts list that a node is allowed to join:

```
# change to the extracted elasticsearch directory
% cd elasticsearch-6.1.1

# start elasticsearch
% bin/elasticsearch
[2018-01-15T20:46:35,408][INFO ][o.e.n.Node ] [] initializing ...
...
[2018-01-15T20:46:36,328][INFO ][o.e.p.PluginsService ] [W6r6s1z] loaded
module [aggs-matrix-stats]
[2018-01-15T20:46:36,329][INFO ][o.e.p.PluginsService ] [W6r6s1z] loaded
module [analysis-common]
[2018-01-15T20:46:36,329][INFO ][o.e.p.PluginsService ] [W6r6s1z] loaded
module [ingest-common]
...
[2018-01-15T20:46:36,330][INFO ][o.e.p.PluginsService ] [W6r6s1z] loaded
module [tribe]
[2018-01-15T20:46:37,491][INFO ][o.e.d.DiscoveryModule ] [W6r6s1z] using
discovery type [zen]
[2018-01-15T20:46:37,929][INFO ][o.e.n.Node ] initialized
[2018-01-15T20:46:37,930][INFO ][o.e.n.Node ] [W6r6s1z] starting ...
[2018-01-15T20:46:38,100][INFO ][o.e.t.TransportService ] [W6r6s1z]
publish_address {127.0.0.1:9300}, bound_addresses {[::1]:9300},
{127.0.0.1:9300}
[2018-01-15T20:46:41,164][INFO ][o.e.c.s.MasterService ] [W6r6s1z] zen-
disco-elected-as-master ([0] nodes joined), reason: new_master
{W6r6s1z}{W6r6s1zTQ96ULo2wq9Tm3w}{ykEtBVl9Sy62mkXOFo892g}{127.0.0.1}{127.0.
0.1:9300}
...
[2018-01-15T20:46:41,196][INFO ][o.e.n.Node ] [W6r6s1z] started
[2018-01-15T20:46:41,239][INFO ][o.e.g.GatewayService ] [W6r6s1z] recovered
[0] indices into cluster_state
```

Note that the first node that is started is automatically elected as a master of the cluster to which other nodes can join:

```
% curl http://localhost:9200
{
  "name" : "W6r6s1z",
  "cluster_name" : "elasticsearch",
  "cluster_uuid" : "g33pKv6XRTaj_yMJLliL0Q",
  "version" : {
    "number" : "6.1.1",
    "build_hash" : "bd92e7f",
    "build_date" : "2017-12-17T20:23:25.338Z",
    "build_snapshot" : false,
    "lucene_version" : "7.1.0",
    "minimum_wire_compatibility_version" : "5.6.0",
    "minimum_index_compatibility_version" : "5.0.0"
  },
  "tagline" : "You Know, for Search"
}
```

Once the Elasticsearch node is up and running, to test the instance send a `GET` request to the default `9200` port on the machine where Elasticsearch is running using cURL, as shown in the preceding example. It should return a response stating the version of the node. Verify that it is the right version, that is, `6.1.1`, for this example.

> For more details on the important settings of Elasticsearch and System, take a look at the Elasticsearch docs for *Important Settings* (`https://www.elastic.co/guide/en/elasticsearch/reference/current/important-settings.html`) and *System Settings* (`https://www.elastic.co/guide/en/elasticsearch/reference/current/setting-system-settings.html`).

The preceding configuration discusses a typical cluster deployment for Elasticsearch. Elasticsearch also provides a concept of **Cross Cluster Search** (`https://www.elastic.co/guide/en/elasticsearch/reference/current/modules-cross-cluster-search.html`) that allows any node to act as a federated client across multiple clusters of Elasticsearch.

> The steps taken in this section use Elasticsearch tarball to set up Elasticsearch cluster, but Elasticsearch provides a number of options to set it up using binaries, including RPM package, Debian package, MSI package for Windows, and a Docker image. For more details, refer to the installation instructions at `https://www.elastic.co/guide/en/elasticsearch/reference/current/install-elasticsearch.html#install-elasticsearch`.

Setting up Kibana

Kibana is the visualization and dashboard interface for Elasticsearch. It allows exploring data using its **Discover module** (`https://www.elastic.co/guide/en/kibana/6.1/discover.html`) and building real-time dashboards. It includes a good number of visualization options (`https://www.elastic.co/guide/en/kibana/current/visualize.html`) that allow users to aggregate data stored within Elasticsearch and visualize them using various charts, such as line, bar, area, maps, and tag clouds. Kibana can be used to build the monitoring dashboard using the various metrics that are captured within Elasticsearch.

To set up Kibana, download the latest version from the Kibana downloads page (`https://www.elastic.co/downloads/kibana`) and extract it as shown in the following example; this book uses Kibana 6.1.1, which can be downloaded from the release page of 6.1.1 (`https://www.elastic.co/downloads/past-releases/kibana-6-1-1`):

```
# download Kibana 6.1.1 tar
% wget
https://artifacts.elastic.co/downloads/kibana/kibana-6.1.1-linux-x86_64.tar
.gz
--
https://artifacts.elastic.co/downloads/kibana/kibana-6.1.1-linux-x86_64.tar
.gz
Resolving artifacts.elastic.co (artifacts.elastic.co)... 54.225.188.6,
23.21.118.61, 54.235.82.130, ...
Connecting to artifacts.elastic.co
(artifacts.elastic.co)|54.225.188.6|:443... connected.
HTTP request sent, awaiting response... 200 OK
Length: 64664051 (62M) [application/x-gzip]
Saving to: 'kibana-6.1.1-linux-x86_64.tar.gz'

kibana-6.1.1-linux-x86_64.tar.gz 100%[===============================>]
61.67M 2.06MB/s in 53s

... (1.10 MB/s) - 'kibana-6.1.1-linux-x86_64.tar.gz' saved
[64664051/64664051]

# extract the downloaded tarball
% tar -xvf kibana-6.1.1-linux-x86_64.tar.gz
...

# make sure that these directories are present
% tree -L 1 kibana-6.1.1-linux-x86_64
kibana-6.1.1-linux-x86_64
├── bin
```

```
├──── config
├──── data
├──── LICENSE.txt
├──── node
├──── node_modules
├──── NOTICE.txt
├──── optimize
├──── package.json
├──── plugins
├──── README.txt
├──── src
├──── ui_framework
└──── webpackShims

10 directories, 4 files
```

Next, configure Kibana instance by setting the following configuration parameters in
the `$KIBANA_HOME/config/kibana.yml` file. The environment
variable—`$KIBANA_HOME`—refers to the extracted Kibana installation folder, that
is, `kibana-6.1.1-linux-x86_64` for the command shown in the preceding code snippet.

Config Parameter	Value	Description
`server.port`	`5601`	Default
`server.host`	`<host_ip>`	Kibana binds to this IP address
`server.basePath`	`<base_prefix_URL>`	Should not end with `/`. Used to map proxy URL prefix, if any
`server.name`	`<name>`	Display name
`elasticsearch.url`	`http://<es_host>:<es_port>`	Elasticsearch URL to connect to; default port is `9200`
`kibana.index`	`<name>`	Index name as created by Kibana in Elasticsearch
`pid.file`	`<path_to_pid_file>`	PID file location
`logging.dest`	`<path_to_log_file>`	File to write Kibana logs

Once all the settings are in place, start Kibana using the command shown in the following
example; ensure that Elasticsearch is already running and accessible to the Kibana node on
the configured `elasticsearch.url` setting, as described in the preceding table.

```
# change to extracted kibana directory
% cd kibana-6.1.1-linux-x86_64
```

```
# start kibana
% bin/kibana
  log [16:41:31.409] [info][status][plugin:kibana@6.1.1] Status changed
from uninitialized to green - Ready
  log [16:41:31.443] [info][status][plugin:elasticsearch@6.1.1] Status
changed from uninitialized to yellow - Waiting for Elasticsearch
  log [16:41:31.461] [info][status][plugin:console@6.1.1] Status changed
from uninitialized to green - Ready
  log [16:41:31.484] [info][status][plugin:metrics@6.1.1] Status changed
from uninitialized to green - Ready
  log [16:41:31.646] [info][status][plugin:timelion@6.1.1] Status changed
from uninitialized to green - Ready
  log [16:41:31.650] [info][listening] Server running at
http://localhost:5601
  log [16:41:31.668] [info][status][plugin:elasticsearch@6.1.1] Status
changed from yellow to green - Ready
```

Once Kibana is up and running, open the URL `http://localhost:5601`, as logged in the preceding messages to open Kibana interface, as shown in the following screenshot; it should show the Kibana home page with options to visualize and explore data:

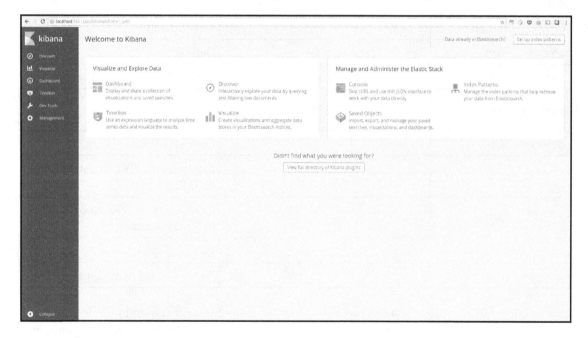

The current configuration of Kibana allows users to explore Elasticsearch in a closed network. Since Kibana provides full control over the underlying Elasticsearch cluster and data stored within it, it is recommended that you enable SSL and also the load-balancing option as defined in the production configuration (`https://www.elastic.co/guide/en/kibana/current/production.html`) for users to connect and access dashboards.

 Kibana not only allows users to explore datasets already stored within Elasticsearch but also supports loading datasets directly into Elasticsearch via its user interface. To learn more about this, follow the **Loading Sample Data** tutorial of Kibana (`https://www.elastic.co/guide/en/kibana/current/tutorial-load-dataset.html`).

Setting up Logstash

Logstash allows users to collect, parse, and transform log messages. It supports a number of input (`https://www.elastic.co/guide/en/logstash/current/input-plugins.html`) and output (`https://www.elastic.co/guide/en/logstash/current/output-plugins.html`) plugins that allow Logstash to collect logs from a variety of sources, parse and transform them, and then write the results to one of the supported plugins. To set up Logstash, download the latest version from the Logstash downloads page (`https://www.elastic.co/downloads/logstash`) and extract it as shown in the following code snippet—this book uses Logstash 6.1.1, which can be downloaded from the release page of 6.1.1 (`https://www.elastic.co/downloads/past-releases/logstash-6-1-1`):

```
# download Logstash 6.1.1 tar
% wget
https://artifacts.elastic.co/downloads/logstash/logstash-6.1.1.tar.gz
-- https://artifacts.elastic.co/downloads/logstash/logstash-6.1.1.tar.gz
Resolving artifacts.elastic.co (artifacts.elastic.co)... 23.21.118.61,
54.243.108.41, 184.72.218.26, ...
Connecting to artifacts.elastic.co
(artifacts.elastic.co)|23.21.118.61|:443... connected.
HTTP request sent, awaiting response... 200 OK
Length: 109795895 (105M) [application/x-gzip]
Saving to: 'logstash-6.1.1.tar.gz'

logstash-6.1.1.tar.gz 100%[==================================>] 104.71M
1.09MB/s in 81s

... (1.30 MB/s) - 'logstash-6.1.1.tar.gz' saved [109795895/109795895]

# extract the downloaded tarball
% tar -xvf logstash-6.1.1.tar.gz
```

```
. . .

# make sure that these directories are present
% tree -L 1 logstash-6.1.1
logstash-6.1.1
├── bin
├── config
├── CONTRIBUTORS
├── data
├── Gemfile
├── Gemfile.lock
├── lib
├── LICENSE
├── logstash-core
├── logstash-core-plugin-api
├── modules
├── NOTICE.TXT
├── tools
└── vendor

9 directories, 5 files
```

The following table lists the primary configuration settings that are required
for Logstash and must be added to the $LOGSTASH_HOME/config/logstash.yml file; the
environment variable—$LOGSTASH_HOME—refers to the extracted Logstash installation
folder, that is, logstash-6.1.1 for the command shown in the preceding code snippet.

Config Parameter	Value	Description
node.name	<name>	Node name to identify the node from output interface. Good to have as a hostname.
path.data	<path_to_data>	One or more paths where Logstash and its plugin keeps the data for any persistence needs.
pipeline.workers	1, 2, 3, 4, and so on	Workers to execute filter and output stages. If deployed on a separate machine, set this to number of CPU cores.
pipeline.output.workers	1, 2, and so on	Number of workers to use per output plugin instance. Defaults to 1.
path.config	<path_to_config>	Location to fetch pipeline configuration for main pipeline.

`http.host`	`<host_ip>`	Bind address for metrics REST endpoint.
`http.port`	`<host_port>`	Bind port for the metrics REST endpoint. Also accepts ranges, such as (9600-9700), to pick the first available port.
`path.logs`	`<path_to_logs>`	Path where Logstash will keep the logs.

The preceding table lists only the primary configuration parameters; for more details and all the supported configuration parameters, refer to Logstash Settings File guide (`https://www.elastic.co/guide/en/logstash/current/logstash-settings-file.html`). Once all the settings are in place, test a sample Logstash pipeline that uses **stdin** (`https://www.elastic.co/guide/en/logstash/current/plugins-inputs-stdin.html`) as its input plugin to receive messages and **stdout** (`https://www.elastic.co/guide/en/logstash/current/plugins-outputs-stdout.html`) as its output plugin to emit the received messages, as follows:

```
# change to extracted logstash directory
% cd logstash-6.1.1

# start logstash pipeline by specifying the configuration
# at command line using the -e flag
% bin/logstash -e 'input { stdin { } } output { stdout {} }'
Sending Logstash's logs to logstash-6.1.1/logs which is now configured via
log4j2.properties
[2018-01-15T23:11:02,245][INFO ][logstash.modules.scaffold] Initializing
module {:module_name=>"netflow",
:directory=>"logstash-6.1.1/modules/netflow/configuration"}
[2018-01-15T23:11:02,257][INFO ][logstash.modules.scaffold] Initializing
module
...
[2018-01-15T23:11:03,872][INFO ][logstash.runner ] Starting Logstash
{"logstash.version"=>"6.1.1"}
[2018-01-15T23:11:04,415][INFO ][logstash.agent ] Successfully started
Logstash API endpoint {:port=>9600}
[2018-01-15T23:11:06,212][INFO ][logstash.pipeline ] Starting pipeline
{:pipeline_id=>"main", "pipeline.workers"=>4, "pipeline.batch.size"=>125,
"pipeline.batch.delay"=>5, "pipeline.max_inflight"=>500,
:thread=>"#<Thread:0x77cbc3e6 run>"}
[2018-01-15T23:11:06,305][INFO ][logstash.pipeline ] Pipeline started
{"pipeline.id"=>"main"}
The stdin plugin is now waiting for input:
```

```
[2018-01-15T23:11:06,413][INFO ][logstash.agent ] Pipelines running
{:count=>1, :pipelines=>["main"]}
hello world
2018-01-15T17:41:19.900Z fc-machine hello world

2018-01-15T17:41:21.707Z fc-machine
Hello Logstash!
2018-01-15T17:41:28.566Z fc-machine Hello Logstash!
Hello ELK!
2018-01-15T17:41:32.255Z fc-machine Hello ELK!
Hello Helping Hands Events!
2018-01-15T17:41:38.685Z fc-machine Hello Helping Hands Events!
```

Logstash may take a few seconds to start the pipeline, so wait for the **Pipeline running** message to be logged. Once the pipeline is running, type a message in the console, and Logstash will echo the same on the console appended with the current timestamp and hostname. This is a very simple pipeline that does not do any transformation, but Logstash allows transformations to be applied on the received messages before they are emitted to the sink. Similar to the basic pipeline shown in the preceding test, the Logstash pipeline configuration is created for each pipeline that is required to be executed by Logstash to capture logs, events, and data, and store them in the target sinks.

 Logstash plugins are implemented primarily in Ruby (https://www.ruby-lang.org/en/). That is why all the job configuration files for Logstash and transformation constructs use syntax of Ruby language.

Using ELK Stack with Collectd

Collectd is a daemon that can be configured to collect metrics from various source plugins, such as Logstash. As compared to Logstash, Collectd is very lightweight and portable, but it does not generate graphs. It can write to RRD files, though, that need a RRDTool (https://en.wikipedia.org/wiki/RRDtool) to read them and generate graphs to visualize the logged data. On the other hand, since Collectd is written in C programming language (https://en.wikipedia.org/wiki/C_(programming_language)), it is also possible to use it to collect metrics from embedded systems as well.

Collectd needs to be built from source. First, download the Collectd 5.8.0 version and extract the same:

```
# download Collectd 5.8.0 tar
% wget
https://storage.googleapis.com/collectd-tarballs/collectd-5.8.0.tar.bz2
```

```
-- https://storage.googleapis.com/collectd-tarballs/collectd-5.8.0.tar.bz2
Resolving storage.googleapis.com (storage.googleapis.com)...
172.217.26.208, 2404:6800:4007:802::2010
Connecting to storage.googleapis.com
(storage.googleapis.com)|172.217.26.208|:443... connected.
HTTP request sent, awaiting response... 200 OK
Length: 1686017 (1.6M) [application/x-bzip]
Saving to: 'collectd-5.8.0.tar.bz2'

collectd-5.8.0.tar.bz2 100%[================================>] 1.61M
2.67MB/s in 0.6s

... (2.67 MB/s) - 'collectd-5.8.0.tar.bz2' saved [1686017/1686017]

# extract the downloaded tarball
% tar -xvf collectd-5.8.0.tar.bz2
...

# make sure that these directories are present
% tree -L 1 collectd-5.8.0
collectd-5.8.0
├── aclocal.m4
├── AUTHORS
├── bindings
├── build-aux
├── ChangeLog
├── configure
├── configure.ac
├── contrib
├── COPYING
├── m4
├── Makefile.am
├── Makefile.in
├── proto
├── README
├── src
├── testwrapper.sh
└── version-gen.sh

6 directories, 11 files
```

Next, install Collectd to a `build` directory, as shown in the following example. In case the configure script requests for missing dependencies, install them before continuing the setup as per the **First steps** wiki (`https://collectd.org/wiki/index.php/First_steps`) of Collectd:

```
# change to extracted collectd directory
```

```
% cd collectd-5.8.0

# configure the target build directory
# give the fully qualified path as prefix
# $COLLECTD_HOME points to collectd-5.8.0 directory
% ./configure --prefix=$COLLECTD_HOME/build
checking build system type... x86_64-unknown-linux-gnu
checking host system type... x86_64-unknown-linux-gnu
checking how to print strings... printf
checking for gcc... gcc
checking whether the C compiler works... yes
checking for C compiler default output file name... a.out
checking for suffix of executables...
...

# install collectd
% sudo make all install
...

# verify the build directories
% tree -L 1 build
build
├── bin
├── etc
├── include
├── lib
├── man
├── sbin
├── share
└── var

8 directories, 0 files

# own the entire collectd directory
# replace <user> with your username
% sudo chown -R <user>:<user> .
```

Once Collectd is installed, the next step is to update the `build/etc/collectd.conf` file with the desired configurations and plugins. The following is a sample `collectd.conf` file to enable `cpu`, `df`, `interface`, `network`, `memory`, `syslog`, `load`, and `swap` plugins; for more details on the available plugins and their configuration, refer to Collectd **Table of Plugins** (`https://collectd.org/wiki/index.php/Table_of_Plugins`).

```
# Base Configuration
# replace all paths below with fully qualified
# path to the extracted collectd-5.8.0 directory
Hostname "helpinghands.com"
```

```
BaseDir "/collectd-5.8.0/build/var/lib/collectd"
PIDFile "/collectd-5.8.0/build/var/run/collectd.pid"
PluginDir "/collectd-5.8.0/build/lib/collectd"
TypesDB "/collectd-5.8.0/build/share/collectd/types.db"
CollectInternalStats true

# Syslog
LoadPlugin syslog
<Plugin syslog>
        LogLevel info
</Plugin>

# Other plug-ins
LoadPlugin cpu
LoadPlugin df
LoadPlugin disk
LoadPlugin interface
LoadPlugin load
LoadPlugin memory
LoadPlugin network
LoadPlugin swap

# Plug-in Config
<Plugin cpu>
  ReportByCpu true
  ReportByState true
  ValuesPercentage false
</Plugin>

# replace device and mount point
# with the device to be monitored
# as shown by df command
<Plugin df>
        Device "/dev/sda9"
        MountPoint "/home"
        FSType "ext4"
        IgnoreSelected false
        ReportByDevice false
        ReportInodes false
        ValuesAbsolute true
        ValuesPercentage false
</Plugin>
<Plugin disk>
        Disk "/^[hs]d[a-f][0-9]?$/"
        IgnoreSelected false
        UseBSDName false
        UdevNameAttr "DEVNAME"
</Plugin>
```

```
# report all interface except lo and sit0
<Plugin interface>
        Interface "lo"
        Interface "sit0"
        IgnoreSelected true
        ReportInactive true
        UniqueName false
</Plugin>
<Plugin load>
        ReportRelative true
</Plugin>
<Plugin memory>
        ValuesAbsolute true
        ValuesPercentage false
</Plugin>
# sends metrics to this port i.e.
# configured in logstash to receive
# the log events to be published
<Plugin network>
        Server "127.0.0.1" "25826"
        <Server "127.0.0.1" "25826">
        </Server>
</Plugin>
<Plugin swap>
        ReportByDevice false
        ReportBytes true
        ValuesAbsolute true
        ValuesPercentage false
</Plugin>
```

Once the configuration file is in place, start Collectd daemon, as shown here:

```
# start collectd daemon with sudo
# some plug-ins require sudo access
% sudo build/sbin/collectd

# make sure it is running
% ps -ef | grep collectd
anuj 27208 1768 0 01:21 ? 00:00:00 build/sbin/collectd
...

# verify syslog to make sure that collectd is up
% tail -f /var/log/syslog
...
Jan 16 01:40:01 localhost collectd[28725]: plugin_load: plugin "syslog"
successfully loaded.
Jan 16 01:40:01 localhost collectd[28725]: plugin_load: plugin "cpu"
successfully loaded.
```

```
Jan 16 01:40:01 localhost collectd[28725]: plugin_load: plugin "df"
successfully loaded.
Jan 16 01:40:01 localhost collectd[28725]: plugin_load: plugin "disk"
successfully loaded.
Jan 16 01:40:01 localhost collectd[28725]: plugin_load: plugin "interface"
successfully loaded.
Jan 16 01:40:01 localhost collectd[28725]: plugin_load: plugin "load"
successfully loaded.
Jan 16 01:40:01 localhost collectd[28725]: plugin_load: plugin "memory"
successfully loaded.
Jan 16 01:40:01 localhost collectd[28725]: plugin_load: plugin "network"
successfully loaded.
Jan 16 01:40:01 localhost collectd[28725]: plugin_load: plugin "swap"
successfully loaded.
...
Jan 16 01:40:01 localhost collectd[28726]: Initialization complete,
entering read-loop.
```

Next, create a Logstash pipeline configuration
file, `$LOGSTASH_HOME/config/helpinghands.conf`, to receive the data from Collectd
using the Collectd Codec (`https://www.elastic.co/guide/en/logstash/current/
plugins-codecs-collectd.html`) plugin and send it to Elasticsearch using its output plugin
(`https://www.elastic.co/guide/en/logstash/current/plugins-outputs-
elasticsearch.html`):

```
input {
  udp {
    port => 25826
    buffer_size => 1452
    codec => collectd {
      id => "helpinghands.com-collectd"
      typesdb => [ "/collectd-5.8.0/build/share/collectd/types.db" ]
    }
  }
}
output {
  elasticsearch {
    id => "helpinghands.com-collectd-es"
    hosts => [ "127.0.0.1:9200" ]
    index => "helpinghands.collectd.instance-%{+YYYY.MM}"
  }
}
```

Next, run the Logstash pipeline to receive data from Collectd process over UDP (https://en.wikipedia.org/wiki/User_Datagram_Protocol) and send it to Elasticsearch. Ensure that the 25826 port specified in the UDP configuration above matches the port of the network plugin of Collectd configuration. Before running Logstash, verify that Elasticsearch and Collectd both are running:

```
# change to $LOGSTASH_HOME directory and run logstash
% bin/logstash -f config/helpinghands.conf
...
Sending Logstash's logs to /logstash-6.1.1/logs which is now configured via
log4j2.properties
[2018-01-16T02:03:57,028][INFO ][logstash.modules.scaffold] Initializing
module {:module_name=>"netflow",
:directory=>"/logstash-6.1.1/modules/netflow/configuration"}
[2018-01-16T02:03:57,057][INFO ][logstash.modules.scaffold] Initializing
module {:module_name=>"fb_apache",
:directory=>"/logstash-6.1.1/modules/fb_apache/configuration"}
...
[2018-01-16T02:03:58,410][INFO ][logstash.runner ] Starting Logstash
{"logstash.version"=>"6.1.1"}
[2018-01-16T02:03:58,935][INFO ][logstash.agent ] Successfully started
Logstash API endpoint {:port=>9600}
[2018-01-16T02:04:02,412][INFO ][logstash.outputs.elasticsearch]
Elasticsearch pool URLs updated {:changes=>{:removed=>[],
:added=>[http://127.0.0.1:9200/]}}
...
[2018-01-16T02:04:03,777][INFO ][logstash.outputs.elasticsearch] New
Elasticsearch output {:class=>"LogStash::Outputs::ElasticSearch",
:hosts=>["//127.0.0.1:9200"]}
...
[2018-01-16T02:04:03,883][INFO ][logstash.pipeline ] Pipeline started
{"pipeline.id"=>"main"}
[2018-01-16T02:04:03,960][INFO ][logstash.inputs.udp ] Starting UDP
listener {:address=>"0.0.0.0:25826"}
[2018-01-16T02:04:03,997][INFO ][logstash.agent ] Pipelines running
{:count=>1, :pipelines=>["main"]}
[2018-01-16T02:04:04,030][INFO ][logstash.inputs.udp ] UDP listener started
{:address=>"0.0.0.0:25826", :receive_buffer_bytes=>"106496",
:queue_size=>"2000"}
```

Once Logstash starts, observe Elasticsearch logs that shows that Logstash has created a new index based on the `helpinghands.collectd.instance-%{+YYYY.MM}` pattern as configured in Logstash's Elasticsearch output plugin. Note that the index name will differ based on the current month and year. Maintaining a time-based index pattern is recommended for indexes that store timeseries datasets. It not only helps in query performance but also helps in backup and cleanup based on the data retention policies of an organization. The following are the log messages that can be observed in Elasticsearch log files for successful creation of the required index for the data captured by Logstash from Collectd:

```
[2018-01-16T02:04:12,054][INFO ][o.e.c.m.MetaDataCreateIndexService]
[W6r6s1z] [helpinghands.collectd.instance-2018.01] creating index, cause
[auto(bulk api)], templates [], shards [5]/[1], mappings []
[2018-01-16T02:04:15,259][INFO ][o.e.c.m.MetaDataMappingService] [W6r6s1z]
[helpinghands.collectd.instance-2018.01/9x0mla-mS0akJLuuUJELZw]
create_mapping [doc]
[2018-01-16T02:04:15,279][INFO ][o.e.c.m.MetaDataMappingService] [W6r6s1z]
[helpinghands.collectd.instance-2018.01/9x0mla-mS0akJLuuUJELZw]
update_mapping [doc]
[2018-01-16T02:04:15,577][INFO ][o.e.c.m.MetaDataMappingService] [W6r6s1z]
[helpinghands.collectd.instance-2018.01/9x0mla-mS0akJLuuUJELZw]
update_mapping [doc]
[2018-01-16T02:04:15,712][INFO ][o.e.c.m.MetaDataMappingService] [W6r6s1z]
[helpinghands.collectd.instance-2018.01/9x0mla-mS0akJLuuUJELZw]
update_mapping [doc]
[2018-01-16T02:04:15,922][INFO ][o.e.c.m.MetaDataMappingService] [W6r6s1z]
[helpinghands.collectd.instance-2018.01/9x0mla-mS0akJLuuUJELZw]
update_mapping [doc]
```

Let the pipeline run and store the machine metrics captured via Collectd–Logstash–Elasticsearch pipeline. Now, open the Kibana interface in the browser using the URL `http://localhost:5601` and click on the **Set up index patterns** button on the top-right corner. It will automatically list the newly created index `helpinghands.collectd.instance-2018.01`, as shown in the following screenshot:

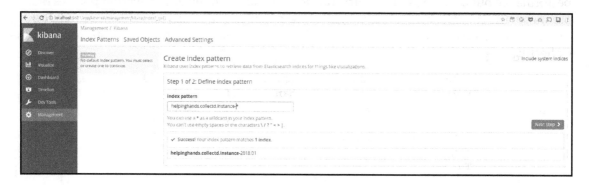

Add the index pattern `helpinghands.collectd.instance-*`, as shown in the preceding screenshot, to include all the indexes created for the metrics captured by Collectd. Click on the **Next step** button on the right-hand side and select **Time filter field name** as `@timestamp`, as shown in the following screenshot:

Next, click on the **Create index pattern** button, as shown in the preceding screenshot. It will show the list of fields that Kibana was able to retrieve from the Elasticsearch index mapping (`https://www.elastic.co/guide/en/elasticsearch/reference/current/mapping.html`). Now, click on **Discover** in the left-hand side menu, and it will show the real-time dashboard of all the messages being captured, as shown in the following screenshot:

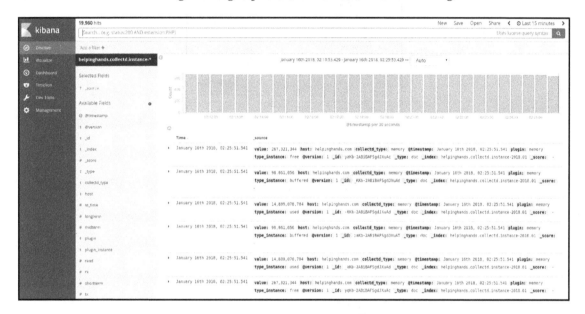

The left-hand side panel of the **Discover** screen lists all the fields being captured. For example, click on **host** and **plugin** fields to see the hosts being monitored and all the plugins for which the data has been captured by Collectd and sent to Elasticsearch via the Logstash pipeline, as shown in the following screenshot:

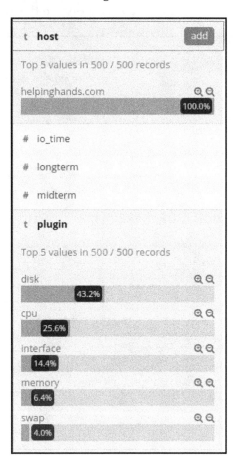

Kibana dashboard allows building dashboard with various visualization options. For example, to take a look at the CPU utilization since Collectd started monitoring it, perform the following steps:

1. Click on **Visualize** in the left panel of the Kibana application
2. Click on the **Create a visualization** button
3. Click on **Line** to choose the line chart
4. Choose the index **helpinghands.collectd.instance-*** pattern from the section on the left
5. Click on the **Add a filter +** option below the search bar at the top
6. Select filter as **plugin.keyword is cpu** and save
7. Click on the *Y*-axis and change **Aggregation** to **Average**
8. Select the field as **Value**
9. Next, click on the **X-Axis** under **Buckets**
10. Choose the **Aggregation** as **Date Histogram**
11. It should by default select the **@timestamp** field
12. Keep the interval as **Auto**
13. Click on the apply changes play icon at the top of the **Metrics** panel
14. It will show the chart on the right-hand side, as shown in the next screenshot
15. Click on the arrow icon at the bottom of the chart area to bring up the table

Once these steps have been performed, you should be able to see the CPU utilization over time for the last 15 minutes (default), as shown in the following screenshot. The created visualization (https://www.elastic.co/guide/en/kibana/current/visualize.html) can be saved and later added to a dashboard (https://www.elastic.co/guide/en/kibana/current/dashboard.html) to build a full-fledged dashboard to monitor all the captured metrics in real time:

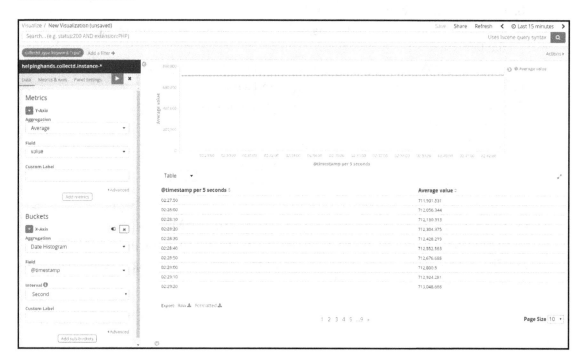

Logging and monitoring guidelines

Microservices of the Helping Hands application must generate both application and audit logs that can be captured by the ELK Stack. Application logs can be generated by the services using the `tools.logging` library of Clojure (https://github.com/clojure/tools.logging) that logs a message in a standard log4j (https://logging.apache.org/log4j/2.x/) style syntax. Logstash works well with most of the common logging formats (https://www.elastic.co/guide/en/logstash/6.1/plugins-inputs-log4j.html), but it is recommended to use structured logging instead.

Structured logs are easier to parse and load within a centralized repository using tools such as Logstash. Libraries such as timbre (`https://github.com/ptaoussanis/timbre`) support structured logging and also allow publishing the logs directly to a remote service instead of logging to a file. In addition to structured logging, consider including predefined standard tags within the log messages, as shown in the following table:

Name	Event
`<service>`	The name of the service, such as `helping-hands.alert`
`<service>-start`	Logged from the main function once the application is up and running
`<service>-init`	Once the service is up and running and it has been successfully initialized with the required configuration
`<service>-stop`	The last statement in the main function before the application exits or is in the shutdown hook
`<service>-config`	Used for configuration-related messages
`<service>-process`	Used for processing-related messages
`<service>-exception`	Used for runtime exception handler and related messages

Tags are particularly useful to filter the log messages originating from a service of interest and also helps to further drill down the logs via specific state level tags, such as log messages generated at startup, during shutdown, or logged as a result of an exception.

In addition to the tags, it is also recommended to always use UTC (`https://en.wikipedia.org/wiki/Coordinated_Universal_Time`) while generating log messages. Since all these log messages are aggregated in a centralized repository, having different timezone makes it challenging to analyze them, as they will be out of sync due to the timezone of the host machines that may be running in different time zones.

Although log messages are quite useful to debug the issues and provide information regarding the state of the application, they affect the performance of the application drastically. So, log judiciously and asynchronously as much as possible. It is also recommended to publish the log events asynchronously to channels, such as Apache Kafka, instead of logging to a file that requires disk I/O. Logstash has an input plugin for Kafka (`https://www.elastic.co/guide/en/logstash/current/plugins-inputs-kafka.html`) that can read events from a Kafka topic and publish it to the target output plugin like that of Elasticsearch (`https://www.elastic.co/guide/en/logstash/current/plugins-outputs-elasticsearch.html`).

Riemann (`http://riemann.io/`) is an alternative to ELK stack. It is used to monitor distributed systems, such as the ones based on microservices-based architecture. Riemann is incredibly fast and can be used to generate alerts in near real time without overwhelming the recipient, using its rollup and throttle constructs (`http://riemann.io/howto.html#roll-up-and-throttle-events`).

Using ELK stack to collect the events and, at the same time, streaming Logstash events via Riemann using Logstash Riemann output plugin (`https://www.elastic.co/guide/en/logstash/current/plugins-outputs-riemann.html`) makes it possible to generate alerts in near real time and also use the goodness of Elasticsearch and Kibana to provide a real-time monitoring dashboard for drill-down analysis.

Deploying microservices at scale

Microservices must be packaged as a self-contained artifact that can be replicated and deployed using a single command. The services should also be lightweight with shorter start times to make sure that they are up and running within seconds. It is recommended to package microservices within a container (`https://en.wikipedia.org/wiki/LXC`) that can then be deployed faster due to its inherent implementation as compared to setting up a bare metal machine with a host operating system and required dependencies. Packaging microservices within containers also makes it possible to move from development to production faster and in an automated fashion.

Introducing Containers and Docker

Linux Containers (**LXC**) is a virtualization method at the operating system level that makes it possible to run multiple isolated Linux systems, also known as containers, on a single host OS using a single Linux Kernel (`https://en.wikipedia.org/wiki/Linux_kernel`). The resources are shared among the containers using cgroups (`https://en.wikipedia.org/wiki/Cgroups`) that do not require virtual machines. Since each container relies on the Linux Kernel of the host OS that is already running, the start time of containers is much lower as compared to a virtual machine that is run by a Hypervisor (`https://en.wikipedia.org/wiki/Hypervisor`).

Docker (`https://en.wikipedia.org/wiki/Docker_(software)`) also provides resource isolation for the containers using Linux cgroups, kernel namespaces (`https://en.wikipedia.org/wiki/Linux_namespaces`), and union mounting option (`https://en.wikipedia.org/wiki/Union_mount`) that helps it to avoid the overhead of starting and maintaining virtual machines. Using Docker container for microservices makes it possible to package the entire service and its dependencies within a container and run on any Linux server.

 Although it is possible to package the entire microservice, including the database within a Docker container, it is recommended that you keep the database out of the Docker container. Reason being that databases may not be the prime candidate for dynamic scale up and scale down as compared to the services themselves.

Setting up Docker

Docker is a software that helps create Docker images that can be used to create one or more containers and run it on the host operating system. The easiest way to set up Docker is to use the setup script provided by Docker for the community edition, as shown here:

```
% wget -qO- https://get.docker.com/ | sh
```

The preceding command will set up Docker, based on the host operating system. Docker also provides prebuilt packages for all the popular operation systems under its **Download** section (`https://www.docker.com/community-edition#/download`). Once installed, add the current user to the `docker` group, as shown here:

```
% sudo usermod -aG docker $USER
```

You may have to start a new login session for group membership to be taken into account. Once done, Docker should be up and running. To test Docker, try listing the running containers using the following command:

```
% docker ps -a
CONTAINER ID IMAGE COMMAND CREATED STATUS PORTS NAMES
```

Since there are no containers running, it will just list the headers. To test running a container, use the `docker run` command, as shown in the following example. It will download the `hello-world` Docker image and run it in a container:

```
% docker run hello-world
Unable to find image 'hello-world:latest' locally
latest: Pulling from library/hello-world
```

```
ca4f61b1923c: Pull complete
Digest:
sha256:66ef312bbac49c39a89aa9bcc3cb4f3c9e7de3788c944158df3ee0176d32b751
Status: Downloaded newer image for hello-world:latest

Hello from Docker!
This message shows that your installation appears to be working correctly.

To generate this message, Docker took the following steps:
 1. The Docker client contacted the Docker daemon.
 2. The Docker daemon pulled the "hello-world" image from the Docker Hub.
    (amd64)
 3. The Docker daemon created a new container from that image which runs
the
    executable that produces the output you are currently reading.
 4. The Docker daemon streamed that output to the Docker client, which sent
it
    to your terminal.

To try something more ambitious, you can run an Ubuntu container with:
 $ docker run -it ubuntu bash

Share images, automate workflows, and more with a free Docker ID:
 https://cloud.docker.com/

For more examples and ideas, visit:
 https://docs.docker.com/engine/userguide/
```

 The preceding output is a result of the execution of the hello-world image. Dumping the entire set of steps that were used by Docker to generate the message is helpful to understand what a single command such as docker run does at the back.

The preceding command downloads the hello-world image, stores it locally, and then runs it within a container. The image just dumps a message with the steps that were used to generate the message on the console and exits. Since, the hello-world image was used for the first time, it was not present on the local machine, and that is the reason the docker command downloaded it first from remote Docker Registry (https://docs.docker.com/registry/). Try running the same command again, and, this time, it will locate the image within the local machine and use it straight away, as shown in the following example. In this case, it just dumps the message and the installation steps as an output of the execution of the hello-world image as before:

```
% docker run hello-world
```

```
Hello from Docker!
This message shows that your installation appears to be working correctly.

To generate this message, Docker took the following steps:
 1. The Docker client contacted the Docker daemon.
 2. The Docker daemon pulled the "hello-world" image from the Docker Hub.
    (amd64)
 3. The Docker daemon created a new container from that image which runs
the
    executable that produces the output you are currently reading.
 4. The Docker daemon streamed that output to the Docker client, which sent
it
    to your terminal.

To try something more ambitious, you can run an Ubuntu container with:
 $ docker run -it ubuntu bash

Share images, automate workflows, and more with a free Docker ID:
 https://cloud.docker.com/

For more examples and ideas, visit:
 https://docs.docker.com/engine/userguide/
```

To list the Docker images available on the local machine, execute the `docker images` command as shown in the following example; it lists all the available images:

```
% docker images
REPOSITORY TAG IMAGE ID CREATED SIZE
hello-world latest f2a91732366c 7 weeks ago 1.85 kB
```

Similarly, to list the Docker containers that were created, use the `docker ps -a` command, as used earlier. This time, it should list the containers that were started using the `hello-world` image, as shown here:

```
% docker ps -a
CONTAINER ID IMAGE COMMAND CREATED STATUS PORTS NAMES
e0e5678ef80a hello-world "/hello" 5 minutes ago Exited (0) 5 minutes ago
happy_rosalind
ea9815d87660 hello-world "/hello" 8 minutes ago Exited (0) 8 minutes ago
fervent_engelbart
```

For more details on the available commands and options, refer to the Docker CLI commands reference guide (`https://docs.docker.com/engine/reference/commandline/docker/`).

For more details on Docker setup and configuration options, take a look at the Docker post installation guide (`https://docs.docker.com/engine/installation/linux/linux-postinstall/`)

Creating a Docker image for Helping Hands

Helping Hands services created in the previous chapters have a `Dockerfile` created as a part of the project template. For example, take a look at the directory structure of the Auth service, as shown in the following example. To run within a Docker container, the `::http/host` key of the `service` definition within the `helping-hands.auth.service` namespace must be set to a fixed IP address or `0.0.0.0` to bind to all the IPv4 addresses available within the container.

```
% tree -L 1
.
├── Capstanfile
├── config
├── Dockerfile
├── project.clj
├── README.md
├── resources
├── src
├── target
└── test

5 directories, 4 files
```

Change the content of the `Dockerfile` for the Auth service, as shown in the following example. It copies both the `config` directory and the stand-alone JAR file of the Auth service of Helping Hands. If the stand-alone JAR is not present in the `target` folder, create it using the `lein uberjar` command that will create a stand-alone JAR in the target directory of the Auth project.

```
FROM java:8-alpine
MAINTAINER Helping Hands <helpinghands@hh.com>

COPY target/helping-hands-auth-0.0.1-SNAPSHOT-standalone.jar /helping-hands/app.jar
COPY config/conf.edn /helping-hands/
```

```
EXPOSE 8080

CMD exec java -Dconf=/helping-hands/conf.edn -jar /helping-hands/app.jar
```

Next, create a Docker image using the `docker build` command, as shown in the following example. The `docker build` command looks for a `Dockerfile` in the same directory where it started from. If `Dockerfile` is present at some other location, explicit path to the `Dockerfile` can be specified using the `-f` flag. For more details on the `docker build` command, refer to the usage instructions (`https://docs.docker.com/engine/reference/builder/#usage`).

```
# build the docker image
% docker build -t helping-hands/auth:0.0.1 .
Sending build context to Docker daemon 48.44 MB
Step 1/6 : FROM java:8-alpine
8-alpine: Pulling from library/java
709515475419: Pull complete
38a1c0aaa6fd: Pull complete
5b58c996e33e: Pull complete
Digest:
sha256:d49bf8c44670834d3dade17f8b84d709e7db47f1887f671a0e098bafa9bae49f
Status: Downloaded newer image for java:8-alpine
 ---> 3fd9dd82815c
Step 2/6 : MAINTAINER Helping Hands <helpinghands@hh.com>
 ---> Running in dd79676d69a4
 ---> 359095b88f32
Removing intermediate container dd79676d69a4
Step 3/6 : COPY target/helping-hands-auth-0.0.1-SNAPSHOT-standalone.jar
/helping-hands/app.jar
 ---> 952111f1c330
Removing intermediate container 888323c4cc30
Step 4/6 : COPY config/conf.edn /helping-hands/
 ---> 3c43dfd4af83
Removing intermediate container 028df1e03d58
Step 5/6 : EXPOSE 8080
 ---> Running in 8cf6c15cab9f
 ---> e79d993e2c67
Removing intermediate container 8cf6c15cab9f
Step 6/6 : CMD exec java -Dconf=/helping-hands/conf.edn -jar /helping-hands/app.jar
 ---> Running in 0b4549cf84f2
 ---> f8c9a7e746f3
Removing intermediate container 0b4549cf84f2
Successfully built f8c9a7e746f3

# list the images to make sure it is available
% docker images
```

```
REPOSITORY TAG IMAGE ID CREATED SIZE
helping-hands/auth 0.0.1 f8c9a7e746f3 17 seconds ago 174 MB
hello-world latest f2a91732366c 7 weeks ago 1.85 kB
java 8-alpine 3fd9dd82815c 10 months ago 145 MB
```

Once the image is created and registered using the specified name and tag, new containers can be created from the same image, as shown here:

```
# create a new container from the tagged image
% docker run -d -p 8080:8080 --name hh_auth_01 helping-hands/auth:0.0.1
286f21a088dd8b6b6d814f1fb5e4d27a59f46b6d8c474160628ffe72d3de2b56

# verify that the container is running
% docker ps -a
CONTAINER ID IMAGE COMMAND CREATED STATUS PORTS NAMES
286f21a088dd helping-hands/auth:0.0.1 "/bin/sh -c 'exec ..." 5 seconds ago
Up 3 seconds 0.0.0.0:8080->8080/tcp hh_auth_01
e0e5678ef80a hello-world "/hello" 51 minutes ago Exited (0) 50 minutes ago
happy_rosalind
ea9815d87660 hello-world "/hello" 54 minutes ago Exited (0) 53 minutes ago
fervent_engelbart
```

Check the log messages generated by Docker to make sure that Auth service is up and running, as shown here:

```
% docker logs 286f21a088dd
Creating your server...
Omniconf configuration:
 {:conf #object[java.io.File 0x47c40b56 "/helping-hands/conf.edn"]}
```

The Auth service can now be accessed directly at the 8080 port as shown in the following example. The port is mapped using the docker run command with -p flag, as used earlier while creating the container.

```
% curl -i "http://localhost:8080/tokens?uid=hhuser&pwd=hhuser"
HTTP/1.1 200 OK
...
Authorization: Bearer
eyJlbmMiOiJBMTI4Q0JDLUhTMjU2IiwiYWxnIjoiQTEyOEtXIn0.1enLmASKP8uqPGvW_bOVcGS
8-0wtR3AS0xxGolaNixXCSaY_7LKqw.RcXp4s0397a3M_EB-
DyFAQ.B6b93-1_grZa7HJee6nkcT4LM3gV7QxmR3CIHxX9ngzFqPyyJTcBWvo2N4TT1Y4gJYgeN
tIyaJsAmvVYCEi7YKyp47bF1wzgFbpjkfVen6y-580kmf5JqaP2vXQmNpFiVRB6FGGqldnAaDKd
BCCrv0HRgGbaxyg_F_05j4G9AktO26hUMfXvmd9woh61Id-1V4xvRZOcn57X6aH-
HL2JuA.hUWvDD61QWmXaRGYCf3YOQ
Transfer-Encoding: chunked
```

To stop the container, use the `docker stop` command, and to delete the container, use the `docker rm` command, as shown here:

```
% docker stop hh_auth_01
hh_alert_01

% docker rm hh_auth_01
hh_alert_01

% docker ps -a
CONTAINER ID IMAGE COMMAND CREATED STATUS PORTS NAMES
e0e5678ef80a hello-world "/hello" 54 minutes ago Exited (0) 54 minutes ago
happy_rosalind
ea9815d87660 hello-world "/hello" 57 minutes ago Exited (0) 57 minutes ago
fervent_engelbart
```

 For more details on how to create effective `Dockerfile`, take a look at the best practices for writing Dockerfiles (`https://docs.docker.com/engine/userguide/eng-image/dockerfile_best-practices/`).

Introducing Kubernetes

Containerizing the services of the Helping Hands application allows them to be deployed across multiple machines faster, but scaling them requires manual effort and involvement of the DevOps team to scale it up and down. Monitoring all the running containers may also become overwhelming over time, as the services may scale to hundreds of instances running containers across the cluster of machines. Although the failure of any service or container can be alerted to the team, but running them manually is a tedious task. Moreover, it is exhaustive and often error-prone to estimate and achieve effective resource utilization and optimally balance the number of running instances of each service manually.

To avoid such manual tasks and ensure that the configured number of services are always running and effectively utilizing the available resources, container orchestration engines are required. Kubernetes is one such open source container orchestration engine that is widely used for automated deployment, scaling, and management of containerized applications such as the services of the Helping Hands application.

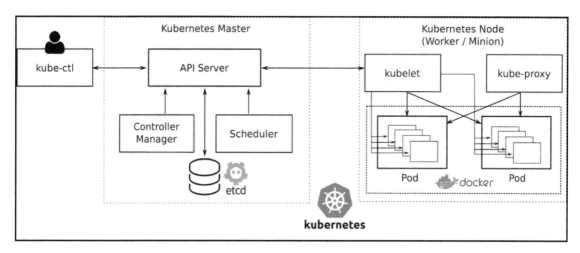

In a Kubernetes deployment, there are two kinds of machines, **Master** and **Node** (previously known as **Minions**). Master instances are the brain of Kubernetes engine that make all the decisions related to the deployment of containers and also respond to various events of failures and new allocation requests. Master instance runs `kube-apiserver` (`https://kubernetes.io/docs/admin/kube-apiserver/`), `etcd` (`https://kubernetes.io/docs/tasks/administer-cluster/configure-upgrade-etcd/`), `kube-controller-manager` (`https://kubernetes.io/docs/admin/kube-controller-manager/`), and `kube-scheduler` (`https://kubernetes.io/docs/admin/kube-scheduler/`). They also run `kube-proxy` (`https://kubernetes.io/docs/admin/kube-proxy/`) to work within the same overlay network as that of nodes. It is recommended to run Master on separate machines that are dedicated for cluster management tasks only.

Nodes, on the other hand, are worker machines in a Kubernetes cluster and runs Pods. A Pod (`https://kubernetes.io/docs/concepts/workloads/pods/pod/`) is a smallest unit of computing that can be created and managed by Kubernetes cluster. It is a group of one or more containers that share network, storage, and a common set of specifications. Each Node runs a Docker service, `kubelet` (`https://kubernetes.io/docs/admin/kubelet/`), and `kube-proxy` and is managed by the master components. The `kubelet` agent runs on each Node and manages the pods that are allocated to the Node. It also reports the status of the pods back to the Kubernetes cluster.

For more details on Kubernetes Master and Node components, take a look at Kubernetes Concepts document at `https://kubernetes.io/docs/concepts/overview/components/`.

Kubernetes has an in-built support for Docker containers. Service such as Automatic Bin Packing (`https://kubernetes.io/docs/concepts/configuration/manage-compute-resources-container/`) for effective utilization of the resources, horizontal scaling (`https://kubernetes.io/docs/tasks/run-application/horizontal-pod-autoscale/`) to scale the services up and down and based on factors such as CPU usage and Self-Healing (`https://kubernetes.io/docs/concepts/workloads/controllers/replicationcontroller/#what-is-a-replicationcontroller`) to automatically restart containers that fail is provided out-of-the-box by Kubernetes.

Kubernetes also supports **Service Discovery** and **Load Balancing** by allocating containers their own IP addresses. It also allocates a common DNS name for a set of containers that allow other external services to just know the DNS name and use the same to reach the service. Kubernetes internally balances the requests among the services running in the containers that are registered with the DNS with the specified name. Rolling Upgrades (`https://kubernetes.io/docs/tutorials/kubernetes-basics/update-intro/`) are also provided by Kubernetes by incrementally upgrading the containers with the new ones. All updates are versioned by Kubernetes, and it allows rollback to any previous stable version.

For more details on Kubernetes, take a look at Kubernetes tutorials that cover all the basic features of Kubernetes with examples from `https://kubernetes.io/docs/tutorials/`.

Getting started with Kubernetes

The simplest way to get started with Kubernetes and run locally on a single machine is to use Minikube (`https://github.com/kubernetes/minikube`). To setup Minikube, use the following installation script:

```
% curl -Lo minikube
https://storage.googleapis.com/minikube/releases/latest/minikube-linux-amd6
4 && chmod +x minikube && sudo mv minikube /usr/local/bin/
```

The preceding command downloads the latest release of Minikube script and makes it available on the path by copying it to the `/usr/local/bin` directory. Minikube also requires `kube-ctl` to interact with the Kubernetes cluster. To set up `kube-ctl`, use the installation script of `kube-ctl`, as shown here:

```
# download kube-ctl script
% curl -LO https://storage.googleapis.com/kubernetes-release/release/$(curl
-s
https://storage.googleapis.com/kubernetes-release/release/stable.txt)/bin/l
inux/amd64/kubectl

# make the script executable
% chmod +x ./kubectl

# make it available on the path
% sudo mv ./kubectl /usr/local/bin/kubectl
```

For more details on how to use the `minikube` command to create a Kubernetes cluster and `kube-ctl` to interact with the Master and deploy containers, take a look at the Minikube project documentation (`https://github.com/kubernetes/minikube`).

Summary

In this chapter, you learned how to prepare microservices for production. We focused on security and monitoring of microservices of the Helping Hands application. We also learned how to deploy and scale microservices using containers. We also discussed orchestration engines such as Kubernetes and how they are useful to orchestrate containers. With this chapter, you are all set to build your next best application using microservices-based architecture and deploy it effectively in production. What will you build next?

Other Books You May Enjoy

If you enjoyed this book, you may be interested in these other books by Packt:

Mastering Microservices with Java 9 - Second Edition
Sourabh Sharma

ISBN: 978-1-78728-144-8

- Use domain-driven design to design and implement microservices
- Secure microservices using Spring Security
- Learn to develop REST service development
- Deploy and test microservices
- Troubleshoot and debug the issues faced during development
- Learning best practices and common principals about microservices

Spring 5.0 Microservices - Second Edition
Rajesh R V

ISBN: 978-1-78712-768-5

- Familiarize yourself with the microservices architecture and its benefits
- Find out how to avoid common challenges and pitfalls while developing microservices
- Use Spring Boot and Spring Cloud to develop microservices
- Handle logging and monitoring microservices
- Leverage Reactive Programming in Spring 5.0 to build modern cloud native applications
- Manage internet-scale microservices using Docker, Mesos, and Marathon
- Gain insights into the latest inclusion of Reactive Streams in Spring and make applications more resilient and scalable

Leave a review - let other readers know what you think

Please share your thoughts on this book with others by leaving a review on the site that you bought it from. If you purchased the book from Amazon, please leave us an honest review on this book's Amazon page. This is vital so that other potential readers can see and use your unbiased opinion to make purchasing decisions, we can understand what our customers think about our products, and our authors can see your feedback on the title that they have worked with Packt to create. It will only take a few minutes of your time, but is valuable to other potential customers, our authors, and Packt. Thank you!

Index

Clojure
  about 70
  history 70
  URL 50, 70
ClojureCLR
  reference link 70
Cloverage
  reference link 79
Codox
  reference link 79
Collectd Codec
  reference link 289
Collectd
  about 284
  ELK stack, using 284
  URL 273
Command Query Responsibility Segregation
    (CQRS) pattern
  about 230
  references 230
  using 230
command side 230
Common Language Runtime (CLR) 70
Common Lisp
  reference link 71
communications protocols
  reference link 128
components
  about 25
  hexagonal architecture 26
  reference link 25
  references 222
Config
  reference link 215
configuration parameters
  defining 214
  using 214
consul
  URL 33
Consumer Group 232, 235
containers
  reference link 19
Context Map
  about 100
  importance 102

context
  designing 150
continuous delivery (CD) 41
continuous integration (CI) 22
contracts
  about 27
  service contracts 31
Coordinated Universal Time
  reference link 297
core business logic 26
core.async
  reference link 100
Counterclockwise
  URL 84
Cross Cluster Search
  about 277
  reference link 277

D

data management
  about 13, 35
  asynchronous events 36
  data, combining 37, 39
  direct lookup 35
  transactions 39
data model 138, 156
data structure
  reference link 100
data transfer
  Avro, using for 246, 247
database adapter 26
database port 26
Datalog to query
  using 145
Datalog
  reference link 145
Datomic query grammar
  reference link 146
Datomic schema
  defining 160
Datomic
  about 136
  architecture 136
  data model 138
  data, transacting 143

www.ingramcontent.com/pod-product-compliance
Lightning Source LLC
Chambersburg PA
CBHW080621060326

40690CB00021B/4776